VIETNAM STUDIES

ALLIED PARTICIPATION IN VIETNAM

by
Lieutenant General Stanley Robert Larsen
and
Brigadier General James Lawton Collins, Jr.

DEPARTMENT OF THE ARMY
WASHINGTON, D.C., 1985

Library of Congress Catalog Card Number: 74-28217

First Printed 1975—CMH Pub 90-5

For sale by the Superintendent of Documents, U.S. Government Printing Office
Washington, D.C. 20402

Foreword

The United States Army has met an unusually complex challenge in Southeast Asia. In conjunction with the other services, the Army has fought in support of a national policy of assisting an emerging nation to develop governmental processes of its own choosing, free of outside coercion. In addition to the usual problems of waging armed conflict, the assignment in Southeast Asia has required superimposing the immensely sophisticated tasks of a modern army upon an underdeveloped environment and adapting them to demands covering a wide spectrum. These involved helping to fulfill the basic needs of an agrarian population, dealing with the frustrations of antiguerrilla operations, and conducting conventional campaigns against well-trained and determined regular units.

It is still necessary for the Army to continue to prepare for other challenges that may lie ahead. While cognizant that history never repeats itself exactly and that no army ever profited from trying to meet a new challenge in terms of the old one, the Army nevertheless stands to benefit immensely from a study of its experience, its shortcomings no less than its achievements.

Aware that some years must elapse before the official histories will provide a detailed and objective analysis of the experience in Southeast Asia, we have sought a forum whereby some of the more salient aspects of that experience can be made available now. At the request of the Chief of Staff, a representative group of senior officers who served in important posts in Vietnam and who still carry a heavy burden of day-to-day responsibilities has prepared a series of monographs. These studies should be of great value in helping the Army develop future operational concepts while at the same time contributing to the historical record and providing the American public with an interim report on the performance of men and officers who have responded, as others have through our history, to exacting and trying demands.

All monographs in the series are based primarily on official records, with additional material from published and unpublished secondary works, from debriefing reports and interviews with key participants, and from the personal experience of the author. To facilitate security clearance, annotation and detailed bibliography have been omitted from the published version; a fully documented account with bibliography is filed with the U.S. Army Center of Military History.

The reader should be reminded that most of the writing was accomplished while the war in Vietnam was at its peak, and the monographs frequently refer to events of the past as if they were taking place in the present.

Lieutenant General Stanley Robert Larsen is well qualified to write the history of the Republic of Korea armed forces in the Vietnam conflict. As Commanding General, I Field Force, Vietnam, from August 1965 to August 1967, he skillfully managed the complex administrative and logistical problems incidental to the arrival of Korean Army and Marine units within his area of command. As the senior U.S. military official in the II Corps Tactical Zone to which the Koreans were assigned, General Larsen was in a good position to observe the abilities and accomplishments of the Korean forces in Vietnam. Drawing on his previous experience as the Deputy Chief of Staff for Plans and Operations of the Eighth U.S. Army in Korea, General Larsen worked closely with the Koreans on joint military operations and on numerous programs designed to win the allegiance of the Vietnamese people. In recognition of his outstanding service and assistance to the Korean armed forces in Vietnam, the Korean government awarded General Larsen the Order of Ulchi, one of its most prestigious decorations.

Brigadier General James Lawton Collins, Jr., presently the Chief of Military History, U.S. Army, has the wealth of experience required to tell the story of allied participation in the Vietnam War. After having served in Korea as the Assistant Commander, I Corps (Group) Artillery, General Collins had two tours of duty in Vietnam that involved close liaison with all nations participating in the allied effort. In 1964 he was assigned as the senior U.S. adviser to the Vietnamese Regional Forces and Popular Forces, and in May 1965 was named Special Assistant to the Commander, U.S. Military Assistance Command, Vietnam. In the latter capacity General Collins was the personal representative of General Westmoreland to the Vietnamese Joint General Staff on all matters pertaining to the co-ordination of U.S., Vietnamese, and allied forces operations. For his outstanding service in Vietnam, the Republic of Vietnam awarded him the National Order and the Army Distinguished Service Medal, two of its most coveted awards.

Washington, D.C.
1 May 1974

VERNE L. BOWERS
Major General, USA
The Adjutant General

Preface

More than forty nations provided assistance to the Republic of Vietnam in its struggle against North Vietnam. This aid ranged from economic and technical assistance to educational and humanitarian contributions. Hundreds of Free World civilians worked in Vietnam as doctors, teachers, and technical specialists. Eight nations also provided military assistance. The flags of these Free World countries—the United States, the Republic of Korea, Thailand, Australia, New Zealand, the Philippines, the Republic of China, and Spain—flew alongside the colors of the Republic of Vietnam at the headquarters of the Free World Military Assistance Forces in Saigon. The military contributions of these nations included combat troops, army medical teams, and individual political warfare advisers. The degree of assistance and co-operation among the concerned Free World nations resulted from years of work and involvement. While many nations expressed sympathy for the plight of South Vietnam, aid did not always come easily, quickly, or to the extent desired. Many nations, beset by their own internal economic and political problems, could do little to help; others did nothing. The story of the efforts of the contributing nations and the efforts to enlist their aid is the subject of this monograph.

The members of the Sixth Army Historical Staff, under the guidance of Mr. Herbert Avedon, Sixth Army Historian, gave generous assistance in putting together those elements of the monograph that refer to Korean activities after 1 August 1967. Without their detailed research and helpful suggestions the story of the Koreans in Vietnam would have taken much longer to complete. The revision of the Korean part of the manuscript owes much to the skill of Lieutenant Colonel Samuel Focer, Headquarters, U.S. Army, Pacific.

For their efforts in researching and drafting other chapters in this volume thanks are due especially to Dr. Richard A. Hunt, who helped to assemble the monograph in its final form, overseeing its progress through the staff and contributing to the first chapter; Lieutenant Colonel John E. Eshelman, U.S. Army, who helped to launch the volume; and Loretto C. Stevens, who gave skilled editorial assistance. Their work and support made the history of the Allied effort in Vietnam immeasurably less difficult to tell.

Washington, D.C.
1 May 1974

STANLEY ROBERT LARSEN
Lieutenant General, U.S. Army

JAMES LAWTON COLLINS, JR.
Brigadier General, U.S. Army

Contents

Chapter		Page
I.	THE BACKGROUND, 1961–1966	1
	Early Negotiations for Aid to Vietnam	2
	Free World Troops in Vietnam, 1965–1966	14
II.	THAILAND	25
	Beginnings of Thai Assistance	26
	Thai Operations	45
	Last Years of Assistance	48
III.	THE PHILIPPINES	52
	History of Philippine Aid	53
	Pacification Efforts	76
	The Thanh Dien Refugee Resettlement Project	83
IV.	AUSTRALIA AND NEW ZEALAND	88
V.	THE REPUBLIC OF CHINA	115
VI.	THE REPUBLIC OF KOREA	120
	The Korean Commitment	120
	Operational Control of Korean Troops	131
	Initial Developments	135
	Results of Korean Combat Operations	147
	Evaluation of Korean Operations	151
	Tactics	154
	Ambushes	156
	Pacification Efforts	157
VII.	NONMILITARY AID TO VIETNAM	160
	Far East	161
	Middle East	163
	Africa	164
	Europe	164
	North America	168
	Latin America	168

	Page
APPENDIX A: LEAFLET ADDRESSED TO THE VIETNAMESE PEOPLE	171
GLOSSARY	175
INDEX	177

Tables

No.
1. Strength of Free World Military Assistance Forces, 1964–1970 — 23
2. Location, Strength, and Mission of New Zealand Forces, June 1969 — 110

Charts

1. Organization of Royal Thai Army Volunteer Force, 25 January 1968 — 39
2. Royal Thai Forces, Vietnam — 43
3. Philippine Civic Action Group, Vietnam — 63
4. Organization of Philippine Contingent, Vietnam — 75
5. Republic of China Military Assistance Group, Vietnam — 118

Maps

1. Royal Thai Forces, Vietnam, August 1969 — 45
2. Concept of Ben Cam Operation, Royal Thai Army Volunteer Force, 24 November–4 December 1969 — 46
3. 1st Philippine Civic Action Group, Vietnam, Disposition, 1967 — 61
4. 1st Philippine Civic Action Group, Vietnam, Tay Ninh Province, 1967 — 84
5. Community Plan, Thanh Dien Resettlement Project — 86
6. Australia–New Zealand Area of Responsibility, Phuoc Tuy Province, 1969 — 102
7. Korean Corps Area of Responsibility, December 1966 — 132

Illustrations

	Page
Soldiers of the Queen's Cobras Conduct a Search and Sweep Mission in Phuoc Tho	33
Troops of Royal Thai Black Panther Division Dock at Newport, Vietnam	44
Royal Thai Flag Is Carried Down Gangplank of USS *Okinagon*	44
Thai Soldiers Board C–130 at Long Thanh for Trip Home	50
Lieutenant General William B. Rosson Presents Meritorious Unit Citation to Thai Panther Division	50
Philippine Security Troops Rebuild a Base Camp Bunker	62
Philippine Civic Action Group Member Distributes Medicines	78
Philippine Group Clears Debris After Viet Cong Mortar Hit	80
Entertainers of Philippine Group Play to Villagers	82
Troops of Royal Australian Regiment After Arrival at Tan Son Nhut Airport	91
Living Quarters at an Australian Fire Support Base	92
Australian Soldier Mans Machine Gun Position	94
Members of Australian Civic Action Team Confer With Village Officials	95
Soldier of Royal Australian Regiment Pauses During Sweep of Cultivated Area Around a Village	100
Members of Royal New Zealand Artillery Carry Out a Fire Mission	104
Australian Civil Affairs Team Member Treats Village Boy	107
Soldier of Royal New Zealand Army Cooks His Lunch	109
Australian Soldier Searches for Enemy in Hoa Long Village	111
Soldier of Royal Australian Regiment With M60	112
Royal Australian Air Force Civic Action Team Moves Out Past Vietnamese Temples to Mung Duc	114
Korean Marines Prepare Defensive Positions	137
Field Command Headquarters of Republic of Korea Force, Vietnam	139
Korean Troops Use Chart to Show Villagers Types of Viet Cong Booby Traps	144
Korean Soldiers Search the Jungle Near Qui Nhon for Viet Cong	147
Color Guard Displays Flags at Ceremonies	154
General Creighton W. Abrams Presents Bronze Stars to Soldiers of the Tiger Division	155
Medic of Tiger Division Treats Village Boy	157
Korean Instructor in Taekwondo Watches Vietnamese Practice After Class	158

All illustrations are from the Department of Defense files. The emblem on the front and back covers of the softback edition symbolizes the Free World Military Assistance Forces in Vietnam.

ALLIED PARTICIPATION
IN VIETNAM

CHAPTER I

The Background, 1961−1966

Putting the contribution of the Free World allies into proper focus requires first of all a knowledge of the negotiations leading to the commitment of allied economic and military aid, and, second, an understanding of why multilateral aid was sought. The context in which the early discussion of possible troop commitments by the United States or the Southeast Asia Treaty Organization took place indicates the assumptions of U.S. policy-makers. They considered Vietnam, like Korea, a testing ground where the Free World had to use its strength against the forceful expansion of communism. As the Korean War had been an effort of Free World allies against North Korean and Chinese Communist aggression, so they saw the Vietnam War as an allied effort against the aggression of the Viet Cong and North Vietnamese, who were aided by the Russian and Chinese Communists. It is not at all surprising that in the early sixties, when the nature of the U.S. commitment to Vietnam was taking shape, the idea of multilateral aid was being considered.

From the earliest discussions in 1961, Free World troop deployments were tied to and contingent upon the deployment of U.S. troops. Thus in the story of aid to South Vietnam, Free World and U.S. military assistance are intertwined and inextricable, especially in the background of the decisions to deploy troops to South Vietnam. To tell the story of Free World participation it is necessary, therefore, to refer to the background of the deployment of U.S. forces.

Throughout 1961 many possible kinds of troop deployment were considered, from unilateral U.S. intervention to a multilateral Southeast Asia Treaty Organization (SEATO) force. In May an *ad hoc* task force appointed by Assistant Secretary of Defense Roswell L. Gilpatric recommended to the National Security Council that the United States should be prepared to fulfill its obligations under the treaty organization, unilaterally if necessary; the State Department redraft of this memorandum also supported the employment of SEATO troops in South Vietnam. The Joint Chiefs of Staff further recommended deployment of sufficient U.S. forces to deter Communist aggression against South Vietnam. These proposals led to a formal request, National Security Action Memorandum 52, directing the Department of Defense to examine the size and composition of possible troop deployments.

In the absence of a decision by the President of the United States, memorandums continued to stream forth. Presidential adviser Walt W. Rostow suggested in October 1961 a 25,000-man SEATO force to guard the South Vietnam–Laos border; the Joint Chiefs modified this, saying the force should be used instead to secure the Central Highlands. The logical and inevitable synthesis of these proposals was made in a memorandum drafted by Under Secretary of State U. Alexis Johnson. Blending Rostow's border control proposal with the Joint Chiefs of Staff's concept of winning control of the highlands, Secretary Johnson advocated his synthesis as the initial twofold mission for U.S. forces in Vietnam and spelled out the U.S. objective: to defeat the Viet Cong and preserve a free non-Communist government in the south.

Early Negotiations for Aid to Vietnam

In an October 1961 message requesting more U.S. aid, sent with the concurrence of U.S. Ambassador to South Vietnam Frederick C. Nolting, Jr., President Ngo Dinh Diem also asked the United States to consider the possibility of having President Chiang Kai-shek send a division of Nationalist Chinese troops to South Vietnam.

No firm decisions were made in 1961. The attention of the United States was focused on Laos, Diem was growing increasingly reluctant to accept additional outside intervention, and the internal security situation in South Vietnam did not then seem acute. By 1964, however, the situation had changed: the Laotian war had apparently been settled by the 1962 Geneva Accords, Diem had been overthrown and killed, the Viet Cong insurgency had grown, and South Vietnam had become politically unstable. There was a growing awareness from 1963 on that the war against the Viet Cong, and later against the North Vietnamese Army, was not going well. The issue of increased U.S. or allied assistance was consequently again brought up in high policy councils, this time with greater urgency.

Signaling the growing need of allied and U.S. assistance for South Vietnam was President Lyndon B. Johnson's public call on 23 April 1964 for "more flags" to come forth to support a beleaguered friend. In a similar move in April, the Ministerial Council of the Southeast Asia Treaty Organization issued a communique declaring the defeat of the Viet Cong essential to Southeast Asia's security and underscoring the necessity for SEATO nations to fulfill their treaty obligations. McGeorge Bundy, Presidential Assistant for National Security Affairs, in a related memorandum dated 25 May, recommended that a high-level Southeast Asia strategy conference be convoked to consult with the SEATO allies of the United States in order to obtain specific force commitments. This proposal of a SEATO conference—a conference that was never held—was the last official attempt to place Free World assistance under the aegis of the Southeast Asia Treaty Organization. Certain members, especially France, were growing more antipathetic to American policy in Vietnam; hence, when the issue of Free World support for South Vietnam surfaced again in December 1964, it was discussed outside the context of SEATO commitments.

When troop commitments to South Vietnam were further discussed at a White House meeting on 1 December 1964, U.S. objectives were reiterated: first, to end Democratic Republic of Vietnam support of Viet Cong operations in South Vietnam; second, to maintain the security of other non-Communist nations in Southeast Asia; and third, to re-establish an independent and secure South Vietnam. The meeting resolved also that aid be sought from "key allies." Thailand was to be asked to support the U.S. program and intensify its own counterinsurgency efforts in Thailand. Prime Minister J. Harold Wilson of England was to be briefed on the U.S. position and his support sought. William P. Bundy of the State Department was to ask Australia and New Zealand for additional help as well as consideration of the possibility of sending small combat units when and if the United States moved to the second phase of its strategy of increasing military pressure against the enemy. The Philippines were to be asked for a commitment of approximately 1,800 men. The conferees decided to press generally and strongly for more outside aid.

A memorandum for the chief of staff of U.S. Military Assistance Command, Vietnam (MACV), implementing the 1 December White House decision, specifically stated that "Australia, New Zealand and the Philippines should be encouraged to provide combat *advisory* personnel now and, in event of U.S. troop deployment in RVN, to provide combatant units to reinforce DMZ Defense."[1]

---

[1] Italics are the author's.

At the time the memorandum was written sixteen countries including the United States were already providing aid—some advisory military but largely economical and technical—to South Vietnam. At the end of December the Philippine, Korean, and Nationalist Chinese governments had made known through diplomatic channels their readiness to provide military assistance to South Vietnam.

The 1 December White House meeting appears to have been crucial in determining the manner of soliciting allied support and the nature of the relationship between the Republic of Vietnam and the allies. President Johnson then strongly felt the need for "new, dramatic, effective" forms of assistance, specifically from Australia, New Zealand, Canada, and the Philippines; Dean Rusk, the Secretary of State, felt that Britain, too, could help. (Inexplicably, aid from the Republic of Korea was not discussed at the December meeting.) It was decided to seek "military and political cooperation" from these allies. General Maxwell D. Taylor, U.S. Ambassador to South Vietnam, was to inform the White House what kind of assistance would be welcome after explaining U.S. policy and consulting with government officials of Vietnam. The parameters of Ambassador Taylor's discussions with the Vietnam government clearly had been laid down at the 1 December White House meeting. Thus the initiative in seeking allied help for Vietnam came first from the United States. The government of Vietnam did have a voice, however, in determining the nature of allied assistance.

In November 1964, prior to Taylor's return to Washington, Major General Nguyen Khanh, the head of state in South Vietnam, had mentioned to him in reference to the more flags appeal that South Vietnam had only a general need for additional manpower for the military and police.[2] Upon his return to South Vietnam in December, acting on his instructions from President Johnson, Taylor emphasized in a 7 December meeting with Vietnam government officials the importance of Free World assistance from the U.S. domestic point of view but stressed that the United States did not want to "internationalize" the war on the pattern of Korea. The issue really involved making Free World support concretely evident. To this principle General Khanh and Brigadier General Cao Van Vien agreed.

It must be kept in mind at this point that aside from tentative probes of the attitudes of the government of Australia and the government of New Zealand no effort was being made to secure

---

[2] This is the only guidance Taylor received from the Vietnamese prior to 1 December 1964 as far as the author can discover.

foreign combat troops, but economic assistance, military advisers, civil affairs personnel, and humanitarian aid were requested. A series of State Department messages dating from May 1964 stressed again and again that no foreign combat troops were being sought.

From the time of the earliest deliberations on the question of troop deployments the United States had conceived of military assistance in its broad aspects in multilateral terms. Significantly the question of allied versus unilateral aid to Vietnam seems to have been resolved by the United States in favor of allied aid. The request for allied aid resulted from U.S. initiatives; the government of South Vietnam seems to have acted merely as the agent transmitting the formal request for assistance.

Chester Cooper, former director of Asian affairs for the White House, fittingly summarized the U.S. quest for more flags in his book, *The Lost Crusade:*

> The "More Flags" campaign had gotten off to a slow start in late 1964. It required the application of considerable pressure for Washington to elicit any meaningful commitments. One of the more exasperating aspects of the search for "More Flags" was the lassitude, even disinterest, of the Saigon Government. In part . . . the South Vietnamese leaders were preoccupied with political jockeying . . . . In addition Saigon appeared to believe that the program was a public relations campaign directed at the American people. As a consequence, it was left to Washington to play the role of supplicant in the quest for Free World support.

Further, the inexperienced and understaffed foreign service of the Vietnam government simply did not have the resources to carry out such a major diplomatic initiative. With political turmoil and war at home, and representation in only a few countries abroad, the Vietnam government was physically unable to obtain aid alone and perforce had to rely on U.S. assistance to obtain outside help. The usual procedure was to have the American embassies in Europe, Asia, and Latin America discuss the subject of aid for South Vietnam with the host countries. The Military Assistance Command, Vietnam, and the U.S. Operations Mission prepared a list of the kind of aid desired. When a country agreed to provide some assistance, the U.S. government then informed the Vietnam government, which in turn made a formal request for aid from the country.

In January 1965 as the United States became more actively engaged in the war in Vietnam, the search for more flags was intensified and the United States gradually in later months began to seek combat units.

To erase the conception that the Vietnam War was purely an American undertaking supported only by non-Asians, the Australians for example, more effort was placed on increased Free World support, especially from nonaligned countries. The focus of diplomatic activities shifted to Latin America, where countries were urged to assist South Vietnam.

Even before January 1965 the United States government had shown interest in obtaining Latin American support in keeping with the President's appeal for more international aid. Conversation with Argentinian and Brazilian officials indicated that Latin American countries would be more inclined to participate on the general basis of support for countries struggling against communism than on the basis of aid specifically earmarked for South Vietnam. The commitment was in principle to support anti-Communist nations against Communist aggression, but not to provide support to South Vietnam in particular.

As a follow-up to the earlier probes, U.S. embassies in all Latin American nations (save Haiti) approached their respective host governments about possible forms of aid for the government of South Vietnam in its struggle against communism. The U.S. government made it clear that each country could determine the best way to assist South Vietnam but suggested that medical and engineering personnel and food and medical supplies would be welcome.

As a result of these U.S. approaches on behalf of the Vietnam government, a number of Latin American governments indicated interest. Honduras and Nicaragua were thinking of a joint medical service team, Brazil of foodstuffs and medical supplies. Ecuador and Peru declined to assist because of their own internal political problems; other Latin American countries were still undecided at the end of January 1965.

After the initial contacts were made, U.S. missions were directed not to pursue further the question of aid to South Vietnam. They could respond positively to any offers of help from Latin Americans and could offer U.S. financial support to underwrite any aid. The restriction on further diplomatic initiatives on behalf of South Vietnam in Latin America was due to unfavorable stories in the Latin American press that accused the United States of exerting pressure to extract aid. Thus the Latin American diplomatic thrust was tempered.

Certain funding guidelines were set. Donor countries were urged to meet as much of the cost of their aid as possible, particularly expenses within the donor country and transportation costs. The U.S. government would consider, on a case basis,

THE BACKGROUND, 1961–1966

financing those costs or a portion thereof necessary to prevent the aid from being withdrawn. Washington would decide the question of cost sharing, and pressed for standardized overseas allowance and maintenance costs, reflecting equal rates for all Free World forces. In the event donors could not meet operating expenses, the Agency for International Development through allocations to the budget would subsidize them. Donors were also asked to furnish the supplies and equipment their projects entailed. In determining the nature of the project, countries were to keep in mind certain criteria, namely that the project be clearly defined, be self-contained, and make a direct contribution to pacification or other priority programs.

Because of the accelerating pace of events and continuing political uncertainty in South Vietnam, the U.S. government began to consider contingencies other than using noncombatants from the allies. In a memorandum of 7 February 1965 to the President, McGeorge Bundy, believing the government of Vietnam would collapse by 1966 without more U.S. help and action, recommended increasing military pressure against the north. Also in early February the Joint Chiefs of Staff suggested deployment of a Marine expeditionary brigade to Da Nang.

The commander of U.S. Military Assistance Command, Vietnam, General William C. Westmoreland, responding to a message from the Joint Chiefs requesting his views on the security situation and possible troop deployments to the most vulnerable areas, indicated in a 17 February message that the security situation was in fact deteriorating, and supported the Joint Chiefs' recommendation that the Marine brigade be sent to Da Nang.

In February 1965, the chairman of the Joint Chiefs notified General Westmoreland that a major policy decision had been made "at the highest level" to "do everything possible to maximize our military efforts to reverse the present unfavorable situation [in South Vietnam]." The foundation was thus laid for steady increases in U.S. and Free World combat troop deployments; it was determined to press forward to attain U.S. limited objectives despite any difficulties.

The Joint Chiefs then expanded, in a 20 February message, their recommendations to include deployment of a Republic of Korea Army division "for counterinsurgency and base security operations. Estimated strength 21,000," as well as additional U.S. troops—Air Force, Army, and Marine Corps. The message also spelled out two stumbling blocks to the recommended deployment. The first problem was the provision of sufficient logistical support and the second the establishment of joint command relationships to provide the Commander, U.S. Military Assistance Command, Vietnam, with effective command of U.S. and allied ground forces so that combat operations could in turn be properly co-ordinated with those of the Army of the Republic of Vietnam. The chairman of the Joint Chiefs again solicited the views of the Commander in Chief, Pacific, and the Commander, U.S. Military Assistance Command, on projected logistical and command arrangements necessary to implement the recommendations of the Joint Chiefs, who had concluded that "the needs of the military situation in SVN have become primary, and direct military action appears to be imperative if defeat is to be avoided."

Ambassador Taylor, in response to the Joint Chiefs' proposals, indicated that he had strong reservations against sending marines to Da Nang, but that he would support General Westmoreland's recommendation for one battalion landing team to provide security for Da Nang. No sooner was the deployment approved, the marines on their way, and Vietnam government consent sought, than the State Department requested Taylor's views on the possible use of an international—that is, a multilateral—force in Vietnam.

The ambassador's first reaction to the idea of an international combat force for northern South Vietnam was not favorable. The Australian envoy to South Vietnam as well as Ambassador Taylor felt that the deployment of such a force might heighten Vietnamese xenophobia and encourage the government of Vietnam to let the U.S. government assume an even greater share of the burden.

The idea of a multilateral or international combat force, of which Ambassador Taylor disapproved, was raised by the Chief of Staff of the Army, General Harold K. Johnson, upon his return from a Vietnam fact-finding trip in March 1965. Specifically in the fourteenth point of his report, General Johnson recommended seeking a commitment from Australia and New Zealand to take responsibility for establishing Regional Forces training centers and thus broadening the international nature of the war against the Communists. The Secretary of Defense concurred but also suggested the deployment of a Korean division. He noted in his concurrence with General Johnson's recommendation that the policy of the United States was now to send anything that would strengthen the position of the government of Vietnam.

General Johnson also attempted to resurrect (without success) the notion of invoking the terms of the Southeast Asia

Treaty Organization to deploy a four-division force across the demilitarized zone, from the South China Sea through Laos to the Mekong River, to stem infiltration.

April 1965, like February, was a crucial and significant time for U.S. policy on the deployment of Free World combat troops. The United States had been, in the months from December 1964 to March 1965, edging toward the commitment of outside combat forces, U.S. and Free World, and a policy of more active support for South Vietnam. In April the United States became committed, at first in principle and then in deed, to sending combat troops to Vietnam and to engaging in a more active and open partnership in the defense of South Vietnam.

On 1 April Free World troop contributions were discussed in a high-level policy meeting at which General Johnson's 21-point proposal, which included soliciting troops from Australia and New Zealand, was approved. Discussion of the desirability of Free World combat forces continued on 3 April while Ambassador Taylor was still in the United States. The President and Secretary of Defense both favored the idea but it was recognized that there were serious political problems in obtaining troops from the Republic of Korea, the only readily available source. Moreover the Vietnam government seemed reluctant to have them. Other officials wanted to ask Australia for a destroyer to work with the Seventh Fleet. Taylor was instructed to explain upon his return to South Vietnam the latest U.S. policy decision and to obtain concurrence and co-operation from the government of Vietnam on possible contributions from other countries. The actual decision to seek Free World combat troops, made earlier, was confirmed on 6 April and embodied in National Security Action Memorandum 328. The State Department was to explore with the Korean, Australian, and New Zealand governments the possibility of rapidly deploying combat elements of their armed forces in conjunction with additional U.S. deployments. Both Australia and the Republic of Korea had already on 3 April 1965 indicated informally their willingness to send combat troops.

The following day, 7 April, in his Johns Hopkins speech, the President, while stressing the desire of the United States for peace and its reluctance to get involved in the Vietnam War, stated that the United States' pressure on North Vietnam as well as its greater military effort was not a change in purpose but a change in what "we believe that purpose requires."

Obviously what was required of the United States to accomplish its purpose in South Vietnam was changing. Even though a survey concluded that the manpower resources of South Vietnam were adequate to support both the "quantitative and qualitative requirements of RVNAF provided the resources were used effectively," there was an apparent need for more troop strength quickly. General Westmoreland had reported on 3 April evidence of the presence of elements of the 325th Division of the People's Army of [North] Vietnam in South Vietnam. This discovery plus the deteriorating security situation in I and II Corps Tactical Zones was the background of both the diplomatic probes to obtain Free World forces and the preparation of a Joint Chiefs plan of action and time schedule to send a two- or three-division force into South Vietnam.

With the basic decision made to commit Free World combat forces when needed, policy and plans began to be formulated to bring about the deployment and to establish command relationships.

In messages to the chairman of the Joint Chiefs and Commander in Chief, Pacific, General Westmoreland outlined his proposed command relationship for the employment of Free World troops. The Korean division, according to General Westmoreland's recommendation, would not be attached to the U.S. Marine Corps expeditionary force but would constitute the major Free World component of an international military security task force to block infiltration through the demilitarized zone. General Westmoreland wanted, however, to deploy the Korean force first around Quang Ngai to provide security for port and base development there. Admiral U. S. Grant Sharp, Commander in Chief, Pacific, directed this on 10 April. Free World units would be attached or assigned to U.S. brigades with combined staff representation to give these forces an international flavor and still allow the United States to retain full authority over its own forces.

General Westmoreland also proposed "a mechanism at the national level to control international forces"—involving the joint exercise of authority by Commander in Chief, Vietnamese Armed Forces, and Commander, U.S. Military Assistance Command, Vietnam—the formation of a small, single, combined staff headed by a U.S. general, a Vietnamese deputy chief of combined staff, and a multinational staff. This staff would develop the parameters of strategic guidance, rules of engagement, and command relationships. The small combined staff which General Westmoreland wanted established would provide staff supervision and direction of multinational forces in the event major multinational forces were assigned to South Vietnam; no national headquarters would stand between the unit commander and the Commander, Military Assistance Command, Vietnam, or Commander in Chief, Vietnam Armed Forces.

In separate meetings later in April with Australian and Vietnamese government officials, the issue of a combined staff was again discussed. At a conference on 28 April, General Westmoreland told General Nguyen Van Thieu and Major General Duong Van Minh that the first mission of Free World forces would be to furnish base security in order to release Vietnamese troops from such tasks; patrols would then be sent outside base areas in co-ordination with Vietnam commanders. Though General Minh had previously favored the combined staff concept, he now stated that he would prefer to have the MACV International Military Assistance Office provide the necessary staff mechanism. The proposal was to be studied further.

Meeting the following day with the Australian Ambassador to South Vietnam, General Westmoreland again broached the question of command arrangements. Pending further guidance, the ambassador was unprepared to say whether it would be possible to incorporate Australian forces with other Free World troops into an international military security task force but indicated his government had been thinking of brigading the Australian battalion with a U.S. unit rather than put the battalion out on its own. The Australian Ambassador was also notified that the MACV International Military Assistance Office was visualized as the staff mechanism for solving problems between the government of Vietnam and Free World forces.

The Korean government, not wanting to have the only Free World combat forces besides the U.S. forces in South Vietnam, expressed the fear that its aid might be seen not as independently and freely given but as the fulfillment of the obligation of a vassal state. These misgivings caused the United States to weigh more carefully the pros and cons of obtaining Korean combat troops before again asking the government of Vietnam to approach the Republic of Korea for combat troops.

On 15 April word had come from Washington that more U.S. troops would definitely be sent because deteriorating conditions in South Vietnam warranted it, and there had not been a negative reaction to the earlier deployments. Ambassador Taylor was somewhat taken aback by this development. During his recent visit to Washington, 28 March–5 April, he had felt that the President was exercising caution and restraint on the subject of possible troop deployments. But after President Johnson's 7 April speech at Johns Hopkins he had noticed that the cables from Washington indicated a strong desire to accelerate deployments. Taylor's response was twofold: he asked first that the decision to send a U.S. brigade to Bien Hoa or Vung Tau be held in abeyance and that the matter be brought up at the Honolulu Conference scheduled later in April; and second, in a separate message, he suggested the kind of instructions and rationale Washington should provide for him to present to the Vietnam government in order to further the new U.S. policy of actually seeking Free World ground combat forces.

Taylor reasoned that in spite of the evidence of U.S.-Vietnam success it had become increasingly clear that the U.S. objective of forcing the Democratic Republic of Vietnam to cease its support of the Viet Cong insurgency "cannot be attained in an acceptable time frame by the methods presently employed." The Joint Chiefs, therefore, after assessing the manpower situation and concluding that the Army of the Republic of Vietnam would have insufficient manpower to master the situation even with mobilization in the foreseeable future, believed that the equivalent of twenty new battalions was needed to prevent the war from dragging "into 1966 and beyond." The government of the United States had accepted the validity of this reasoning and offered to help the Vietnam government raise these forces, stated Taylor, "provided we can get a reasonable degree of participation from other third countries. If the GVN will make urgent representation to them, we believe, it will be entirely possible to obtain the following contributions: Korea, one regimental combat team; Australia, one infantry battalion; New Zealand, one battery and one company of tanks; Philippine Islands, one battalion." The United States would provide necessary logistic and combat support. Taylor concluded that such arguments would, when presented to the Vietnam government, give him the means of getting South Vietnam to resolve the question of Free World support.

The points raised by Taylor were resolved at the Honolulu Conference of 20 April 1965 at which time the deployment of one Australian battalion at Vung Tau and one Korean regimental combat team (three battalions) at Quang Ngai was approved. The instructions Taylor proposed as the basis for raising the issue of Free World forces were accepted verbatim. These instructions noted in closing that "you [Taylor] will seek the concurrence of the GVN to the foregoing program, recognizing that a large number of questions such as command relationships, concepts of employment and disposition of forces must be worked out subsequently."

The one revision of the Honolulu Conference decisions was to ask the Republic of Korea for a division and not a regimental combat team; it was expected in South Vietnam in mid-June.

The Honolulu Conference also introduced a general concept of operations by U.S. and allied ground combat forces in support of Republic of Vietnam Armed Forces. A number of assumptions undergirded the discussion: national forces would retain command identity; the United States would not place its forces under the operational control of the Vietnam armed forces as allied commanders, though the Republic of Vietnam might in a special case place its forces under U.S. operational control; and allied forces would accept operational control by U.S. commanders, and combat units would normally be placed under operational control of U.S. commanders at brigade level or higher. The mission of U.S. and allied forces was "to render advice and/or combat support to RVNAF."

General Westmoreland in early May set forth the "procedures and command relationship" involved in commitments of additional U.S. ground forces, and the underlying concept of an international military security task force first discussed in April. According to this concept allied forces were to be "brigaded" with U.S. forces under a U.S. commander and a combined staff. The U.S. brigade would be the nucleus of the international security force, which would be employed in a manner similar to that of a U.S. brigade. The mission of allied forces was set down in three stages. The first stage was base security; the second, after the bases were secure, was deep patrolling and offensive operations involving reconnaissance and moves against Viet Cong bases and areas; and the third was search missions for enemy units farther afield in co-ordination with Vietnam armed forces. The Commander, U.S. Military Assistance Command, Vietnam, would assume operational control of U.S. and allied forces upon their arrival in Vietnam. General Westmoreland reiterated that U.S. forces would not be placed under operational control or command of allied commanders.

The international security force concept *per se*, which envisioned a multinational force blocking infiltration through the demilitarized zone, and the attendant concept of brigading Free World and U.S. units were later dropped. Other countries and the Republic of Vietnam had shown little interest, there were many political problems, and, most significantly, the bulk of enemy infiltration skirted the demilitarized zone and came through Laos. The concept of a three-stage mission was retained.

Nonetheless, planning for command and control arrangements of Free World forces continued into May 1965. From June to October 1964 Free World activities had been handled by a small staff section within the Military Assistance Command, Vietnam—J–5, the Plans and Policy Directorate. As the scope of the Free World contributions, military and technical, grew, the need for a separate staff section just for Free World affairs became apparent. As a first step General Westmoreland in December 1964 had established the International Military Assistance Office under the staff supervision of the USMACV assistant chief of staff, J–5. In May 1965 after the decision to seek Free World combat forces had been taken, further plans were made to effect smooth-functioning command relationships. Generals Westmoreland and Minh, in discussing the subject of a combined staff, brought up earlier in April, envisaged this time a staff which would prepare studies, analysis, and guidance for U.S. and Vietnam field commands through the respective chains of command—a combined staff, not a combined headquarters. General Westmoreland felt it premature to propose creation of a combined co-ordinating staff. At the same time he appointed Brigadier General James L. Collins, Jr., as his special representative to the Vietnam Joint General Staff on all matters pertaining to the co-ordination of U.S., Vietnam, and other Free World forces operations. This was about as far as General Westmoreland was willing to go at the time on the matter of command arrangements.

Free World Troops in Vietnam, 1965–1966

In May 1965 Free World commitments began to be honored as other governments agreed officially to send troops and prepared to deploy them. The first to help with this expansion was the government of Australia. Australia agreed in May to send a task force to South Vietnam composed of Headquarters, Royal Australian Regiment, plus the 79th Signal Troop and a logistical support company. Arriving in South Vietnam during the early part of June, this contingent, attached to the U.S. 173d Airborne Brigade, operated from Bien Hoa. A military working arrangement had already been signed between the Commander, Australian Armed Forces, Vietnam, and General Westmoreland that provided for operational control of the Australian troops by the Commander, U.S. Military Assistance Command, Vietnam, and also for complete U.S. administrative and logistical support. In September a financial working arrangement was concluded that provided for the Australian government to repay the United

States for support on a reimbursable basis. At the end of September the Australians augmented their infantry battalion with a 105-mm. howitzer battery, a field engineer troop, and an air reconnaissance flight. With the addition of another signal troop, the year-end Australian strength in South Vietnam reached 1,557.

It was also in May 1965 that the government of New Zealand decided to replace its engineer detachment with a combat force and announced the decision to deploy a 105-mm. howitzer battery. The battery arrived in Vietnam on 21 July and was attached to the U.S. 173d Airborne Brigade. Its primary mission was to support the Australian battalion. Like the Australians, the New Zealanders were also under the operational control of General Westmoreland, with the United States providing administrative and logistical support on a reimbursable basis. At the end of 1965, 119 New Zealanders were fighting alongside their Australian comrades.

General Westmoreland's long-range goal was for the nations of Australia and New Zealand to deploy a full Australian–New Zealand Army Corps (ANZAC) brigade during the coming year. As a short-range objective, he hoped for the immediate deployment of an additional Australian battalion. This matter was still unresolved by the end of the year.

After the United States, the nation providing the greatest amount of assistance to South Vietnam in 1965 was the Republic of Korea. In January, after an official request, the Korean government deployed a task force consisting of an army engineer battalion with necessary support and self-defense troops for work in the field of civic action. The main party of this "Dove Unit," as it was called, arrived on 16 March and was based at Di An in Bien Hoa Province. The military working arrangement between General Westmoreland and the Korean commander, Major General Chae Myung-Shin, stated that the task force would function under the operating parameters established by the Free World Military Assistance Policy Council. The council consisted of the chief of staff of the U.S. Military Assistance Command, Vietnam, Major General Richard G. Stilwell (later replaced by the commander himself); the senior Korean commander; and the chief of the Joint General Staff, Brigadier General Cao Van Vien, who was the council chairman. The council provided operational guidance for, not control of, Free World forces. The working agreement also stated that the Korean unit would be responsive to the over-all commander in any given area.

In response to further requests by both the U.S. and Vietnam governments, the Korean government on 12 August approved deployment of an Army infantry division (understrength), one Marine Corps regiment, and one field support command composed of Army and Marine elements with normal support troops. Prior to their arrival in South Vietnam, a new Military Assistance Policy Council would continue to provide operational guidelines and the United States would furnish logistical support. The Republic of Korea Capital Infantry Division (understrength), and the Republic of Korea 2d Marine Brigade were completely deployed by early November of 1965 and given security duties at Cam Ranh Bay and Qui Nhon. Following discussions between the Korean commander and General Westmoreland, it was determined that the U.S. Commanding General, Field Forces, Vietnam, would have *de facto* operational control over the Korean forces, although orders would be phrased as requests. (Since the command and control arrangements for Korean units were unlike those for any other Free World troop contributors, they will be treated separately and in detail.) Korean troop strength was now raised to 20,620, with considerable discussion regarding further increases.

The Republic of the Philippines, Thailand, and the Republic of China also had given aid, but only in the form of noncombatants to act in either advisory or civic action roles. Throughout 1965 efforts were made to obtain additional Philippine representation, specifically a 2,000-man civic action group. As a result of domestic political problems, however, the Philippine government failed to make a decision on this matter.

At the end of 1965, a new drive was under way in Washington to encourage Free World nations to increase the amount of their aid or, in some cases, to begin aid to Vietnam. As a result of these efforts Free World contributions to South Vietnam increased significantly in 1966. Much of the aid resulted from negotiations and the urgings of the United States in the previous year. Only now did these efforts bear fruit. Most nations still preferred to provide civic action and medical assistance as opposed to active military assistance. Fear of adverse world public opinion specifically affected the decisions of the German Federal Republic and the Republic of China as to the kind of assistance offered or the kind that could be accepted. Germany was concerned with the possibility of renewed Soviet pressure on Berlin, while the entry of the Republic of China into Vietnam might bring about a Chinese Communist reaction in the Formosa Strait. India and Canada were also limited in the kind of assistance they could give because of their membership in the International Control Commission. The Republic of the Philippines and the Republic of Korea found their proposals meeting opposition from within their respective national legislative bodies. Some of this opposition was due to political instability in South Vietnam from March through June 1966. Countries were reluctant to send aid when the future of South Vietnam seemed uncertain and perilous.

While political bickering over the Vietnam issue occupied some elements of the Korean government, less publicized efforts were well under way to increase the number of Korean units in South Vietnam. On 8 January 1966 the U.S. Ambassador in Seoul was instructed by the Secretary of State to begin prompt negotiations to obtain a Korean regiment for deployment to South Vietnam by April, and a Korean division for deployment by July. These units were to be accompanied by the necessary combat support and combat service support elements.

During the course of the negotiations, three major points developed by the Korean government and agreed to by the United States were that Korean defense capability would not be jeopardized, that the expenses of deploying additional forces to South Vietnam would not constitute an excessive economic burden to the Korean people, and that the Republic of Korea would receive preferential treatment to maximize its economic benefits.

President Chung Hee Park of Korea on 29 January approved, subject to ratification by the Korean National Assembly, the South Vietnamese request for an additional Korean regiment and division. In response to this announcement the United States agreed to finance all additional costs and equip as necessary the extra forces deployed to South Vietnam; assume the costs of overseas allowances at the agreed upon scale; provide death and disability gratuities resulting from casualties; and equip, train, and finance the replacements for the forces deployed to South Vietnam. After several weeks of debate and behind-the-scenes political maneuvering, the Korean National Assembly passed the bill authorizing the dispatch of additional troops to South Vietnam.

On 17 February 1966, the Royal Thai Military Assistance Group, Vietnam, was activated, with the Thai Air Force contingent becoming a subordinate element of that group. In March a military working arrangement was signed between the U.S. Military Assistance Command, Vietnam, and the Royal Thai Military Assistance Group, Vietnam.

By March the Joint General Staff had developed a tentative Korean force structure and presented it to the Chief, Korean

Military Assistance Group. The major components of this force provided for one infantry division and one regiment, headquarters augmentation to the Republic of Korea Forces, Vietnam, logistical headquarters units, one engineer battalion, one evacuation hospital and associated medical units, ordnance direct support and ammunition units, quartermaster service, signal units, and transportation units—a total of 23,488 men.

More help was forthcoming when on 8 March the government of Australia announced it would increase its one-battalion force to a two-battalion task force with a headquarters, special air service squadron, armor, artillery, signal, supply and transport, field ambulance, and ordnance and shop units. Low key discussions had been under way since December 1965, but fear of criticism had prevented the subject from being made public. This commitment would raise the Australian troop strength to over 4,500.

Concurrently the MACV staff and an Australian joint services planning team were striving to develop new military working arrangements and a plan for the deployment of the task force. The agreement, signed on 17 March, confirmed the employment of the task force in Phuoc Tuy Province. The advance party for the 1st Australian Task force left for South Vietnam on 12 April, the main body following in several increments.

Soon after the action of Australia, the New Zealand government decided to increase modestly its contingent in South Vietnam. Despite Australian election year pressures, the artillery battery supporting the Australian forces was to be brought up to strength by adding two more 105-mm. howitzers and twenty-seven men. In addition, the surgical team at Qui Nhon was to be increased from seven to thirteen men.

In preparation for the influx of Free World forces, President Johnson signed into law on 25 March 1966 a Department of Defense supplemental appropriations bill which transferred the responsibility for Military Assistance Program funding from the Office of the Secretary of Defense to the various services in South Vietnam. The change in budgeting and funding had little or no impact on support procedures in Vietnam, but it did allow Free World Military Assistance Forces to be supported by corresponding U.S. services rather than through the normal Military Assistance Program channels. This was done for ease of planning and to provide some relief to the Vietnamese logistics system, which was having a difficult enough time in accomplishing the support mission for its own forces.

In early April the Joint Chiefs of Staff asked the Commander in Chief, Pacific, about the possibility of increased Free World assistance to South Vietnam. The basis of this inquiry was a Joint Chiefs study to determine what additional support would be useful and what support Free World nations could be expected to provide. It was hoped that shortfalls in certain types of U.S. units decided upon at the Honolulu Conference held earlier in the year could be filled by Free World nations. Several problem areas required co-ordination before a request to a nation could be made. The first consideration was a unit's ability to contribute favorably to the progress of the war, with immediate and noticeable effect. Other problem areas were command and control, security, areas of operation, linguistic barriers, special situations engendered by nationality, religious customs, degree of acceptability in South Vietnam, and the donor nation's ability to house air units. Finally, the Free World units should be operationally, logistically, and administratively within the means of support of the United States, South Vietnam, or the Free World country providing the assistance.

Headquarters, MACV, provided the Commander in Chief, Pacific, Admiral Sharp, with a list of units it believed the Free World Military Assistance Forces could realistically provide. The Army list consisted of varying numbers of infantry battalions; antiaircraft battalions; field artillery battalions; engineer construction companies, light equipment companies, port construction companies, dump truck companies, asphalt platoons, and miscellaneous engineer support detachments; medical evacuation units; petroleum depot units; transportation units; and tugboat crews. The Air Force pointed out a need for F-100, F-104, F-5, and B-57 squadrons; possibly Free World forces to man an F-5 squadron at Bien Hoa; light observation units and qualified men for use in forward air control; and air liaison officers and duty officers for command centers and transport squadrons or flights. It was recognized, however, that the introduction of additional air force units would require the construction of more facilities. The Navy pointed out a need for additional surface patrol craft for coastal operations, additional craft of the destroyer type for naval gunfire missions, more patrol aircraft, survey ships to meet the demands of hydrographic surveys, and logistics lift craft. In analyzing the list of Asian nations that might be able or willing to contribute, the Commander in Chief, Pacific, noted that Thailand and Malaysia were committed fully in their own particular areas. The Republic of Korea had provided all that could be expected, and further increases would not produce sufficient returns for the amount of U.S. investment required. Both Japan and the Republic of China were capable of supplying more assistance in all of the categories, but once again political considerations and fear of Chinese Communist escalation of the war limited their support.

It was also in April 1966 that the U.S. Mission in Saigon put in abeyance indefinitely the concept of inviting military observer teams from selected African countries to South Vietnam. These observers were to have been used to advise and assist in counterinsurgency warfare. The idea had been advanced as early as August 1965 but never got off the ground. Efforts to get other military observers to South Vietnam did continue, however. Both Greek and Dutch military officers showed interest, but the same could not be said for the Greek government. The U.S. Ambassador in Athens suggested that if one or more of the other North Atlantic Treaty Organization nations were to take the first step, the Greek government would probably follow suit. The government of the Netherlands appeared to favor the idea and as a result a joint invitation from Vietnam and the United States was sent to the Dutch Minister of Defense. However, the invitation to send Dutch military observers to Vietnam was never issued. In late September a group of observers from the Japanese Self-Defense Force visited South Vietnam and toured various installations. The visit was sponsored by the Japanese Embassy, and the U.S. Military Assistance Command, Vietnam, provided the transportation within Vietnam.

While the military situation seemed to be sorting itself out, the political turmoil in South Vietnam caused concern within the Korean government over the advisability of increasing the Korean commitment. Some influential government officials and segments of the press suggested that it might be wise to delay the deployment of additional troops until after the Vietnam elections. When the United States pointed out the adverse effect such a decision would have, the Korean Minister of Defense on 25 May reaffirmed the Korean commitment to South Vietnam.

Philippine assistance to Vietnam came closer to being a reality when the Philippine Vietnam aid bill was passed in June. Unexpected opposition to this measure and the election of a new president the previous November had all contributed to months of delay. In addition, the original plan of Diosdada Macapagal, the defeated candidate for president, who favored a combat force, was altered to provide a task force tailored to carry out a civic action mission. Consisting of an engineer construction battalion, medical and rural community development teams, a security battalion, a field artillery battery, and logistics and headquarters elements, the task force was to number 2,068 men and to carry the designation 1st Philippine Civic Action Group, Vietnam. It was not until mid-October 1966 that the last of these troops settled into their base camp on the outskirts of Tay Ninh City.

As the enemy threat grew, methods for utilizing Free World forces were considered. At the Mission Council meeting of 1 August 1966, General Westmoreland discussed the large-scale infiltration of the 324 B Division of the North Vietnam Army through the demilitarized zone and possible means to counter it. One was the formation of a multinational force to operate in the area south of the demilitarized zone. A brigade-size unit of Korean, Australian, New Zealand, and U.S. (KANZUS) troops, was conceived to support the 1st Vietnam Army Division. The brigade would be commanded by a U.S. Marine Corps general officer and would consist of two U.S. Marine battalions and one Korean infantry battalion; the headquarters would provide spaces for incorporating token contributions from Australia and New Zealand. The U.S. commander was to have operational control over the Vietnamese Army forces also, but this control was to be exercised under the guise of "operational co-ordination" to avoid offending the sensibilities of the Vietnamese. The principal value of this organization was that it would be an international force confronting the invasion from the north. General Westmoreland suggested also that the International Control Commission could place observers with the force. Since a unit of this type would be expected to co-operate closely with the commission, positions held by the force would be accessible for visits by the commission.

The Mission Council responded favorably to the concept and believed that if an international force could be developed and possibly could be deployed under the auspices of the International Control Commission that the U.S. position in the event of peace negotiations might be improved. The Joint Chiefs were requested to study the proposal and, if in agreement, to ask the U.S. government to approach the governments concerned to obtain their views and concurrence. The U.S. Ambassador to South Vietnam, Henry Cabot Lodge, pursued the same end with an identical message to the Secretary of State. All U.S. ambassadors to the nations consulted concurred in the project and were favorably impressed with the proposal.

On 21 August General Westmoreland requested that State and Defense Department approval of and guidance for the KANZUS project be speeded up. The stationing of any sizable force in northern Quang Tri Province would have to be accomplished by 1 October; otherwise the beginning of the northeast monsoon would seriously hinder base camp construction, establishment and stocking of supply points, upgrading of lines of communication, and other actions necessary for adequate logistical and administrative support. Also, only minimum time was available for the assembly and shakedown of elements of the force.

Other difficulties arose. Exception was taken to the name KANZUS as being necessarily restrictive to the nations participating and it was proposed that a name be devised that would signify broad participation in this international force. The ground rules for operations in the area of the demilitarized zone also had to be considered, and it was recommended that the force have the necessary authority to maneuver in the South Vietnamese portion of the zone.

As September ended it was apparent that the proposed KANZUS force was insufficient to meet the enemy threat in northern I Corps, which was now on the order of three divisions. To counter this multidivisional threat, which could be supported indefinitely from adjacent enemy havens, a force of greater strength and capability than KANZUS was required. A MACV study concluded that the concept of an international force was valid but recommended that implementation be delayed until after the monsoon season.

In early October 1966, General Westmoreland was asked to comment on the feasibility of employing the British Gurkha Brigade in South Vietnam. The Gurkhas, professional soldiers from Nepal, had been a part of the British Army since 1815. Excellent soldiers, they had established an outstanding reputation in every campaign in which they participated. Since World War II, the Gurkhas had been employed on the Malay Peninsula and Borneo and all but 500 of the 14,500 Gurkhas then on active duty were still in the area. Speculation that the Gurkhas would be phased out of British service was confirmed in discussions between the U.S. Army attaché in London and the Adjutant General of the British Army; the Adjutant General was unable to say when, except that the phase-out would commence within the year and could be completed within three years. Among other problems was whether it was desirable to employ the Gurkhas in South Vietnam. Gurkha units were formed and trained on the British system, and, above platoon level, were led by British officers. The Gurkha Brigade consisted of eight infantry battalions, one engineer battalion, one signal battalion, and other sup-

Table 1—STRENGTH OF FREE WORLD MILITARY ASSISTANCE FORCES
1964–1970

(Strength by Calendar Year)

Country	1964	1965	1966	1967	1968	1969	1970
Australia							
Strength	200	1,557	4,525	6,818	7,661	7,672	6,763
Number of maneuver battalions	----	1	2	2	3	3	3
Korea							
Strength	200	20,620	45,566	47,829	50,003	48,869	48,537
Number of maneuver battalions	----	10	22	22	22	22	22
Thailand							
Strength	0	16	244	2,205	6,005	11,568	11,586
Number of maneuver battalions	----	0	0	1	3	6	6
New Zealand							
Strength	30	119	155	534	516	552	441
The Philippines							
Strength	17	72	2,061	2,020	1,576	189	74
Republic of China							
Strength	20	20	23	31	29	29	31
Spain							
Strength	0	0	13	13	12	10	7
Total strength	467	22,404	52,566	59,450	65,802	68,889	67,444
Total maneuver battalions	0	11	24	25	28	31	31

port elements, all of which would have made a welcome addition to the allied effort. There were, however, several important factors to be considered in using Gurkha units in South Vietnam. Besides American antipathy toward the use of mercenaries, there was the possibility that the Gurkhas would be reluctant to serve under other than British leadership. Further, employing Gurkhas in South Vietnam could become the focal point of a new Communist propaganda compaign.

If the Gurkhas were made available, General Westmoreland's concept of employment was to use the brigade on operations similar to those it had been conducting. The principal advantage of having the brigade would be the addition of highly trained and disciplined troops, experienced in counterguerrilla operations. All questions, however, became moot when the United Kingdom decided not to phase out the Gurkha Brigade before 1969. At that time British defense policy and troop requirements beyond 1969 would be reviewed.

Loss of the Gurkha force was more than offset by another increase in Korean troops. The 9th Korean Division, brought in during the period from 5 September to 8 October, was placed in the Ninh Hoa area at the junction of Highways 1 and 21. Of the 9th Korean Division, known as the White Horse Division, the 28th Regiment was stationed in the Tuy Hoa area, the 29th Regiment on the mainland side to protect Cam Ranh Bay.

The contributions of the Free World Military Assistance Forces increased after the end of fiscal year 1965. The time of the greatest buildup was during fiscal year 1966, after which there was a leveling off period with a decrease in strength. (*Table 1*)

Beginning with the arrival by late 1966 of sizable Free World contingents, the story of the contribution of individual Free World countries can best be told on an individual case basis.

CHAPTER II
Thailand

The decision of Thailand to participate actively in the defense of Vietnam represented a departure from the country's traditional policy of nonintervention. At first this participation was minimal, but as the situation in South Vietnam worsened Thailand reappraised its role in Southeast Asian affairs.

Thailand's interest in increasing the size of its contribution to South Vietnam was in part a desire to assume a more responsible role in the active defense of Southeast Asia; it was also an opportunity to accelerate modernization of the Thai armed forces. Equally important, from the Thai point of view, was the domestic political gain from the visible deployment of a modern air defense system, and the international gain from a stronger voice at the peace table because of Thai participation on the battlefield. For the United States the increased force strength was desirable, but the real significance of the increase was that another Southeast Asian nation was accepting a larger role in the defense of South Vietnam. Some officials in Washington also believed that public acceptance of a further buildup of U.S. forces would be eased as a result of a Thai contribution. Secretary of Defense Robert S. McNamara was even more specific when he stated that from a political point of view a Thai contribution was almost mandatory.

How determined U.S. efforts were to increase Thai participation can be judged by a message to Thai Prime Minister Kittikachorn Thanom from President Johnson which said in part:

... In this situation I must express to you my own deep personal conviction that prospects of peace in Vietnam will be greatly increased in measure that necessary efforts of United States are supported and shared by other nations which share our purposes and our concerns. I am very much aware of and deeply appreciative of steady support you and your Government are providing. The role of your pilots and artillerymen in opposing Communist aggressors in Laos; arrangements for utilization of certain Thai bases by American air units; and ... steadfast statements which you have made in support of our effort in Southeast Asia are but most outstanding examples of what I have in mind. It is, nevertheless, my hope that Thailand will find ways of increasing the scale and scope of its assistance to Vietnam, as a renewed demonstration of Free World determination to work together to repel Communist aggression. It is, of course, for you to weigh and decide what it is practicable for you to do without undermining vital programs designed to thwart Communist designs on Thailand itself. . . .

Beginnings of Thai Assistance

The first contribution to the Vietnam War effort by Thailand was made on 29 September 1964, when a sixteen-man Royal Thai Air Force contingent arrived in Vietnam to assist in flying and maintaining some of the cargo aircraft operated by the South Vietnamese Air Force. As an adjunct to this program, the Royal Thai Air Force also provided jet aircraft transition training to Vietnamese pilots.

The status of this early mission changed little until the Royal Thai Military Assistance Group, Vietnam, was activated on 17 February 1966 and a Thai Air Force lieutenant colonel was designated as commander. The Royal Thai Air Force contingent then became a subordinate element of the Royal Thai Military Assistance Group, Vietnam.

In March the commander of the Thai contingent asked the U.S. Military Assistance Command to furnish one T-33 jet trainer from its assets to be used for jet transition training previously given South Vietnamese pilots in Thailand. This training program had been suspended the preceding month because of a shortage of T-33's in the Royal Thai Air Force. The Thais had also requested two C-123 aircraft with Royal Thai Air Force markings to allow the Thai contingent to function as an integral unit and to show the Thai flag more prominently in South Vietnam. General Westmoreland replied that jet transition training for Vietnamese pilots was proceeding satisfactorily and that a T-33 could not be spared from MACV resources. He suggested that the aircraft be procured through the Military Assistance Program in Thailand. However, MACV did grant the request for C-123's; the commander of the Pacific Air Force was asked to provide the aircraft. The commander stated that C-123 aircraft were not available from the United States and recommended bringing Thai pilots to South Vietnam to fly two C-123's owned and maintained by the United States but carrying Thai markings. Arrangements were made to have these pilots in Vietnam not later than 15 July, assuming the Thai crew members could meet the minimum proficiency standards by that time. The crews, consisting of twenty-one men, became operational on 22 July 1966 and were attached to the U.S. 315th Air Commando Wing for C−123 operations. Five men remained with the Vietnamese Air Force, where they were assigned to fly C−47 aircraft. The Royal Thai Air Force strength in South Vietnam was now twenty-seven.

On 30 December 1966 four newspapers in Bangkok carried front page stories saying that the Thai government was considering the deployment of a battalion combat team of 700 to 800 men to South Vietnam. A favorable response had been expected from the Thai people, but the reality far exceeded the expectation. In Bangkok alone, more than 5,000 men volunteered, including some twenty Buddhist monks and the prime minister's son. One 31-year-old monk, when asked why he was volunteering for military duty, said: "The communists are nearing our home. I have to give up my yellow robe to fight them. In that way I serve both my country and my religion."

On the morning of 3 January 1967 the Thai government made official a speculation that had appeared in the press several days earlier; it announced that a reinforced Thai battalion would be sent to fight in South Vietnam. The following reasons for this decision were given:

Thailand is situated near Vietnam and it will be the next target of communists, as they have already proclaimed. This is why Thailand realizes the necessity to send Military units to help oppose communist aggression when it is still at a distance from our country. The government has therefore decided to send a combat unit, one battalion strong, to take an active part in the fighting in South Vietnam in the near future.

This combat unit, which will be composed of nearly 1,000 men, including infantry, heavy artillery, armored cars, and a quartermaster unit will be able to take part in the fighting independently with no need to depend on any other supporting units.

This decision can be said to show far-sightedness in a calm and thorough manner, and it is based on proper military principles. The time has come when we Thais must awake and take action to oppose aggression when it is still at a distance from our country. This being a practical way to reduce danger to the minimum, and to extinguish a fire that has already broken out before it reaches our home. Or it could be said to be the closing of sluice-gates to prevent the water from pouring out in torrents, torrents of red waves that would completely innundate our whole country.

Opposing aggression when it is still at a distance is a practical measure to prevent our own country being turned into a battlefield. It will protect our home from total destruction, and safeguard our crops from any danger threatening. Our people will be able to continue enjoying normal peace and happiness in their daily life with no fear of any hardships, because the battlefield is still far away from our country.

Should we wait until the aggressors reach the gates of our homeland before we take any measures to oppose them, it would be no different from waiting for a conflagration to spread and reach our house, not taking any action to help put it out. That is why we must take action to help put out this conflagration, even being willing to run any risk to stave off disaster. We must not risk the lives of our people, including babies, or run the risk of having to evacuate them from their homes, causing untold hardship to all the people, everywhere. Food will be scarce and very high-priced.

It is therefore most proper and suitable in every way for us to send combat forces to fight shoulder-to-shoulder with other countries in opposition to aggression, especially at a time when that aggression is still far away from our country. This is a decision reached that is most proper and suitable, when considered from a military, a political and an economic angle.

This decision led to a number of problems for the United States. The first was the amount of logistical support to be given Thailand. The United States assumed that the Thai unit would resemble the one proposed, that is, a group of about 1,000 men, organized into infantry, artillery, armored car, and quartermaster elements, and able to fight independently of other supporting forces. Assurances had been given to the Thai Prime Minister that support for the force would be in addition to support for the Thai forces in Thailand, and would be similar to that given the Thai forces already in South Vietnam. These assurances were an essential part of the Thai decision to deploy additional troops. Thus the Department of Defense authorized service funding support for equipment and facilities used by Thai units in South Vietnam, and for overseas allowances, within the guidelines established for support of the Koreans. Death gratuities were payable by the United States and no undue economic burden was to be imposed on the contributing nation.

With the Thai troop proposal now in motion, the Commander in Chief, Pacific, felt that U.S. Military Assistance Command, Vietnam, and U.S. Military Assistance Command, Thailand, should begin discussions on organization, training, equipment, and other support problems pertaining to the deployment of the Thai unit. The U.S. Embassy in Bangkok, however, was of a different mind. The ambassador pointed out that General Westmoreland had asked for a regimental combat team. This request had been seconded by the Commander in Chief, Pacific, the Secretary of State, and the Secretary of Defense. The ambassador said he still hoped to obtain a regimental-size unit but did not believe negotiations had reached the stage where detailed discussions as suggested by the Commander in Chief, Pacific, should be undertaken.

In the meantime representatives of the Vietnam and the Thai military assistance commands met and held discussions during the period 27-30 January 1967 on various aspects of the pending deployment. In February the commitment of Thai troops was affirmed and on 13 March the unit began training. The Thai contingent would eventually be located with and under the operational control of the 9th U.S. Infantry Division. On 15 March representatives of the Royal Thai Army and U.S. Military Assistance Command, Thailand, met with the MACV staff to finalize the unit's tables of organization and equipment and allowances. Discussions were held also on training, equipage, and deployment matters. The approved table of organization and equipment provided for a regimental combat team (minus certain elements) with a strength of 3,307, a 5 percent overstrength. The staff of the regimental combat team, with its augmentation, was capable of conducting field operations and of securing a base camp. Organizationally, the unit consisted of a headquarters company with a communications platoon, an aviation platoon, an M113 platoon, a psychological operations platoon, a heavy weapons platoon with a machine gun section, and a four-tube 81-mm. mortar section; a service company consisting of a personnel and special services platoon and supply and transport, maintenance, and military police platoons; four rifle companies; a reinforced engineer combat company; a medical company; a cavalry reconnaissance troop of two reconnaissance platoons and an M113 platoon; and a six-tube 105-mm. howitzer battery. On 18 March the approved table of organization and equipment was signed by representatives of MACV and the Royal Thai Army.

During the above discussions, the Royal Thai Army agreed to equip one of the two authorized M113 platoons with sixteen of the Thai Army's own armored personnel carriers (APC's) provided by the Military Assistance Program; the United States would furnish APC's for the remaining platoon. This was necessary because all APC's scheduled through the fourth quarter of fiscal year 1967 were programed to replace battle losses and fill the cyclic rebuild program for U.S. forces. Subsequently, however, the Royal Thai Army re-evaluated its earlier proposal and decided to deploy only the platoon from headquarters company, which was to be equipped with APC's furnished from U.S. project stocks. The platoon of APC's in the reconnaissance troop would not be deployed with Thai-owned APC's. The Royal Thai Army was agreeable to activating the platoon and using sixteen of its APC's for training, but insisted on picking up sixteen APC's to be supplied upon the platoon's arrival in South Vietnam. If this was not possible, the Thais did not plan to activate the reconnaissance platoon until the United States made a firm commitment on the availability of the equipment. In view of this circumstance, MACV recommended that an additional sixteen M113's be released from project stocks for training and subsequent deployment with the regiment.

Thai naval assistance was also sought. In the latter part of May, MACV decided that the South Vietnamese Navy would be unable to utilize effectively the motor gunboat (PGM) 107 scheduled for completion in July. It was then recommended that the boat be diverted to the Royal Thai Navy and used as a Free World contribution. The Military Assistance Command, Thailand, objected, however, and preferred that the boat be transferred to the Thai Navy under the Military Assistance Program as a requirement for a later year. Since the Thai Navy was already operating two ships in South Vietnam, a request by the United States to operate a third might be considered inappropriate, particularly in view of the personnel problems confronting the Thais, and the ever-present insurgency threat facing Thailand from the sea. Since Thailand wanted to improve its Navy, the Thais saw no advantage in manning a ship that was not their own. In addition, the U.S. Navy advisory group in Thailand had been continuously stressing the need for modernization of the Thai Navy. To suggest that the Thais contribute another Free World ship would appear contradictory. A more acceptable approach, the U.S. Navy group reasoned, would be to offer the PGM–107 as a grant in aid of a future year, and then request Thai assistance in the coastal effort, known as MARKET TIME, by relieving the other PGM when it was due for maintenance and crew rotation in Thailand. This approach would give additional Royal Thai Navy crews training in coastal warfare, increase the prestige of the Thai Navy, and meet the continuing need for a Thai presence in South Vietnam. Overtures to the Thai government confirmed the validity of the Navy group's reasoning. The Thais did not wish to man the new PGM–107 as an additional Free World contribution.

Equipment problems were not limited to APC's and PGM's. The original plan of the Joint Chiefs of Staff for allocation of the M16 rifle for the period November 1966 through June 1967 provided 4,000 rifles for the Thais. A phased delivery of 1,000 weapons monthly was to begin in March. In February 1967, however, the Commander in Chief, Pacific, deferred further issue of the M16 rifle to other than U.S. units. Complicating this decision was the fact that the Military Assistance Command, Thailand, had already informed the Royal Thai Army of the original delivery date. Plans had been made to arm the Royal

Thai Army Volunteer Regiment with the first weapons received, which would have permitted training before deployment. An acceptable alternative would have been to issue M16's to the Thai regiment after it deployed to South Vietnam, had any weapons been available in Thailand for training; but all M16 rifles in Thailand were in the hands of infantry and special forces elements already engaged with the insurgents in northeast Thailand. Failure to provide the rifles any later than April would, in the view of the commander of the Thai Military Assistance Command, have repercussions. Aware also of the sensitivity of the Koreans, who were being equipped after other Free World forces, the commander recommended that 900 of the M16's be authorized to equip the Thai regiment and to support its predeployment training. The Commander in Chief, Pacific, concurred and recommended to the Joint Chiefs that the 900 rifles be provided from the March production. Even with the special issue of M16's, it was still necessary to make available another weapon to round out the issue. The logical choice was the M14, and as a result 900 M14's with spare parts were requested; two factors, however, dictated against this choice. The first was the demand for this weapon to support the training base in the continental United States, and the second was the fact that the Koreans were equipped with M1's. Issuing M14's to the Thais might have political consequences. As a compromise the Thais were issued the M2 carbine.

The liaison arrangements and groundwork for deployment of the Thai unit were completed in July. Following a liaison visit by members of the 9th U.S. Infantry Division, the Royal Thai Army Volunteer Regiment was invited to send liaison men and observers to the 9th Division. As part of the training program in preparation for the scheduled September deployment, five groups of key men from the Thai regiment visited the 9th Infantry Division between 6 and 21 July 1967. Numbering between thirty-four and thirty-eight men, each group was composed of squad leaders, platoon sergeants, platoon leaders, company executive officers, company commanders, and selected staff officers. Each group stayed six days while the men worked with and observed their counterparts. During the period 12 to 14 July, the commander of the Royal Thai Army Volunteer Regiment, accompanied by three staff officers, visited the 9th U.S. Division headquarters.

Debate over the date of deployment of Thai troops to Vietnam arose when on 5 July the Thai government announced a plan to commit the Royal Thai Army Volunteer Regiment against the Communist insurgents in northeast Thailand. The purpose of this move was to build up the regiment's morale and give it combat experience before it went to South Vietnam. At MACV headquarters the plan was viewed with disfavor for several reasons. An operation in northeast Thailand would delay deployment of the regiment in Vietnam from one week to two months. The additional use of the equipment would increase the probability that replacement or extensive maintenance would be necessary prior to deployment. Further, the bulk of the equipment programed for the Thai regiment had been taken from contingency stocks, thus giving the Thais priority over other Free World forces, and in some instances over U.S. forces, in order to insure early deployment of the regiment. The Thai regiment was dependent, moreover, on the 9th Division for logistical support; therefore supplies and equipment scheduled to arrive after 15 August had been ordered to Bearcat where the 9th Division was providing storage and security. Delay in the arrival of the Thai regiment would only further complicate problems attendant in the existing arrangements. Finally, several operations had been planned around the Thai unit and delay would cause cancellation, rescheduling, and extensive replanning. Logistical, training, and operational requirements in South Vietnam had been planned in great detail to accommodate the Thai force on the agreed deployment dates, and any delay in that deployment would result in a waste of efforts and resources.

The weight of these arguments apparently had its effect, for on 27 July the Military Assistance Command, Thailand, reported that the Thai government had canceled its plans to deploy the regiment to the northeastern part of the country.

The deployment of the Royal Thai Army Volunteer Regiment (the Queen's Cobras) to South Vietnam was divided into four phases. Acting as the regiment's quartering party, the engineer company left Bangkok by Royal Thai Navy LST on 11 July 1967 and arrived at Newport Army Terminal on 15 July. After unloading its equipment the company traveled by convoy to Bearcat, where it began work on the base camp. The advance party traveled by air to Bearcat on 20 August. The main body of the Queen's Cobras Regiment arrived during the period 19–23 September 1967. The last unit to reach Vietnam was the APC platoon, which had completed its training on 25 September and was airlifted to South Vietnam on 28 November.

Following a series of small unilateral and larger combined operations with Vietnamese units, the Thai regiment launched Operation NARASUAN in October 1967. In this, their first large-

SOLDIER'S OF THE QUEEN'S COBRAS *conduct a search and sweep mission in Phuoc Tho, November 1967.*

scale separate operation, the Thai troops assisted in the pacification of the Nhon Trach District of Bien Hoa Province and killed 145 of the enemy. The Thai soldier was found to be a resourceful and determined fighting man who displayed a great deal of pride in his profession. In addition to participating in combat operations, the Thai units were especially active in civic action projects within their area of responsibility. During Operation NARASUAN the Thais built a hospital, constructed 48 kilometers of new roads, and treated nearly 49,000 civilian patients through their medical units.

Even before all elements of the Royal Thai Volunteer Regiment had arrived in Vietnam, efforts were being made to increase again the size of the Thai contribution. By mid-1967 the Thai government had unilaterally begun consideration of the deployment of additional forces to South Vietnam. On 8 September the Thai government submitted a request for extensive military assistance to the American Embassy at Bangkok. Specific items in the request were related directly to the provision of an additional army force for South Vietnam. The Thai Prime Minister proposed a one-brigade group at a strength of 10,800 men. This organization was to be composed of three infantry battalions, one artillery battalion, one engineer battalion, and other supporting units as required.

In an apparently related move, meanwhile, the chairman of the Joint Chiefs had requested the Joint General Staff to assess the Thai military situation. This assessment was to include a review of the security situation in Thailand, the military organization, and the ability of the Thais to send additional troops to South Vietnam. In turn the Joint General Staff asked for the views of the U.S. Military Assistance Command, Thailand, not later than 20 September 1967 concerning Thai capability. The Joint Staff wished to know how long it would take the Thai government to provide the following troop levels, including necessary supporting troops, to Vietnam: 5,000 troops (approximately two infantry battalions, reinforced); 15,000 troops (approximately four infantry battalions, reinforced); 20,000 or more troops (approximately eight infantry battalions, reinforced, or more). The staff also wanted to know the effect that furnishing troops at each level would have on Thai internal security.

The commander of the U.S. Military Assistance Command, Thailand, Major General Hal D. McCown, concluded that the Royal Thai Army could provide a 5,000-man force without incurring an unacceptable risk to Thailand's internal security. He also believed it possible for Thailand to deploy a 10,000-man (two-brigade) force, but the organization, training, and deployment had to be incremental to allow the Royal Thai Army to recover from the deployment of one brigade. In addition, he held that it was impractical to attempt to raise a force of 15,000 or larger because of the probable attrition of the training base. In forming the Royal Thai Army Volunteer Regiment, the Thai Army had drawn 97 percent of its men from existing units, despite the talk of maximizing the use of volunteers. There was every indication that it would follow the same pattern in providing additional forces to South Vietnam. Such a draw-down by the Royal Thai Army of its limited number of trained men was acceptable for a force of 5,000 and marginally acceptable for 10,000, but unacceptable for a force greater than 10,000.

With these comments as a basis, Admiral Sharp went back to the Joint Chiefs with his recommendation, which stated:

> Present negotiations with the Thais have centered around a deployment of a total 10,000 man force. CINCPAC concurs that this is probably the largest force the Thais could provide without incurring an unacceptable sacrifice in the trained base of the Thai Army and accepting more than undue risk insofar as the Thais' ability to effectively counter the present insurgency.

Concurrently, General Westmoreland was being queried on the ability of the United States to support the various troop levels under consideration. In making this appraisal he assumed that MACV would have to provide maintenance support for all new equipment not in the Thai Army inventory and all backup support above division and brigade level, including direct support units. Other maintenance requirements, such as organic support, including supply distribution, transportation, and service functions, the Thais would handle. In considering the various force levels he envisioned a brigade-size force (5,000 men) that would be attached to a U.S. division for support. As such, the support command of the parent U.S. division would require a minimum augmentation of 50 men to provide for the additional maintenance requirements. Attaching a force of 10,000 men or more to a U.S. division would be impractical. A U.S. support battalion—approximately 600 men, including a headquarters company, a maintenance and support company, a reinforced medical company, and a transportation truck company— would be required for direct support of a Thai force of that size. A Thai force of 15,000 to 20,000 would also need a special support command, including a headquarters company, a medical company, a supply and transport company, and a division maintenance battalion. The estimated strength of this command would be

1,000 to 1,200 men, requiring an increase in general support troops.

At that time there were no U.S. combat service support units available in Vietnam to meet such requirements. Alternate methods for obtaining additional support units were to readjust forces within approved force ceilings, to increase civilian substitution in military spaces, or to increase the U.S. force ceiling. Any attempt to provide logistical support for the Thai forces within the existing troop ceiling would have to be at the expense of U.S. combat troops. Thus, General Westmoreland considered an increase in the U.S. force ceiling the only practical course of action.

In response to a request by Major General Hirunsiri Cholard, Director of Operations, Royal Thai Army, and with the backing of the American Ambassador in Bangkok, Graham Martin, bilateral discussions began on 3 November 1967 concerning the organization for the Thai add-on force. General Westmoreland gave the following guidance. The missions assigned to the force would be the same type as the missions being assigned to the Royal Thai Army Volunteer Regiment. The area of employment would be generally the same. Reconnaissance elements should be heavy on long-range reconnaissance patrolling. Because of terrain limitations the units should not have tanks. Armored personnel carriers should be limited to the number required to lift the rifle elements of four rifle companies and should not exceed forty-eight. The use of organic medium artillery should be considered; 4.2-inch mortars are not recommended. An organic signal company should be included. The force should consist of at least six battalions of infantry with four companies each. There should be no organic airmobile companies; support will be provided by U.S. aviation units. There should be one engineer company per brigade.

General Westmoreland's interest in whether the force would be two separate brigades or a single force was also brought up in the discussion that followed. On this point General Cholard replied that the guidance from his superiors was emphatic—the force should be a single self-sufficient force with one commander.

The U.S. Ambassador to Thailand, Mr. Martin, established additional guidelines. On 9 November 1967 he advised the Thai government by letter of the action the U.S. government was prepared to take to assist in the deployment of additional Thai troops to South Vietnam and to improve the capability of the Royal Thai armed forces in Thailand. In substance the United States agreed to

Fully equip and provide logistical support for the forces going to South Vietnam. The equipment would be retained by the Royal Thai government upon final withdrawal of Thai forces from South Vietnam.

Assume the cost of overseas allowance at the rates now paid by the U.S. government to the Royal Thai Army Volunteer Regiment in South Vietnam.

Provide equipment and consumables for rotational training in an amount sufficient to meet the agreed requirements of forces in training for deployment; and undertake the repair and rehabilitation of facilities required for such rotational training. The equipment would be retained by the Royal Thai government following the final withdrawal of Thai forces from South Vietnam.

Assume additional costs associated with the preparation, training, maintenance, equipment transportation, supply and mustering out of the additional forces to be sent to South Vietnam.

Assist in maintaining the capability and in accelerating the modernization of the Royal Thai armed forces—including the additional helicopters and other key items—as well as increase to $75 million both the Military Assistance Program for fiscal year 1968 and the program planning for 1969.

Deploy to Thailand a Hawk battery manned by U.S. personnel to participate in the training of Thai troops to man the battery. Provide the Thai government with equipment for the battery and assume certain costs associated with the battery's deployment.

Further discussion between U.S. Military Assistance Command representatives of Vietnam and Thailand set a force size between 10,598 and 12,200 for consideration. As a result of suggestions from the commander of the U.S. Military Assistance Command, Thailand, General McCown, and General Westmoreland, the Thai representatives began to refer to the add-on force as a division. The Royal Thai Army asked for the following revisions to the U.S. concept for the organization of the division: add a division artillery headquarters; revise the reconnaissance squadron to consist of three platoons of mechanized troops and one long-range reconnaissance platoon (the U.S. concept was one mechanized troop and two reconnaissance platoons); add one antiaircraft battalion with eighteen M42's, organized for a ground security role; add a separate replacement company, which would carry the 5 percent overstrength of the division; upgrade the medical unit from a company to a battalion; and upgrade the support unit from a battalion to a group.

The last two requests were designed to upgrade ranks. General Westmoreland had two exceptions to the proposed revisions: first, three mechanized troops were acceptable but the total number of APC's should not exceed forty-eight; and second,

MACV would provide the antiaircraft ground security support through each field force. The M42's would not be authorized.

As the conference in Bangkok continued, general agreement was reached on the training and deployment of the Thai division. The first of two increments would comprise 59 percent of the division and consist of one brigade headquarters, three infantry battalions, the engineer battalion minus one company, the reconnaissance squadron minus one mechanized troop, division artillery headquarters, one 105-mm. howitzer battalion, one 155-mm. howitzer battery, and necessary support, including a slice of division headquarters. The cadre training was tentatively scheduled to begin on 22 January 1968 with deployment to begin on 15 July 1968. The second increment would then consist of the second brigade headquarters, three infantry battalions, one engineer company, one mechanized troop, the second 105-mm. howitzer battalion, the 155-mm. howitzer battalion minus one battery, and necessary support, including the remainder of the division headquarters. Assuming the dates for the first increment held true, the second increment would begin training on 5 August 1968 and deploy on 27 January 1969.

Work continued on the new Thai force structure and another goal was met when a briefing team from U.S. Military Assistance Command, Thailand, presented on 28 November 1967 the proposed Thai augmentation force and advisory requirements to General Creighton B. Abrams, then Deputy Commander, U.S. Military Assistance Command, Vietnam. The basic organization was approved and representatives from both MACV and U.S. Army, Vietnam, returned to Thailand with the briefing team to assist in developing the new tables of organization and equipment and allowances. Concurrently, action was taken to initiate funding for table of organization and construction needs in order to meet the training and deployment dates agreed upon earlier. The final tables for the Royal Thai Army Volunteer Force (the Black Panther Division) were approved on 10 January 1968. The force totaled 11,266 men, including a 5 percent overstrength. (*Chart 1*)

For the final stages of the Thai training, Military Assistance Command, Thailand, proposed that Military Assistance Command, Vietnam, provide 120 advisers. These advisers would deploy with the Royal Thai Army Volunteer Force and the majority would remain with the Thai units while the units were in South Vietnam. General Abrams questioned the size of the requirement and it was subsequently reduced to 81, with 48 needed for the first increment. These 48 advisers were deployed in May 1968.

CHART 1—ORGANIZATION OF ROYAL THAI ARMY VOLUNTEER FORCE
25 JANUARY 1968

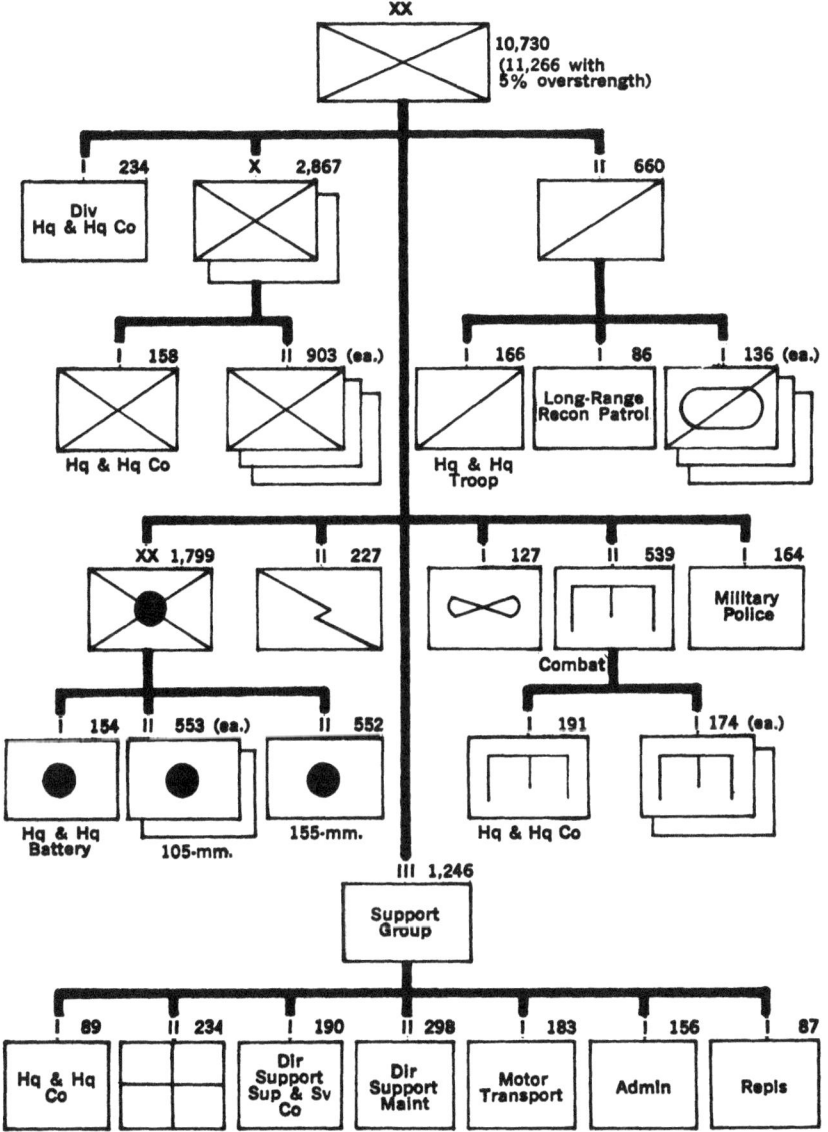

Both the U.S. and Thai governments were anxious to speed up the deployment of additional Thai forces to South Vietnam. In this regard, the State Department queried the American Ambassador in Bangkok on the possibility of the Thais' augmenting some exisiting battalions and sending them to South Vietnam early in 1968 under the command of the Royal Thai Army Volunteer Regiment. As a parallel example, the State Department pointed out that the United States was expediting the deployment of infantry forces to the level of 525,000, and in some cases units were having to complete their final training in South Vietnam.

General Westmoreland did not concur with the concept of expediting the Thai augmentation forces to the point of curtailing their training. He believed that forces deployed to South Vietnam should be equipped and ready to accomplish unit missions upon arrival in their area of operations. Although an exception had been made in the case of certain U.S. units, General Westmoreland did not agree in the case of Free World Military Assistance Forces units. He held it essential that, with the exception of limited orientation in Vietnam, Free World units be fully trained prior to deployment. Lacking full training, it would be necessary to divert troops from essential missions until the Free World troops were operational. The threat of a successful enemy attack on partially trained troops and the resultant adverse political consequences for the Free World effort had to be kept in mind.

For different but equally important reasons, the American Ambassador in Bangkok and the Military Assistance Command, Thailand, also viewed the State Department proposal with disfavor. The ambassador pointed out that the Thais were interested in an early deployment as shown by the one-month adjustment in deployment dates, but the suggestion of augmented battalions was impractical. The Thai government had repeatedly announced that the formation of the volunteer division would not detract from Thailand's ability to deal with internal security problems, and that the volunteer division would be a new and additional Army unit. Deploying an existing battalion would not be in accordance with the firm internal security commitment the Thai government had made to the Thai nation.

The Military Assistance Command, Thailand, also opposed early deployment, believing that the early deployment of one infantry battalion would have a serious impact on the activation, training, and deployment of the division. One of the most difficult problems to be faced in forming the division would be the provision of trained cadre and specialists. To drain the Royal Thai Army of some 900 trained infantrymen at the same time the volunteer division was being formed would seriously handicap the division.

Nonetheless, the idea of hastening deployment persisted. In view of the high-level interest in accelerating the deployment of the Thai forces to South Vietnam, General Westmoreland suggested that an initial infantry battalion might be deployed six weeks early in accordance with the following concept: select the "best" of the three battalions being trained in the first increment of the Royal Thai Army Division, and send it to Bearcat upon completion of its company training. When it arrives at Bearcat, attach it to the Royal Thai Army Volunteer Regiment, which will partially stand down from active combat. The Thai regiment will be given the mission of completing the battalion phase of the unit's training. Other parts of the training will be completed after the arrival of the complete increment. This concept assumes that the battalion will be equipped and trained in accordance with the planned schedule and that the proposal will be acceptable to the Thai government. If this concept is approved, the deployment of the battalion could be accelerated by about six weeks, and would take place around 3 June 1968. The recommendation was not accepted and the schedule remained as planned.

The question of U.S. support troops for the Thais was further discussed. The U.S. Military Assistance Command, Vietnam, and the U.S. Army, Vietnam, both opposed the idea of supplying U.S. troops to assist in the training of the Royal Thai Army Volunteer Force; the United States was already committed to provide all required support for the activation, training, and deployment of the Thai force. Besides, the Thai Military Assistance Command had even identified certain additional forces required on a permanent basis to support this commitment. Admiral Sharp had concurred with the idea of additional forces and forwarded it to the Joint Chiefs. The Department of the Army had then proposed that the additional forces be provided by the U.S. Army, Vietnam, force structure to meet the required dates of January and March 1968. The Department of the Army would then replace these forces beginning in September 1968 from the training base of the continental United States. The Joint Chiefs requested Admiral Sharp's views on the Department of the Army proposal and Admiral Sharp in turn queried General Westmoreland. General Westmoreland replied that U.S. Army, Vietnam, was unable to provide the required spaces either on a temporary or permanent basis and that furthermore the requirement had to be filled from other than MACV assets. U.S. Army, Pacific, made a counterproposal, concurred in by Department of the Army, which asked U.S. Army, Vietnam, for 335 of the 776 men required. The remaining spaces would be filled from U.S. Army, Pacific, resources outside of South Vietnam or from the continental United States. Admiral Sharp recommended adoption of the counterproposal and the Joint Chiefs of Staff issued instructions to implement the plan.

In conjunction with the deployment of the Thai volunteers, in April 1968 the Thai supreme command proposed an increase in the size of the Thai headquarters in South Vietnam from 35 to 228 men. There were several reasons for this request: the primary one was the requirement to administer a larger force. (*Chart 2*) The supreme command also wished to change the functioning of the Royal Thai Forces, Vietnam, from a headquarters designed to perform limited liaison to one conceived along conventional J-staff lines. The proposed organization, developed from experience and from recommendations from the Vietnam headquarters, would correct shortcomings in many areas such as security, public information, and legal and medical affairs. General Westmoreland, while agreeing in principle, still had to determine if the Military Assistance Command, Thailand, approved of the planned increase and whether the approval of the increase by the American Embassy at Bangkok and the U.S. government was necessary. The Thailand command and the embassy both concurred in the planned headquarters increase, but the diplomatic mission in Thailand did not have the authority to approve the augmentation. Military Assistance Command, Thailand, recommended to Admiral Sharp that General Westmoreland be provided with the authorization to approve a proposed table of distribution and allowances for the enlarged Thai headquarters. This authorization was given and the applicable tables were approved on 19 June 1968. The deployment of the new headquarters began with the arrival of the advance party on 1 July 1968 and was completed on 15 July.

Thai troops quickly followed. The first increment of the Thai division known as the Black Panther Division (5,700 men) arrived in South Vietnam in late July 1968 and was deployed in the Bearcat area. The second increment of 5,704 men began deployment in January 1969 and completed the move on 25 February. This increment contained the division headquarters and headquarters company (rear), the 2d Infantry Brigade of three infantry battalions, two artillery battalions, and the remainder of the

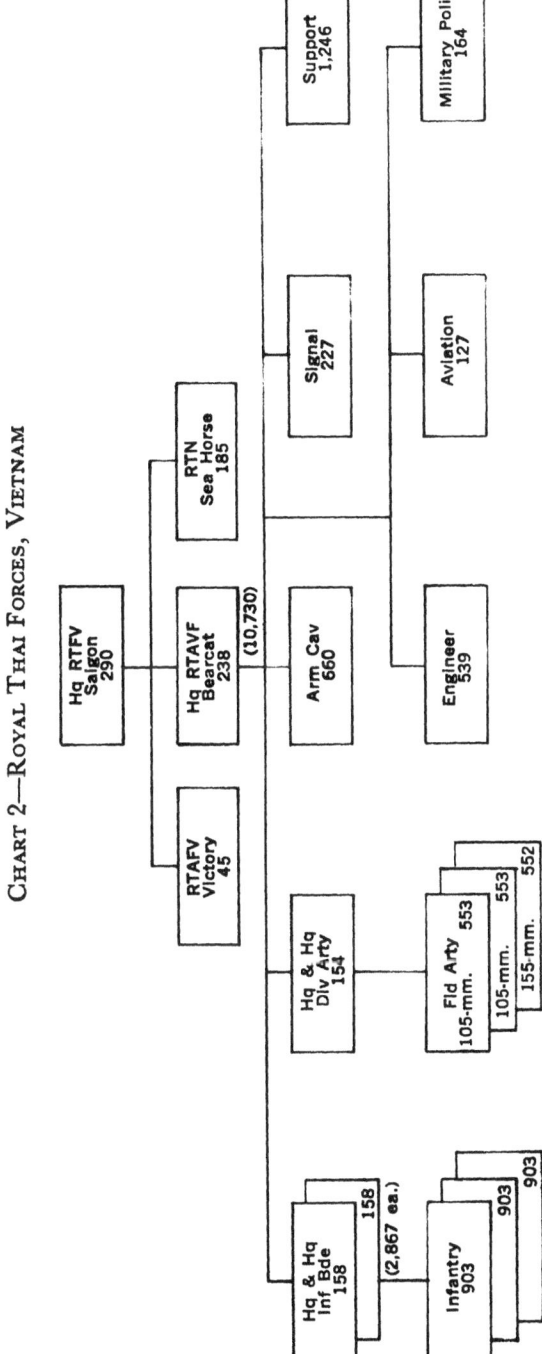

CHART 2—ROYAL THAI FORCES, VIETNAM

Troops of Royal Thai Black Panther Division *dock at Newport, Vietnam, July 1968, above. Royal Thai flag is carried down gangplank of USS Okinagon, below.*

division combat, combat support, and combat service support elements. The division was under the operational control of the Commanding General, II Field Force, Vietnam.

The third increment of the Royal Thai Volunteer Force was deployed to South Vietnam during July and August to replace the first increment, which returned to Thailand. The last of the third increment closed into Bearcat on 12 August 1969. The replacement brigade assumed the designation of 1st Brigade. In addition, the headquarters of the Royal Thai Army Volunteer Force completed its annual rotation. Throughout all of this there was little, if any, loss of momentum in the conduct of field operations. (*Map 1*)

Thai Operations

The area of operations assigned to the Thais was characterized by a low level of enemy action because the land was used by the Viet Cong primarily as a source of food and clothing. Moving constantly and constructing new base camps, the enemy had little time for offensive action. As a result, enemy operations conducted in the Thai area of interest were not as significant as

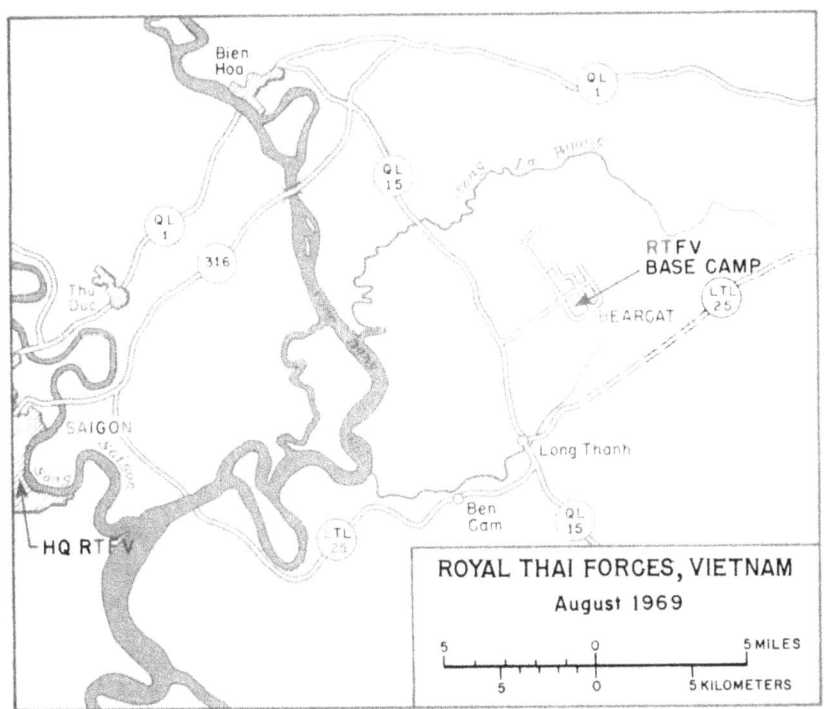

MAP 1

enemy operations elsewhere. Nonetheless, the Thais themselves could launch effective operations. A typical well-planned and successful Thai operation was a search and clear mission conducted by the 2d and 3d Battalions of the 2d Brigade, Royal Thai Army Volunteer Force. It took place in the vicinity of Ben Cam in the Nhon Trach District of Bien Hoa Province during the period 24 November 1969–4 December 1969.

The mission required that an enemy area to the south of Ben Cam village be sealed and then swept free of local guerrillas. Using six rifle companies, the Thais sealed an area bounded on the north by Highway 25, on the west by an engineer-cut path in the vicinity of Ben Cam village, and to the east by another man-made path some forty meters in width. The southern boundary consisted of a trail running from Fire Support Base Tak westward. *(Map 2)* Once the blocking forces were in position, the troop elements to the west began a sweep on a line approximately 500 meters wide. After this force had been moved eastward some 500 meters the southern blocking force was moved a like distance to the north. This process was repeated until the objective area was reduced to a one kilometer square. Kit Carson Scouts and one former enemy turned informer assisted the

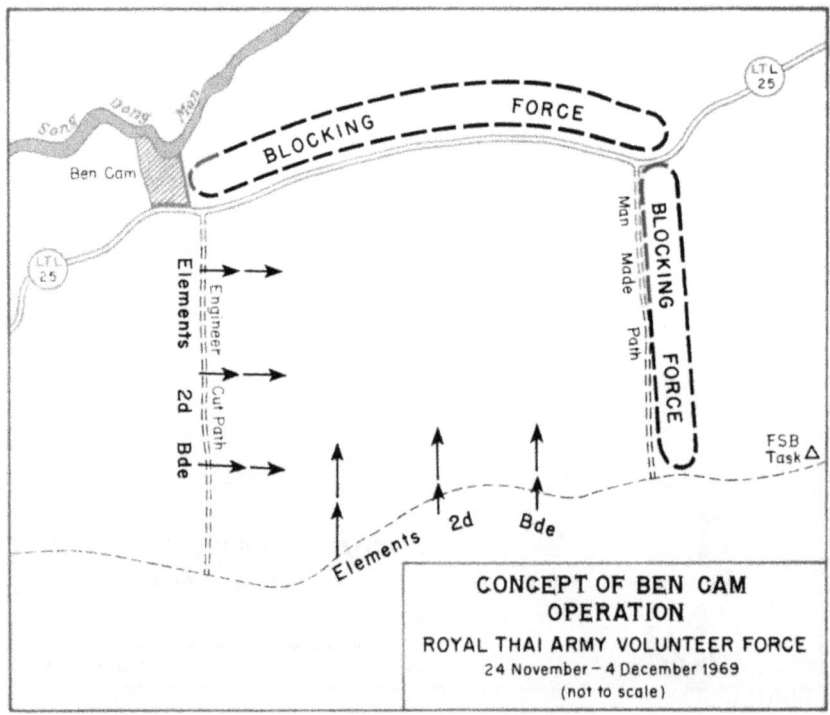

MAP 2

search through the bunker complexes. As a result of these measures only two casualties were suffered from booby traps.

Two engineer bulldozers and two platoons of engineer troops were used throughout the sealing operation. Their mission consisted of cutting north-south, east-west trails in the area swept by the advancing troops. A route was selected to be cut and the engineers then cleared the jungle area with bangalore torpedoes. Bulldozers followed and increased the width of the cut to forty meters. Infantry elements provided security for the engineers during these operations.

Throughout the maneuver the advance of the infantry troops was on line and void of gaps as the sweeps forced the enemy toward the center. Thai night security was outstanding. On three successive occasions the Viet Cong tried to break out of the trap, and in all three instances they were repulsed. Intelligence reported that seven Viet Cong were wounded during these attempts.

In conjunction with the tactical operations, the U.S.-Thai team conducted psychological operations. All returnees under the *Chieu Hoi* (open arms) amnesty program were fully interviewed and in 60 percent of the cases tapes of these interviews were made. These tapes were normally played back to the Viet Cong within four hours. The themes were basically a plea to the Viet Cong to return to the fold of the government while it was still possible, to eliminate their leaders and rally, to receive medical care, and to bring their weapons. When Viet Cong rallied without their weapons, a weapons leaflet was dropped and the next returnees brought in weapons. Once all means of drawing the enemy out had been used and continued efforts were unsuccessful, a C-47 aircraft with miniguns was employed to saturate totally the sealed square kilometer area.

The results of this operation were 14 of the enemy killed, 6 prisoners, and 12 returnees. Some 21 small arms and 2 crew-served weapons were also captured.

While air support was used in the last stage of this particular operation, the Thais in general made limited use of air power. Liaison officers of the U.S. Air Force participating in other Thai operations found that planned air strikes were more readily accepted by Thai ground commanders than close tactical air support. The Thai Army division headquarters requested one planned strike every day. The request was made so automatically and as a matter of routine that it seemed to U.S. troops in the tactical air control party that the Thais were accepting the planned strikes out of typical Thai politeness.

For close-in troop support, helicopter and fixed-wing gunships were preferred. Requests for fighter-bombers were very rare. One air liaison officer stated that Thai ground commanders did not consider close air support a necessity during an engagement. They tended to request it only after contact had been broken off and friendly troops were a safe distance away from the strike. Thus, it became the job of the liaison officer to educate the ground commanders. With one of the two Thai brigades rotating every six months, the education process was a continuing one. As part of the education program, the U.S. Army and Air Force conducted a bombing and napalm demonstration with the Thai observers placed three kilometers away. Even at this distance the results were very palpable and unnerving. Thereafter, as a result of this experience, Thai commanders invariably pulled their troops back approximately three kilometers away from the target before calling in air strikes.

Last Years of Assistance

In December 1969 the effects of the withdrawal of the Philippine Civic Action Group, Vietnam, and publicity given the activities of the Symington Subcommittee were felt in Thailand as elsewhere. The United States had welcomed the decision of the Thai government to contribute troops to South Vietnam and was willing to compensate it by logistical support and payment of certain allowances to Thai forces for duty out of the country. These facts led to charges and countercharges regarding the expenditures of funds supporting the Thai division. On 19 December the Bangkok press reported that some twenty government party members of the Thai parliament had signed a letter to the prime minister urging the withdrawal of Thai troops from South Vietnam. The reasons given were that the situation in South Vietnam had improved as a result of the U.S. Vietnamization program and other aid, as evidenced by U.S. cutbacks, and that difficult domestic economic and security problems existed in Thailand. No reference was made to the "mercenary" and "subsidy" charges of the previous few days. On 21 December Thai Foreign Minister Thanat Khoman told newsmen that he had considered the withdrawal of Thai troops "because the United States recently issued another announcement regarding further withdrawals." He also stated that the subject had been discussed with South Vietnamese Foreign Minister Tran Chan Thanh, and had been under consideration for some time. The minister was cautious on the subject: "Before any action can be taken we will have to consider it thoroughly and carefully from all angles.

We must not do anything or reach any decision in a hurry, neither must we follow blindly in anybody's footsteps."

Two days later there was an apparent reversal of policy. After a cabinet meeting aimed at developing a unified position, the deputy prime minister announced:

Thailand will not pull any of her fighting men out of South Vietnam. . . . Thailand has never contemplated such a move. . . . The operation of Thai troops in South Vietnam is considered more advantageous than withdrawing them. If we plan to withdraw, we would have to consult with GVN since we sent troops there in response to an appeal from them. It is true that several countries are withdrawing troops from South Vietnam but our case is different.

In addition to ground forces, the Thais had an air force contingent in South Vietnam. While never large, the Thai air force contingent achieved its greatest strength in late 1970. The total number of Thais serving with the Victory Flight, as their Vietnam transport operation was designated, had grown from the original sixteen to forty-five. Three pilots and five flight engineers flew with the Vietnamese in the Vietnam Air Force C–47's; nine pilots, seven flight engineers, and three loadmasters were flying C–123K's with the U.S. Air Force 19th Tactical Airlift Squadron which, like the Vietnamese 415th Squadron, was equipped with C–47's and located at Tan Son Nhut. The remaining members of the flight had jobs on the ground in intelligence, communications, flight engineering, loading, and operations. Normally there was an equal balance between officers and enlisted men.

The subject of a Thai troop withdrawal, which arose in December 1969 and was seemingly resolved then, came up again three months later. In a meeting with the U.S. Ambassador in March, the Thai Prime Minister indicated that in light of continued U.S. and allied reductions, there was considerable pressure from the Thai parliament to withdraw. He stated that "When the people feel very strongly about a situation, the government must do something to ease the situation." Little occurred until the following November when the Thai government announced it was planning to withdraw its forces from South Vietnam by 1972. The decision was related to the deterioration of security in Laos and Cambodia and the growth of internal insurgency in Thailand, as well as the U.S. pullback.

The withdrawal plans were based on a rotational phase-out. The fifth increment would not be replaced after its return to Thailand in August 1971. The sixth increment would deploy as planned in January 1971 and withdraw one year later to com-

GENERAL ROSSON PRESENTS MERITORIOUS UNIT CITATION *to Thai Panther Division.*

plete the redeployment. Thai Navy and Air Force units would withdraw sometime before January 1972. The composition of the remaining residual force would be taken up in Thai–South Vietnamese discussions held later. A token Thai force of a noncombatant nature was under consideration.

The withdrawal plans were confirmed and even elaborated upon through a Royal Thai government announcement to the United States and South Vietnam on 26 March 1971. The Thais proposed that one-half of the Panther Division be withdrawn in July 1971, and the remaining half in February 1972; this plan was in line with their earlier proposals. The three LST's (landing ships, tank) of the Sea Horse unit would be withdrawn in April 1972 and Victory Flight would be pulled out by increments during the period April—December 1971. After July 1971 the Headquarters, Royal Thai Forces, Vietnam, would be reduced to 204 men. It would remain at that strength until its withdrawal in April 1972, after which only a token force would remain.

CHAPTER III

The Philippines

The Philippine nation assisted the Republic of South Vietnam for many years. As early as 1953 a group of Philippine doctors and nurses arrived in Vietnam to provide medical assistance to the hamlets and villages throughout the republic. This project, known as Operation BROTHERHOOD, was mainly financed and sponsored by private organizations within the Philippines. Years later the Philippine government, a member of the United Nations and the Southeast Asia Treaty Organization, increased Philippine aid to Vietnam out of a sense of obligation to contribute to the South Vietnamese fight against communism. On 21 July 1964 the Congress of the Philippines passed a law that authorized the President to send additional economic and technical assistance to the Republic of Vietnam. The law was implemented through the dispatch to Vietnam of a group of thirty-four physicians, surgeons, nurses, psychologists, and rural development workers from the armed forces. Four such groups in turn served with dedication during the period 1964–1966.

In addition, and as a part of the Free World Assistance Program, sixteen Philippine Army officers arrived in Vietnam on 16 August 1964 to assist in the III Corps advisory effort in psychological warfare and civil affairs. They were to act in co-ordination with the U.S. Military Assistance Command, Vietnam. Initially the officers were assigned in pairs to the three civil affairs platoons and three psychological warfare companies in the provinces of Binh Duong, Gia Dinh, and Long An, respectively. Of the remaining four, one functioned as the officer in charge, while one each worked with the Psychological Warfare Directorate, the III Corps Psychological Operation Center, and the 1st Psychological Warfare Battalion.

The efforts of the sixteen Philippine officers were directed at a lower governmental level than those of their U.S. allies. Traveling and working with their South Vietnamese counterparts, these officers ensured that the psychological warfare and civil affairs portion of the pacification plan was being carried out. During the time they were in the field, the Philippine officers made an important contribution to the psychological warfare effort. Their success prompted the South Vietnamese to ask for another group of sixteen officers.

History of Philippine Aid

Discussions between the U.S. and Philippine governments regarding an even larger Philippine contribution to South Vietnam began in the fall of 1964. Philippine officials in Washington who arranged for the visit of President Diosdada Macapagal to the United States suggested that the Philippine government was prepared, under certain conditions, to play a greater role in South Vietnam; however, there was a wide variety of opinion in the United States as to the nature and extent of this additional aid. In Washington, U.S. military officials believed that the Philippines should make contributions such as aircraft crews to support the Vietnamese Air Force; a special forces company; engineer platoons; medical platoons; technical personnel in the fields of communications, ordnance, transportation, and maintenance; and Marine and Navy personnel to assist South Vietnam in training its junk fleet and in other counterinsurgency operations. On the other hand, U.S. civilian officials were inclined to believe that the Philippines should contribute medical and civic action workers and agricultural experts, and supply fertilizer.

In the course of his state visit to the United States, President Macapagal discussed a Philippine military contribution with President Johnson and Secretary of Defense McNamara. In response to President Macapagal's suggestion that his government increase its aid, Secretary McNamara replied that the United States would, along with the Philippine government, consider what further contributions it could make to the South Vietnamese counterinsurgency effort, and to what extent the United States could supplement the Philippine military budget.

Underlying his offer was President Macapagal's desire to make the Philippine military establishment "more flexible" in meeting a potential "threat from the South," Indonesia. For this reason he and his advisers pressed for an increase in the Military Assistance Program. Secretary McNamara reiterated his concern over the unsuitably low budget support the Philippine government provided its armed forces and held out the strong possibility that any increase in U.S. aid would be contingent on an increase in the Philippine defense budget. During the discussion President Macapagal indicated that Philippine readiness to respond in South Vietnam would be related to the presence of other friendly Asians in Vietnam.

Following the Macapagal state visit, the U.S. State Department directed the ambassadors in Saigon and Manila to meet with Major General Lloyd H. Gomes, Chief, Joint U.S. Military Assistance Group, Philippines, and General Westmoreland to compare South Vietnam's needs with the ability of the Philippines to fill them. Also on the agenda were such subjects as the specific units that might be deployed, timing, phasing, priorities, and funding details. The State Department thought that for significant impact any Philippine contingent should number approximately 1,000.

Washington, always anxious to increase the amount of assistance to Vietnam from other countries, saw the Philippines as another contributor. General Westmoreland, however, was quick to warn all concerned of the multiple logistics problems which would be encountered if adequate lead time was not given. Experience had shown that Vietnamese logistical support for Free World forces could not be depended upon, and the existing MACV logistical organization and resources could not absorb any substantial increase without additional resources and adequate time for planning and phasing of the deployment.

A staff meeting held on 14 December 1964 by the Joint U.S. Military Assistance Group, Philippines, and Headquarters, Armed Forces, Philippines, discussed the employment of Philippine forces in South Vietnam. The Philippine representatives stipulated that the United States fund the entire Philippine undertaking; replace all ground force equipment deployed on an item-for-item or equivalent basis; and agree to employ the Filipinos on strictly defensive civic action operations in the Bien Hoa area. Special forces and medical personnel could operate in the Tay Ninh area provided they were not near the Cambodian border. The Philippine representatives also revealed the size and composition of the task force they had in mind. President Macapagal had originally thought of sending a combat force to South Vietnam; Ferdinand E. Marcos, then head of the Liberal party, had strongly gone on record as opposing sending any force at all. Accordingly these early discussions restricted the role of the Philippines to a defensive civic action mission with the force tailored to fulfill that mission. The task force strength recommended was approximately 2,480 and was to include an infantry battalion, reinforced, an engineer battalion, reinforced, a support company, civic action personnel, a Navy contingent, and an Air Force contingent.

Early in 1965 the number of participants in discussions of Philippine aid was increased when the government of South Vietnam officially requested more aid from the Philippines. The fate of this request was uncertain for several months. President Marcos, elected in the fall of the year, had been explicit on the subject of Vietnam aid some months earlier. Only after he had studied the situation did he modify his position by saying, "No, I will not send, I will not permit the sending of any combat forces. But I will get behind the idea of sending a civic action force." Once again the task force concept was modified to make the final product a mixture of an engineer construction battalion and medical and civic action teams with their own security support.

During the first half of 1966 President Marcos pressed for passage of a bill based on the civic action task force concept that permitted the force to be sent to South Vietnam. The legislation also provided for an allocation of funds for this purpose up to thirty-five million pesos ($8,950,000). The bill easily passed the House of Representatives but encountered opposition in the Philippine Senate. After much debate, delay, and extra sessions, the Senate passed the bill on 4 June by a vote of fifteen to eight. The bill was then referred to a joint House and Senate conference committee where it stayed until 9 June; President Marcos signed it on 18 June. The bill permitted the dispatch of a 2,000-man civic action group consisting of an engineer construction battalion, medical and rural community development teams, a security battalion, a field artillery battery, a logistics support company, and a headquarters element. The force was to undertake socio-economic projects mutually agreed upon by the Philippines and South Vietnam.

The preamble of the bill clearly stated the reasons for the decision of the Philippine Congress to expand the Philippine people's commitment in South Vietnam. Similar sentiments were contained in a statement by President Marcos who said: "I repeat that if we send engineers to Vietnam this will be because we choose to act on the long-held convictions of the Philippine people, that the option for liberty must be kept for every nation, that our own security requires that democracy be given the chance to develop freely and successfully in our own part of the world."

Not discounting these patriotic motives, it must be pointed out that in return for Philippine support the U.S. Military Assistance Program granted aid to the Philippines in those areas suggested by President Marcos. Included were four river patrol craft for antismuggling operations, M14 rifles and machine guns for one constabulary battalion combat team, and equipment for three engineer battalions. This aid was in addition to the previous commitments for one destroyer escort and several other patrol craft. Also being considered was the provision of one F-5 squadron and helicopter units. The unit was meanwhile assembling. On 1 June 650 officers and enlisted men began training at Fort Magsaysay while at other military areas groups of volunteers were awaiting transportation to Fort Magsaysay.

In the original planning the Philippine Civic Action Group had anticipated deploying approximately 120 days after the Philippine Congress passed the bill. This figure was based on a 60-day period for transport of the group's engineer equipment to the Philippines, including 15 days for deprocessing and movement to a training area, 45 days of training with the equipment, and 15 days for processing and transporting the unit to Vietnam. President Marcos, unhappy about the lengthy lead time required for the departure of his troops, felt that opponents of the bill would continue their opposition as long as the troops remained in the Philippines. In response, the U.S. Military Assistance Command, Vietnam, pointed out that the deployment date could be moved up considerably if the training equipment could be made available in less than the 45 days scheduled, but apparently this was not possible. A Joint Chiefs of Staff proposal that the Philippine Civic Action Group, Vietnam, conduct all individual and unit training in South Vietnam MACV considered infeasible. MACV pointed out that if an untrained unit was deployed to Vietnam, U.S. or Free World tactical forces would be obliged to provide security forces at a time when they would be otherwise committed to tactical operations. In addition, if an inadequately trained Philippine civic action group was attacked and did sustain significant casualties, the far-reaching political implications could adversely affect both the Philippine and the United States governments. An alternate proposal made by the Commander in Chief, Pacific, was that an advance planning group be sent, to arrive within 30 days following passage of the bill, with the advance party to arrive within a 60-day period and the main body at the end of 90 days. This proposal was believed to have merit, but only if it was absolutely necessary to deploy the Philippine group earlier than planned. Recognizing the importance of the training, President Marcos accepted the four-month timetable.

In the course of their training, the Filipinos were assisted by two U.S. mobile training teams. One team from the United States Army, Vietnam, assisted in training with M16 rifles and tactics peculiar to operations in South Vietnam. A second team from the U.S. Eighth Army in Korea conducted training on M113 driving and maintenance. During the training period in the Philippines, the Philippine group experienced some difficulties because of limited funds, lack of equipment, and interruptions caused by parades and ceremonies. Even though schedules were disrupted, however, the training was useful and had a steadying influence on the civic action group's later activities.

U.S. support for the Philippine Civic Action Group, Vietnam, as it was finally worked out was approximately $36 million, most of which was for the purchase, operation, and maintenance of heavy equipment such as bulldozers and trucks. While the Philippine government paid the group its regular wages, the United States was committed to the payment of an overseas allowance and per diem at the rate of $1 for each person. The additional daily overseas allowance was paid according to rank.

Brigadier General	$6.00
Colonel	5.00
Lieutenant Colonel	5.00
Major	4.50
Captain	4.00
1st Lieutenant	3.50
2nd Lieutenant	3.00
Master Sergeant	1.50
Sergeant 1st Class	.50
Corporal	.20
Private First Class/Private	.10

The United States further agreed to furnish the Filipinos in Vietnam with additional material, transportation, and other support. Class I supplies, subsistence (not to exceed the value of subsistence to U.S. troops), was provided through the U.S. logistic system except for rice—800 grams per man per day—and salt—15 grams per man per day—which were furnished through the Vietnamese armed forces supply system. Special Philippine dietary and other items not included in the U.S. ration were purchased by the Philippine Civic Action Group. The United States provided only transportation for these last items from ports in the Philippines to Vietnam.

All Class II and IV general supplies were furnished through the U.S. logistical system with the following exceptions: items common to the Philippine group and the Vietnamese armed forces but not used by the U.S. forces in Vietnam were supported through the Vietnam armed forces supply system; items peculiar to the Philippine group were supplied through the Philippine group supply system; a stockage level of forty-five days of third echelon repair parts was authorized to support those items of equipment provided through the Vietnamese armed forces supply system.

Class III supplies—petroleum, oil, and lubricants—were

provided through the U.S. logistic system.

Class IV, ammunition—all items of ammunition and pyrotechnics—were provided through the U.S. logistical system.

Maintenance through the third echelon was performed by the Philippine group as far as it was able. Equipment maintenance beyond the capacity of the Philippine group or the Vietnamese armed forces was provided by U.S. Military Assistance Command, Vietnam. Equipment that became unserviceable and too costly to repair either through combat use, fair wear and tear, or other reasonable cause was replaced by the appropriate U.S. or Vietnamese armed forces agency.

Transportation between Vietnam and the Philippines was provided by MACV for members of the Philippine group traveling in connection with Philippine group activities. Movements of personnel and equipment were made under the same conditions and system of priorities that applied to U.S. units. This transportation included such authorized travel as the rotation of Philippine group personnel, recall of personnel to the Philippines, return of the dead, and movement of inspection teams in connection with Philippine group activities. Philippine group transportation facilities were used whenever available.

Other support accorded members of the Philippine Civic Action Group, Vietnam, by the Commander, U.S. Military Assistance Command, Vietnam, consisted of permission to use U.S. mess, billeting, club, religious, exchange, commissary, and mail facilities, and to participate in U.S. military recreation programs.

The United States assisted the Philippine group in recovery of the dead and provided mortuary service. The United States further agreed to the provision of death gratuities for members to be administered along the same general lines as the payment of such gratuities to Korean troops.

As support and training questions were being resolved, General Ernesto S. Mata, chief of staff of the Armed Forces of the Philippines and nine other officers arrived in Saigon on 20 July 1966 for three days of talk and an inspection tour. In an unpublicized visit, General Mata emphasized to General Westmoreland the feelings of President Marcos about the strength of the Philippine Civic Action Group. Marcos believed that its organic firepower was inadequate, particularly in the areas of automatic weapons, large mortars, and artillery and that the security battalion did not have the armor and could not carry out the armed reconnaissance that was standard in a comparable U.S. unit. He therefore wanted assurance of quick and effective reinforcement from nearby U.S. and South Vietnamese combat elements in case of large-scale attacks on Philippine installations.

Most of these points were academic because MACV had some three days earlier authorized the Philippine group seventeen additional APC's (armored personnel carriers), six 105-mm. howitzers, eight 4.2-inch mortars, two M41 tanks, and 630 M16 rifles.

With the signing of the military working agreements between the Republic of the Philippines and the United States (Mata-Westmoreland Agreement, 20 July 1966) and between the Republic of the Philippines and the Republic of Vietnam (Mata-Tam Agreement, 3 August 1966), the way was clear to implement the provisions of the bill.

The military working agreements specified that tasks for the Philippine Civic Action Group, Vietnam, would be determined by the Free World Military Assistance Policy Council. Pursuant to these agreements the Philippine group's basic mission was "to render civic action assistance to the Republic of Vietnam by construction, rehabilitation, and development of public works, utilities, and structures, and by providing technical advice on other socio-economic activities." Command and control was vested in the Commanding General, Philippine Civic Action group, Vietnam. The Philippine rural health teams and provincial hospital medical and surgical teams were to provide services on a mission basis in co-ordination with the Ministry of Public Health of the government of South Vietnam and the U.S. Agency for International Development.

In considering the employment of the Philippine Civic Action Group, Vietnam, MACV had decided that Long An Province was unsuitable because its compartmented terrain precluded maximum use of the group and that the land in Hau Nghia Province was preferable. Partly because of the support of the Philippine military attaché for the Hau Nghia location, the area around the town of Bao Trai (Kiem Cuong) was selected. On 1 June, however, General Westmoreland directed that a staff study be conducted to determine the feasibility of relocating the Philippine group in Tay Ninh Province. He believed that the operations of the U.S. 25th Infantry Division around Bao Trai would make it unnecessary to use the Philippine group in that area. In addition there was a certain historical affinity between Cambodia and the Philippines, and the new site would place the Philippine group near the Cambodian border. This suggestion of a border site for the Filipinos was met with some misgivings by the government of South Vietnam; the Vietnamese Minister of Defense, Lieutenant General Nguyen Huu Co, believed that there was a security risk in stationing a unit so close to War Zone C, but he added that it would be a great advantage if the group could provide support for the 100,000 loyal Cao Dai, members of a politically oriented religious sect, in Tay Ninh Province.

Initially opposed to the change in locations, the Philippine government sent the commanding general of the Philippine Forces in Vietnam, Brigadier General Gaudencio V. Tobias, to survey the situation. He was given detailed briefings by the province chiefs of both Hau Nghia and Tay Ninh Province, and made a ground and air reconnaissance of each province. Members of the 25th U.S. Infantry Division and II Field Force, Vietnam, briefed him on the support and security to be provided the Philippine group. Among the reasons given for the selection of Tay Ninh instead of Hau Nghia was the lower rate of Viet Cong incidents in Tay Ninh.

The new location was approved. *(Map 3)* The Philippine Civic Action Group, Vietnam, agreed to provide its own local security, upon arrival, while U.S. forces would provide area security until the Philippine security battalion could assume the responsibility. In the future the Philippine group would be included in all mutual security arrangements in and around Tay Ninh City, would be supported by 105-mm. and 155-mm. units from their base locations, and would receive contingency support from the nearby 175-mm. guns. The security situation was further improved when the 196th Light Infantry Brigade was stationed in Tay Ninh.

The first element of the Philippine Civic Action Group arrived in South Vietnam on 28 July 1966 to survey and lay out the proposed base camp in Tay Ninh. On 16 August the first element was followed by an advance planning group of 100 officers and men charged with the task of co-ordinating with several Vietnamese and U.S. military agencies involved in the reception, transport, and support of the rest of the group. Among this advance planning group were three civic action teams which initiated medical and dental projects within the surrounding hamlets. During their first seven weeks of operations, these teams treated an average of 2,000 medical and dental patients per week. The next increment of the Philippine group, the third, arrived on 9 September 1966 and consisted of sixty drivers, maintenance specialists, and cooks.

With the arrival of General Tobias and his staff on 14 September 1966, the Philippine Civic Action Group, Vietnam, became firmly and fully established. Two days later 741 men who had recently arrived from the Philippines were airlifted from Cam Ranh Bay to the Tay Ninh base camp, which was by this time sufficiently well prepared to handle large groups. Next to

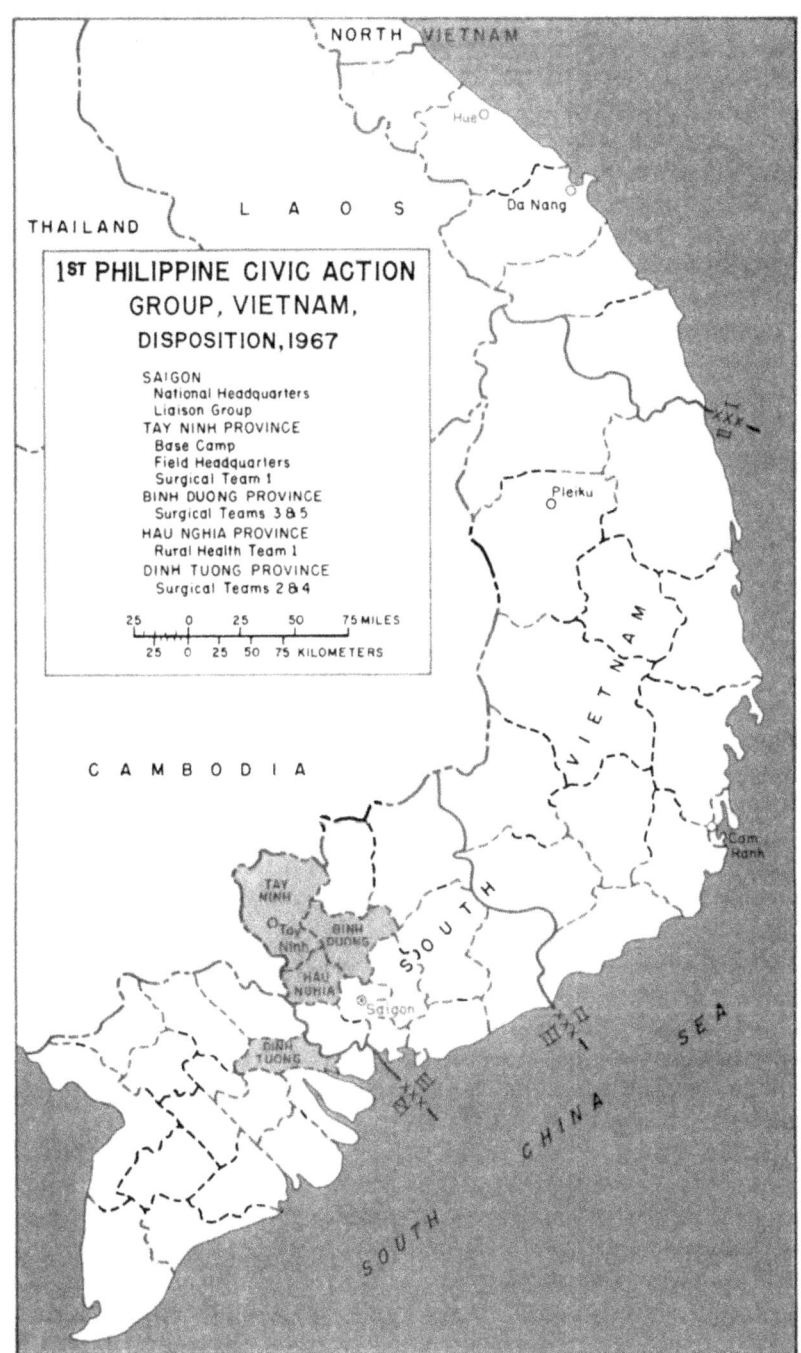

MAP 3

PHILIPPINE SECURITY TROOPS REBUILD A BASE CAMP BUNKER

arrive at Tay Ninh was a group of doctors, nurses, and artillerymen. Arriving on 26 September, they were the first to make the trip by air from Manila to Tay Ninh via Saigon. The two surgical teams in this group were sent to the provincial hospitals of Dinh Tuong at My Tho and Binh Duong at Phu Cuong, while a rural medical team was sent to Bao Trai, capital of Hau Nghia Province.

Additional assets came to the 1st Philippine Civic Action Group, Vietnam, when on 1 October operational and administrative control of the twenty doctors, nurses, and medical technicians of the Philippine contingent was turned over to General Tobias. By mid-October the Philippine Civic Action Group had reached full strength. (*Chart 3*)

From 15 to 19 October 1966 the Philippine armed forces accomplished the biggest air movement in their history. During this period the remainder of the Philippine Civic Action Group was transported directly from Manila International Airport to the Tay Ninh West airport adjacent to the Philippine group base camp. In accordance with instructions from President Marcos the troops departed during the early morning hours. It was his wish that the Philippine group be dispatched as quietly as possible, without publicity or opportunities for large gatherings at

CHART 3—PHILIPPINE CIVIC ACTION GROUP, VIETNAM

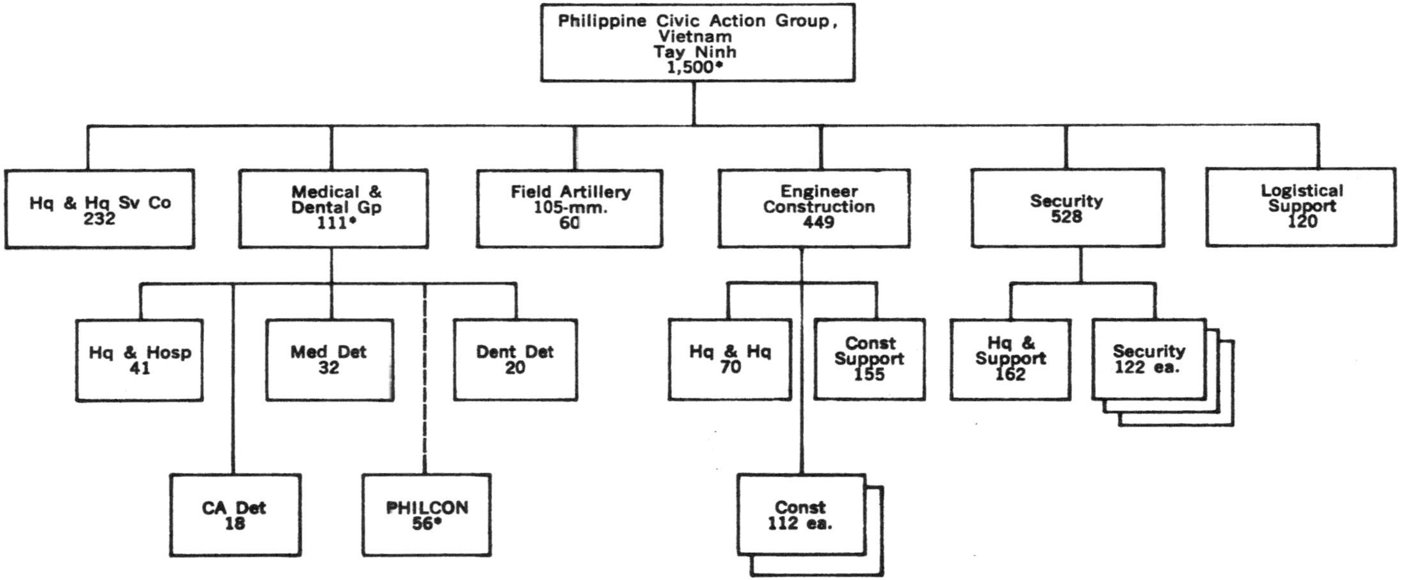

↑ *Philippine Contingent strength is not included in Philippine Civic Action Group, Vietnam, table of organization totals because support came from a separate Republic of the Philippines appropriation.

loading areas. With the arrival in Vietnam of these elements the group was at its full strength of 2,068.

During this early period the Philippine group's main effort was directed toward the construction of a base camp that would serve both as a secure area and as a model community eventually to be turned over to the people of Tay Ninh. This community, which was soon to contain over 200 prefabricated buildings, was the Philippine group's first major construction effort.

Toward the end of September, the group began limited engineering work, making road repairs in some of the hamlets bordering the eastern side of Thanh Dien forest. Once a Viet Cong stronghold, this forested area became the site of the second major Philippine group project. In time, portions of the forest would be cleared, and roads and bridges built to open about 4,500 hectares of farmlands for refugee families from all over Tay Ninh Province.

In an effort to facilitate the execution of this mission, the Philippine Civic Action Group produced and distributed more than 83,000 leaflets in the Vietnam language containing the text of Republic Act 4664 (aid-to-Vietnam bill) and explaining the Philippine presence in Vietnam and the humanitarian missions to be accomplished. (*See Appendix A.*)

It was also in September that the Philippine group suffered its first casualties. While on convoy duty to Saigon, seven enlisted men were wounded by a claymore mine at Tra Vo in Tay Ninh.

Seasonal rains throughout September and early October restricted the use of heavy construction equipment, but despite the adverse weather conditions some engineering work was still carried out.

On 1 December 1966 the clearing of the resettlement site at Thanh Dien forest began. A task force designated BAYANIHAN and composed of elements of one reinforced engineer construction company, one reinforced security company, one explosive ordnance disposal team, one artillery forward observer team, and two civic action teams had the mission of clearing the project site. External security for the task force was provided by four Vietnamese Regional Forces or Popular Forces companies. In this operation the explosive ordnance disposal team was extremely busy since almost every inch of the area had to be cleared of mines, booby traps, and duds. In addition, Task Force BAYANIHAN was subjected to harassing fire from mortars, rifle grenades, and snipers on four separate occasions during the month of December.

In December also, at the request of Philippine President

Marcos, General Westmoreland visited Manila, where he praised the excellent performance of the Philippine Civic Action Group, Vietnam, and suggested that if the Philippine government wanted to increase its contribution to South Vietnam it might consider providing a squadron of UH–1D helicopters for civic action work. Another possibility was Philippine assistance in training a South Vietnamese constabulary similar to the Philippine constabulary; some Philippine advisers could go to South Vietnam while some Vietnamese cadres could be placed with the Philippine constabulary for training in the Philippines.

President Marcos appeared genuinely interested in the idea of forming a helicopter squadron, particularly if his country was to be permitted to keep the aircraft after the completion of the Vietnam mission. He was also in favor of the U.S. proposal to train additional helicopter pilots with the thought that they might be available for duty in South Vietnam, and showed interest in the proposal to have ten helicopters in Vietnam while six were retained in the Philippines for training purposes. But Marcos was not yet ready to approve the entire project, even though the U.S. Embassy in Manila and General Gomes, Chief, Joint U.S. Military Assistance Group, Philippines, concurred in the project and recommended its implementation. Both the ambassador and General Gomes were aware, however, of limiting factors. The Philippine Military Assistance Program could not absorb funding for the squadron without destroying its current program. Furthermore, all of the initial training would have to be conducted in the United States because there were no facilities available in the Philippines.

General Westmoreland believed that a Philippine helicopter squadron would be a welcome addition to Free World forces in South Vietnam, especially if it could support civic action missions of the expanding Philippine program. He preferred a squadron of twenty-five helicopters with the exact table of equipment to be determined through discussions with the Philippine Civic Action Group. The squadron would have to be equipped with UH–1D's since production of UH–1B helicopters was being curtailed, but there were not enought helicopters in Vietnam to do this without affecting existing operations. If the aircraft could not be supplied from sources outside Vietnam, then the squadron would have to be equipped first with H–34 helicopters and then with UH–1D helicopters the following year. The usual ten hours of transition flying would be required to qualify Philippine H–34 pilots in the Huey aircraft. Philippine Air Force helicopter squadrons were capable of organic third and fourth echelon maintenance, and except for the supply of spare parts no significant maintenance problems were anticipated.

Admiral Sharp, Commander in Chief, Pacific, believed the MACV concept to be practical, but was quick to point out that worldwide demands for the UH–1 were such that accelerated deliveries to the Philippine government were unlikely. In light of the aircraft shortages, the limited capability of the Philippine Air Force, and the lukewarm attitude of the Philippine government, Admiral Sharp viewed the plan as impractical. The proposal was again reviewed by the Secretary of State and the Secretary of Defense, who concluded that a Philippine helicopter squadron to support the Philippine Civic Action Group could not be justified and would be an uneconomical use of the limited helicopter resources. The use of Philippine pilots in South Vietnam to support operations of the Philippine group, however, would be militarily beneficial. Washington finally decided that U.S. authorities should neither raise the question of a Philippine helicopter squadron nor take the initiative in obtaining Philippine pilots to serve with U.S. units supporting the Philippine group. Should the Philippine government again raise the question, however, the U.S. response would be that a careful review of the helicopter inventory and competing high priority military requirements appeared to preclude the formation of a separate Philippine squadron in the near future.

While high-level discussions of additional Philippine support were taking place, work continued on the Philippine pacification effort, the Thanh Dien Resettlement Project. Indeed its establishment and presence had bred complications. By January 1967 the Viet Cong began to realize that the project was a threat to their cause. Harassment of work parties became more frequent and intense. In cases where innocent civilians were not involved, the task force returned the enemy's fire with all available organic and supporting weapons. Even with these interruptions work progressed on the resettlement project and related tasks and the first refugee families were resettled in early April.

Enemy opposition to the Philippine group intensified. The Viet Cong attacked the Thanh Dien area both directly and indirectly. In addition to attacks by fire and a propaganda campaign, attempts were made to infiltrate the Philippine equipment park at Hiep Hoa although attacks had little effect.

In the Philippines developments indicated that there would be extended debate over the appropriation for the Philippine Civic Action Group, Vietnam, for the next fiscal year. Although the appropriation bill had passed in the House by an overwhelming vote (81–7) the previous year and more closely in the Senate (15–8), indications pointed to increased opposition. It was contended by one opposition block that the 35-million-peso allocation could be better spent on Philippine roads and irrigation.

The new appropriations bill for the Philippine Civic Action Group, Vietnam, went before the Philippine Congress in March 1967. Speaker of the House Cornelio T. Villereal and other congressmen suggested tying the bill to an over-all review of U.S.-Philippine relations, with particular emphasis on the fulfillment of U.S. military aid commitments. Possibly in an attempt to bolster the bill's chances, South Vietnamese Prime Minister Nguyen Cao Ky asked President Marcos to consider extending the tour of duty and enlarging and expanding the activities of the Philippine group. Ky's note, written in the first person, reached President Marcos on 13 March and began with an expression of appreciation for the Philippine group's efforts. President Marcos responded to the note during his surprise visit to South Vietnam.

Accompanied by General Mata, now Secretary of National Defense, and others, on 16 July Marcos arrived at the Philippine group's base camp at Tay Ninh. During his stay the Philippine president made a presentation of awards, was briefed by General Tobias, and toured the Thanh Dien Resettlement Project. News of his nine-hour visit became known during the afternoon of 16 July and by that evening Filippinos were expressing their admiration for Marcos and comparing his sudden and well-kept secret trip to that made by President Johnson the previous year. In response to press questions of whether the Philippines would increase their participation in Vietnam, Marcos said:

> No, there is no plan to increase our participation. But it has been suggested by some elements here in the Philippines that we should increase such participation. There are many factors to consider; and therefore, as I said, right now there is no plan to increase our participation but, of course a continuing study is being made on all these problems, and this is one of those problems . . . .

General Westmoreland learned in August 1967 that there were plans for replacement forces. The Philippine government was then assembling volunteers for the second Philippine Civic Action Group, Vietnam, at Fort Magsaysay. The planning dates, all tentative, indicated that the advance party would leave for South Vietnam around 30 September 1967. A portion of the main force of about 600 officers and men would arrive on 20 October 1967, with the remainder reaching Vietnam before 16 December 1967. Final deployment dates were to be made firm in

December. In discussions with the Philippine government, General Gomes pressed for maximum training of the second civic action group, using returning group members and equipment, and suggested that Philippine mobile training teams should be introduced early in the training phase. This would permit training to be conducted by men who were familiar with the equipment, procedures, and area of operations in South Vietnam. With regard to other aspects of the training, the Philippine armed forces were insistent that MACV provide mobile training teams for instruction on U.S. supply procedures and the U.S. Army equipment records system.

General Westmoreland concurred in the training proposal of General Gomes, particularly since the mission of the Philippine Civic Action Group, Vietnam, had not changed. He suggested that the procedure for deployment utilize the overlap of personnel on the individual and small unit level to give on-the-job training to the second civic action group without an undue loss of operating efficiency. The training plan not only permitted the job orientation of the replacement force in Vietnam, but also maintained continuity of the established relationships with the Vietnamese and the Americans, minimized a surge in airlift requirements and facilitated redeployment of returning aircraft, and reduced security considerations associated with assembly and movement of large groups.

In spite of the advantage of individual and small unit rotation, the Philippine government could not support financially any extended overlap and only a two-day period was envisioned. Once a deployment date was set, the entire unit was to be rotated as quickly as possible, depending upon the availability of aircraft.

Preparation for the relief of the Philippine Civic Action Group began on 27 September 1967, when the first group of military training teams was sent to the Philippines to assist in the training of the replacement units.

In November 1967 the American Embassy in Manila established parameters for Philippine armed forces proposals that might lead to additional Philippine contributions to Vietnam, especially engineer units. It was almost certain that whatever contributions were made, the armed forces of the Philippines would insist on some form of Philippine command structure to provide command and control of their units. Units that could be substituted for U.S. personnel spaces would be organized under a Philippine logistical support group with a small headquarters for command and control. The logistical group would contain one to three engineer construction battalions and might also include the engineer unit then in South Vietnam.

The Philippine Navy and Air Force made their own proposals. The Philippine Navy proposed in order of priority: crews totaling 400 for LST's (landing ships, tank) or 224 officers and men to operate a sixteen LCM (landing craft, mechanized) board group, or 100 officers and men to operate a division of twelve PCF's (coastal patrol craft or Swift craft) in Operation MARKET TIME, or 100 officers and men to operate a division of four PGM's (motor gunboats) in MARKET TIME.[1]

Using U.S. aircraft and equipment, the Philippine Air Force proposed to operate in a support role in South Vietnam. A squadron of twelve aircraft, preferably C–7A's (Caribous) or C–123's (Providers), was considered. On the basis of sixty flying hours per month for aircraft and no base support requirements, the squadron would have required 50 officers and 203 enlisted men.

After considering the proposals, the State Department believed the best force from the standpoint of both South Vietnam and the Philippines would be three Philippine Army engineer battalions of about 2,100 officers and men. The United States would accept the idea of a Philippine security support force if the Republic of the Philippines insisted but did not want the spaces for the security force to come from the engineer battalions.

The 14 November Philippine Senate elections meanwhile would have a bearing on the future status of the Philippine Civic Action Group, Vietnam. The matter of whether or not to retain the group was injected into the campaign by the opposition Liberal party candidates, who termed the group's presence in Vietnam a diversion of needed funds from domestic Philippine requirements. President Marcos sought to remove the issue from the campaign by postponing his request for an appropriation for the Philippine Civic Action Group in the expectation that his Nationalist party would retain control of the Senate.

The outcome of the election was that the Nacionalista party captured six of the eight contested Senate seats. Marcos lost little time in introducing a $9 million appropriation bill for the continued deployment of the Philippine Civic Action Group, but the bill, while easily passing the House, came under fire not only from members of the Liberal party but also from elements of the ruling Nacionalista party. Senate opposition stemmed in part from a small minority critical of U.S. policies in Vietnam and of

---

[1] On 1 April 1967 the PGM or motor gunboat was redesignated the PG or patrol gunboat. On 14 August 1968 the PCF or patrol craft, coastal (fast), was renamed patrol craft, inshore, although it was still called the PCF.

the presence of U.S. bases in the Philippines. It was also possible that a good share of the opposition resulted from factional maneuvering for control of the Senate itself.

In an effort to placate its critics, the Marcos administration introduced a revised bill that extended the Philippines Civic Action Group, Vietnam, for that calendar year. The bill also reduced the engineer elements and increased proportionally the number of medical personnel.

Since funds to support the group were practically exhausted, the government intended to make a token troop withdrawal to forestall criticism of spending without appropriation and to point out to the Senate that the group was at the end of its rope. Unless Congress did something soon the Marcos administration would have to pull the entire unit out for lack of funds. The goal was to restore the force to full strength when the new appropriations bill was passed, but when the regular session of Congress ended there was still no action on the appropriations bill. A special Congressional session convened on 8 July, but had no more luck than its predecessor at passing the appropriations bill. The strength of the Philippine group in Vietnam had declined over the months to about 1,800 because returning troops were not being replaced.

It was not surprising then that the armed forces of the Philippines informed the American Embassy in Manila on 31 July 1968 that it had the day before issued instructions to reduce the Philippine unit in Vietnam from 1,735 men to 1,500; in accordance with instructions from President Marcos, the reduction was to be accomplished by 15 August. There was speculation that this action may have been a political compromise on the part of President Marcos against pressures for an even greater reduction of the Philippine Civic Action Group. The Philippine President's decision was serious enough to cause the American Embassy in Manila to ask General Gomes to see Mr. Mata, the Philippine Secretary of Defense, as soon as possible. The American Ambassador wished to express to Mr. Mata his concern that this reduction would be badly misinterpreted outside the Philippines. In light of his own conversation with President Marcos, the ambassador further wished General Gomes to confirm personally with the Philippine President that the purported reduction really represented Marcos' views.

General Gomes met with Mata on 3 August and examined in detail the various arguments against a reduction in the current size of the Philippine group in Vietnam. Mata indicated that he fully appreciated the U.S. position on this matter. On 8 August the Philippine Secretary of Defense informed General Gomes that he had talked with President Marcos; the order for the reduction of the Philippine group stood. The following day the American Embassy received a message from the Western Pacific Transportation Office containing an official request from the Philippine Civic Action Group, Vietnam, for a special airlift on 10, 11, 12, and 13 August 1968 to return home 235 members of the Philippine group.

In a news story released on 5 September 1968, Philippine armed forces chief Manuel Yan hinted that the replacement unit then in training would take the place of the Philippine group in Vietnam sometime that month. Yan reportedly told newsmen that financing of the replacement unit would come from the Philippine armed forces regular budget which had already absorbed financing of the civic action group. These were funds made available from other savings in the national budget. He further stated that the mission of the replacement unit was the same as that of the Philippine Civic Action Group, Vietnam, but that greater emphasis would be placed on medical and dental services. In addition, the table of equipment had been changed to increase the number of surgical and rural health teams by five each. To achieve this increase there was a corresponding reduction in the number of men assigned to the engineer battalion. In order to maintain the capabilities of the engineer construction battalion, men assigned to the security battalion were being cross-trained in engineer skills. Philippine Civic Action Group members who had completed a two-year tour in South Vietnam were replaced during the period 16 September – 15 October 1968. The strength reduction and table of equipment change were intended to re-emphasize the noncombatant role of the group to the Philippine Congress and the Philippine people.

On 17 September, the offical designation of the Philippine Civic Action Group, Republic of Vietnam, I, was changed to Philippine Civic Action Group, Republic of Vietnam. This was merely an administrative change within the armed forces of the Philippines.

In the Philippines, after the 1968 reduction, the issue of the Philippine group in Vietnam was temporarily out of the public eye. President Marcos had apparently decided that the Philippine national interest was best served by the group's continued presence in South Vietnam. This presence would guarantee a Philippine right to sit at the Vietnam settlement table and to claim a share of the war surplus material. Domestic critics in the

Philippines, however, soon began calling for a complete withdrawal of the unit. Some members of the Philippine Congress wanted to "punish" the United States for imagined support of Malaysia during the Sabah crises. Other critics felt that there was a legitimate need for the unit at home to oppose a Huk insurgency in central Luzon. Still others considered that supporting even the modest cost of maintaining the civic action group in Vietnam was a continuing financial burden. Since the required funds had been refused by the Philippine Congress, the group was being financed by regular armed forces funds plus $17 million for engineer equipment and $1.5 million annual support provided by the United States.

When the new table of equipment was approved in February 1969 little attention was given to the occasion either by the press or by the public and there were no significant displays of feeling against the Philippine group in Vietnam. In March, however, the Nacionalista party House caucus voted to withdraw the civic action group and replace it with a medical contingent. At the same time approaches were being made to U.S. officials for complete financing of the Philippine Civic Action Group by the United States. This situation raised the question of whether the United States should pick up the entire cost of the Philippine Civic Action Group or be prepared to see the group pull out.

A review revealed that while the Philippine group had done a "passable job" on those construction jobs it had completed, the group could have done more, and that South Vietnamese or U.S. resources could have accomplished the same results. The security battalion and artillery battery had not been assigned offensive missions and had thus contributed nothing to the power of the U.S. Military Assistance Command, Vietnam, to carry on offensive operations. The Philippine force did provide a degree of security to the population of the Tay Ninh City area in which it worked, but since Philippine units engaged in combat only in self-defense, the secure area did not extend beyond the immediate vicinity of the Philippine base camp or work sites. As for any psychological impact, the trade-off was between the loss of some allied solidarity—tempered by the fact that a contingent would remain in South Vietnam—and the resentment that many Vietnamese felt against the Philippine force. This resentment was strengthened by the traditional Vietnamese xenophobia and reluctance to accept assistance from a nation which had its own problems of internal corruption, underdevelopment, and even limited insurgency. In mid-April the U.S. Embassy stated:

> On balance, therefore, we feel that we should not ourselves take any

initiative to maintain PHILCAG in Vietnam. If we relent and acquiesce to the Philippine demands that we pick up the entire check, we will only serve to make it impossible to demand that PHILCAG improve its performance, since one does not preface an effort to shape up a unit by begging them to stay.

The State Department took notice of the embassy position but hoped "for a continuation of the present situation." It was believed that with 1969 an election year in the Philippines, the subject of the Philippine Civic Action Group, Vietnam, could be kept at a low key if the United States would contribute to the discussion by clarifying the choices available to the Philippines.

The existing situation was temporary and lasted only until 5 June, when the Philippine Senate passed its version of the national budget. The budget included funds for the Philippine Civic Action Group but restricted spending to the support of a "phased withdrawal." As the Philippine presidential campaign developed, by early October the civic action group had become a critical issue. President Marcos announced to the press the day after the election a proposed meeting to discuss a plan by which a small medical team would be maintained in South Vietnam. He also indicated that he would not ask Congress for further funding. On 14 November the following communication was received at the U.S. Embassy in Manila:

> Excellency: I have the honor to inform you that the Philippine Government has decided to withdraw the Philippine Civic Action Group (PHILCAG) from Vietnam. This decision is taken pursuant to the recommendation of the Foreign Policy Council. Accept, excellency, the renewed assurances of my highest consideration. Signed Carlos P. Romulo, Secretary of Foreign Affairs.

The most immediate problem caused by the announced withdrawal of the Philippine group was its possible impact on other contributing countries. The first effects were noticed in Thailand when on 20 November the Thai Foreign Minister, General Thanat Khoman, discussed the withdrawal with U.S. Ambassador Ellsworth Bunker. The minister expressed his bewilderment that the Free World allies had not been consulted before the Philippine decision to withdraw and indicated that the future of the other contributors to South Vietnam would be a subject for early discussions with other allies. Some Free World forces voiced the suspicion that the United States had been informed beforehand of the Philippine government's most recent action.

Redeployment planning for the Philippine force began on 25 November 1969. The advance party was transported by U.S. C–130 aircraft in two increments, the first on 1 December and the second a week later. The main body, moved by Philippine LST's between 13 and 15 December. Upon its departure the base camp at Tay Ninh was transferred to the U.S. 25th Infantry Division. Headquarters, Philippine Civic Action Group, Vietnam, was then reopened at Camp Bonaficio, Philippines.

When the main body departed, an equipment retrograde team of forty-four men remained behind to turn in U.S. and South Vietnamese equipment formerly in the hands of the Philippine group. On 21 January 1970 most of the team departed, leaving only fourteen people to complete the documentation of the equipment turned in. The last of this group left Vietnam on 15 February. The residual force was redesignated Philippine Contingent, Vietnam, and consisted of a headquarters element, four Military Assistance Program excess material teams, and four medical and dental teams. (*Chart 4*) All members of the contingent belonged to the armed forces of the Philippines, and the unit had an authorized strength of 131. Of these 131, there were 66 qualified medical, dental, and surgical doctors and technicians assigned to teams based in the cities of Tay Ninh, My Tho, Phu Cuong, and Bao Trai. The Military Assistance Program element consisted of 36 logistic specialists with four excess material teams of nine members each. The teams were located in Long Binh, Da Nang, Qui Nhon, and Cam Ranh Bay. The balance of the contingent was assigned to command and administrative duties at the national headquarters in Saigon.

The U.S. Military Assistance Command, in co-ordination with the Chief, Joint General Staff, Republic of Vietnam Armed Forces, provided security for the Philippine contingent. Members of the Philippine headquarters were assigned to U.S. billets in the Saigon area and the operational elements were located within South Vietnamese or U.S. installations. In keeping with former policy, members of the Philippine contingent carried arms only for the purpose of self-defense in the event of enemy attack. The Philippine contingent did not engage in offensive military operations.

The cycle was now completed. In 1964 the first unit of the Philippine Contingent, Vietnam, consisting of medical, dental, and surgical teams had arrived in South Vietnam. When the Philippine Civic Action Group, Vietnam, I, arrived in 1966, the original contingent was attached to this larger force with its capabilities integrated into the civic action mission. At the beginning of 1970 Philippine Contingent, Vietnam, became the Philippine designation of the rear party of the Philippine Civic Action Group. Basically it was the former Philippine Contingent, Vietnam, element and with no change in mission.

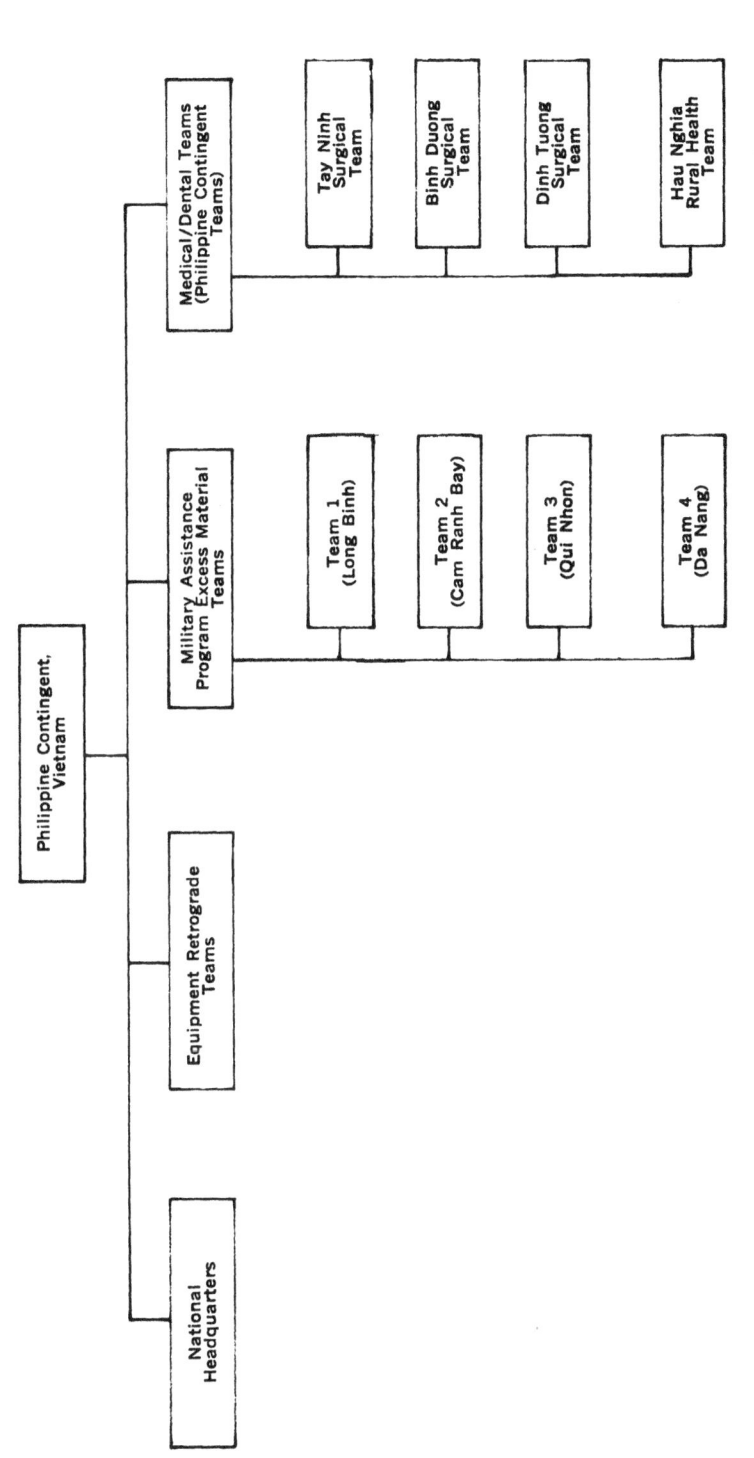

CHART 4—ORGANIZATION OF PHILIPPINE CONTINGENT, VIETNAM

During its existence the Philippine group in Vietnam made certain tangible contributions that will bear listing. Under the Engineering Civic Action Program it constructed 116.4 kilometers of road, 11 bridges, 169 buildings, 10 towers, 194 culverts, and 54 refugee centers. It also cleared 778 hectares of forest land; converted 2,225 hectares to community projects; and turned 10 hectares into demonstration farms. Under the Miscellaneous Environmental Improvement Program it rehabilitated, repaired, or engaged in minor construction work on 2 airstrips; 94 kilometers of roads; 47 buildings; 12 outposts; and 245 wells. It also trained 32 persons in use and maintenance of equipment; 138 in health education; and gave vocational training to 217. It resettled 1,065 families, distributed 162,623 pounds of food boxes, and sponsored 14 hamlets. Under the Medical Civic Action Program, the Philippine Group contributed 724,715 medical missions, 218,609 dental missions, and 35,844 surgical missions.

In discussing the value of the Philippine Civic Action Group during its stay in South Vietnam, President Thieu remarked: PHILCAGV has greatly contributed to the revolutionary development program of the Republic of Vietnam. Their untiring efforts also helped bring under government control many people previously living under Communist rule and . . . [gave] them confidence in the national cause.

Pacification Efforts

The pacification efforts of the Philippine Civic Action Group, Vietnam, are impossible to separate from a general history of the unit since pacification was an integral part, if not the whole, of the group's mission. There are certain aspects of the day-to-day operations, however, that can be clearly identified as pacification-oriented and as such can be separated from the basic study.

The Philippine Civic Action Group, Vietnam, came into being when the Philippine Congress passed a bill that authorized the government to send a contingent of engineer construction, medical, and rural development workers to South Vietnam. Briefly, their mission was to assist the Republic of Vietnam by the construction, rehabilitation, and development of public works, utilities, and buildings, and by offering technical advice on socioeconomic activities.

To accomplish this mission, a 2,000-man force was organized with an engineer construction battalion as its nucleus. Other units included a headquarters company with five civic action teams, a headquarters service company, a security battalion, and a field artillery battery. Attached to this force were six surgical teams and one rural health team which had been working in Vietnam under an earlier Philippine assistance program.

The plan called for the deployment of the Philippine Civic Action Group to Tay Ninh Province where it would clear the Thanh Dien forest, which for years had been a Viet Cong base area near the provincial capital. In addition, the group was to prepare the site for a refugee resettlement village of 1,000 families and at the same time conduct extensive civic action projects in the surrounding area.

The Philippine advance party arrived in Vietnam on 16 August 1966 to co-ordinate the arrival of the main body. With this group were three civic action teams that immediately began to conduct medical and dental programs in the area surrounding the base camp.

After the arrival of the main body in October 1966, work commenced in full. The first major project was the construction of the base camp on the eastern side of Tay Ninh West airfield. The construction was planned so that the base camp could be converted into another refugee resettlement village after the withdrawal of the Philippine Civic Action Group, Vietnam; 150 permanent prefabricated buildings of Philippine design were constructed, along with ten kilometers of road, a drainage system, and an electic lighting system.

The completed complex was more elaborate than was needed for a Vietnamese village, and most observers believed that in the long term the site could have been used more productively as a major training facility. Some American observers criticized the amount of work and materials which went into the construction of the base camp. Some said that by any standards, it was one of the "plushest" military camps in South Vietnam. It appeared to some that the Philippine Civic Action Group was intent on building a showplace that would impress visitors, especially those from the Philippines, and by so doing offset criticism leveled against the Philippine presence in South Vietnam. Much of the time and material used in the base camp construction, the critics felt, could have been better used on projects outside the camp.

Several alternate proposals for the use of the site were made early in the camp's history. One was that it be turned over to the South Vietnamese as a base camp for government troops; but this was not practical since there were few regular troops in the Tay Ninh area. A second proposal, more serious at the time because it had been expressed publicly by the province chief, was that the camp be used as the nucleus of a new university. When

Philippine Civic Action Group Member Distributes Medicines

questioned about the complexity and enormity of such a project and the vast amount of funds that would be required, the province chief replied that the Americans would help him. Another suggestion, which also suffered from a lack of funds, was that an agricultural college be established. The only proposal to merit further attention was the suggestion by the Chief of Staff, Philippine Civic Action Group, Vietnam, that the site be converted into a civil affairs training center.

The Philippine group did not begin to clear Thanh Dien Forest until December 1966 because of the efforts required to secure the base camp. Military operations had to be conducted by U.S. and South Vietnamese forces to clear the forest of Viet Cong. Meanwhile plans for projects were prepared and small-scale action activities were carried out, including the repair of some twenty-five kilometers of road, renovation of dispensaries and schools, construction of playgrounds, and implementation of medical civic action programs. One psychologically important activity was the repair and upgrading of thirty-five kilometers of roadways feeding the Long Ha market area, adjacent to the Cao Dai Holy See. This project did much to gain acceptance of the

Philippine Civic Action Group, Vietnam, by the Cao Dai sect.

Two formal organizations were created to co-ordinate Philippine activities with U.S. forces and South Vietnamese officials in Tay Ninh. The first of these, the Tay Ninh Friendship Council, consisted of the Tay Ninh province chief, the commanding general of the 196th Infantry Brigade, and the commanding general of the Philippine Civic Action Group, Vietnam. The council convened only a few times and then ceased its formal activities when other and more informal channels of co-ordination were found.

The Tay Ninh Friendship Council did produce, nonetheless, a document outlining the responsibilities for co-ordinating the activities and interests of the members. Titled the "Agreement of Mutual Assistance and Cooperation between PHILCAGV, US 196th Brigade and Tay Ninh Province," this document created a Civic Action Committee, the second formal organization. The province chief of Tay Ninh acted as chairman of the committee, which was composed of a senior representative from the Philippine group; the deputy province chief of administration; a representative from the U.S. Agency for International Development; a representative from the Joint U.S. Public Affairs Office; the secretary general for rural reconstruction; the chief of information and of the *Chieu Hoi* amnesty program; the chief of social welfare; the chief of economic services; the chief of health services; the chief of education services; the U.S. S–5 adviser to the Tay Ninh sector; the S–5 of the U.S. 196th Infantry Brigade; the Vietnamese S–5 of the Tay Ninh sector; another representative from the Philippine group; and the chief of any district concerned.

The committee hoped to meet at least once a month, but the organization proved too cumbersome and was difficult to convene. Hence, it rarely met and was of little significance in assisting the co-ordination between the Philippine group and Tay Ninh Province officials. In actual practice, the Philippine Civic Action Group resorted to more informal face-to-face means of contact. Co-ordination and co-operation were in turn left to *ad hoc* arrangements and personal relationships developed between Philippine officers and the Vietnamese officials.

In carrying out various civic action projects, the Philippine group introduced several new pacification techniques to the Republic of Vietnam. The group first explained the Philippine mission in South Vietnam to the local population in leaflets outlining the text of the Philippine Congress resolution which had sent the Philippine Civic Action Group to Vietnam. Philippine

PHILIPPINE GROUP CLEARS DEBRIS AFTER VIET CONG MORTAR HIT

civic action teams in the rural areas continually stressed their role: to build and not to fight. As a result the people were more receptive to the Philippine efforts than they would have been toward similar activities carried out by a combat unit.

The Philippine civic action teams were efficiently organized and adequately staffed to carry on numerous activities in any one hamlet on a given day. Typically, a Philippine civic action team would arrive in a hamlet and set up a bathing station and clothing distribution point for children; distribute school kits to children and teachers' kits to instructors; distribute food to the poor; and deliver kits to be used for prefabricated schools, or perhaps for a new hamlet office or a maternity dispensary. Subsequently, with the help of the hamlet residents, the Philippine team would erect the structures. The medical members of the civic action team then would set up a clinic which included instruments for minor surgery and special examining chairs. Simple dentistry work was then routinely provided and could be greatly appreciated by the inhabitants because of its rarity. Many times, modest engineering projects such as the repair of a hamlet road would be carried out.

In addition to the planned visit of an entire civic action team, each company-size unit was required to sponsor a hamlet in the Philippine area of interest and to conduct its own civic action program of modest projects on a permanent basis. Consequently, each of these units became intimately acquainted with a hamlet and its residents. The projects carried out were always small, but were well chosen for psychological impact. Requests for projects originated with the hamlet residents who were asked for advice by the unit. Philippine soldiers and the people then worked alongside each other to complete the project.

The major engineering undertaking of the Philippine Civic Action Group, the Thanh Dien Refugee Resettlement Project, provided much valuable experience that could be applied elsewhere in South Vietnam. The actual clearing of the forest was very similar to U.S. Rome Plow operations conducted elsewhere, but the difference lay in the fact that the Philippine engineers then developed the cleared land by constructing a model village.

Although the Philippine mission did not include the destruction of the Viet Cong, this did not prevent the group from implementing an active and productive campaign of psychological warfare designed to support the *Chieu Hoi* program. When a civic action team moved into an area, Philippine civic action group intelligence tried to identify the families with Viet Cong members. Attempts were then made to win over these families in order to encourage them to rally to the government cause and persuade their relatives to rally.

The security plans for the Philippine group as a noncombatant force were defensive in nature. The engineering projects were protected by Vietnamese Regional Forces or Popular Forces outposts during the hours of darkness and by their own security troops during the day. In addition, when an area had been chosen for a major project, all the neighboring hamlets received extensive civic action attention in order to develop a favorable atmosphere in the vicinity of the project. The idea was to generate good will among the people and thus perhaps to receive early warning of any impending Viet Cong incursion. Philippine units operated only within range of friendly artillery, and liaison officers were situated at the Tay Ninh sector tactical operations center and the tactical operations centers of nearby U.S. forces. These locations were also linked to the headquarters of the Philippine group by several means of communications.

The Philippine civic action efforts won the friendship and appreciation of many people in Tay Ninh Province. As Asians, the members of the Philippine group were well qualified to un-

ENTERTAINERS OF PHILIPPINE GROUP PLAY TO VILLAGERS

derstand and communicate with the Vietnamese people. They were not the target of anti-European feelings that were a legacy of the colonial period.

Other Vietnamese in Tay Ninh were less favorable toward the Philippine civic action group for several reasons. Reports made by the rural technical team of CORDS (Civil Operations Revolutionary Development Support) indicated that some people disapproved of what they termed "black marketeering and womanizing" by Philippine members. Prominent civilian and government persons in Tay Ninh Province expressed similar views. During a confidential conversation in July 1967 the Tay Ninh province chief commented unfavorably on the extent of the Filipinos' amorous activities and cited the numerous reports he had received of Filipino soldiers selling post exchange items and stolen material on the local black market. The province chief also claimed that the Vietnamese considered the Filipinos to come from an inferior culture without Vietnam's long history. This attitude, shared by other Vietnamese, had not been expressed overtly, but there were indications that this feeling constituted a barrier affecting the co-operation between provincial officials and Philippine officers.

The Thanh Dien Refugee Resettlement Project

The Thanh Dien Refugee Resettlement Project, undertaken by the Philippine Civic Action Group, Vietnam, at the suggestion of the province chief of Tay Ninh, involved the clearing of about 4,500 hectares of forested area for agricultural use, the development of 100 hectares for residential lots, and the construction of 41 kilometers of road. In addition, a bridge was constructed that linked Thanh Dien and a newly created hamlet, Phuoc Dien (Happy Riceland), with Highway 22. This resettlement site became the home of some 1,000 refugee families.

A Viet Cong stronghold for twenty years, the Thanh Dien forest was the home of the C-40 Regional Viet Cong Company, two Viet Cong guerrilla squads, and one Viet Cong special mission squad. Their presence in the Thanh Dien forest area threatened Tay Ninh City, the provincial capital, as well as the villages and hamlets of Phuoc Ninh District along Route 13 in the north and the villages and hamlets of Phu Khuong District along Highway 22 in the east. By clearing the Thanh Dien forest it was believed that the Viet Cong could be driven south. Government control would then extend up to the Vam Co Dong River.

Before work could begin, the forest had to be swept of organized resistance. This was accomplished before the project starting date by the U.S. 196th Light Infantry Brigade and units of the Vietnamese Regional Forces and Popular Forces through extensive search and clear operations.

The Philippine Civic Action Group began work on the project with Task Force BAYANIHAN on 1 December 1967. The force consisted of one reinforced engineer construction company, one reinforced security company, one explosive ordnance demolition team, one artillery forward observer team, and two civic action teams. Task Force BAYANIHAN approached the project area from the pacified hamlet of Ap Thanh Trung and then proceeded westward along an oxcart trail previously used only by Viet Cong and Viet Cong sympathizers. (Map 4) The troops literally inched across the forested area, defending themselves against enemy snipers and sappers and always keeping a close vigil for mines and booby traps. During this stage of the operation three to four Regional Forces companies provided outer security and protected the task force.

Despite this protection and the exercise of great caution, Task Force BAYANIHAN was, during the first six months of work, subjected on eight occasions to harassing fire from small arms, grenade launchers, and mortars; two Philippine enlisted men

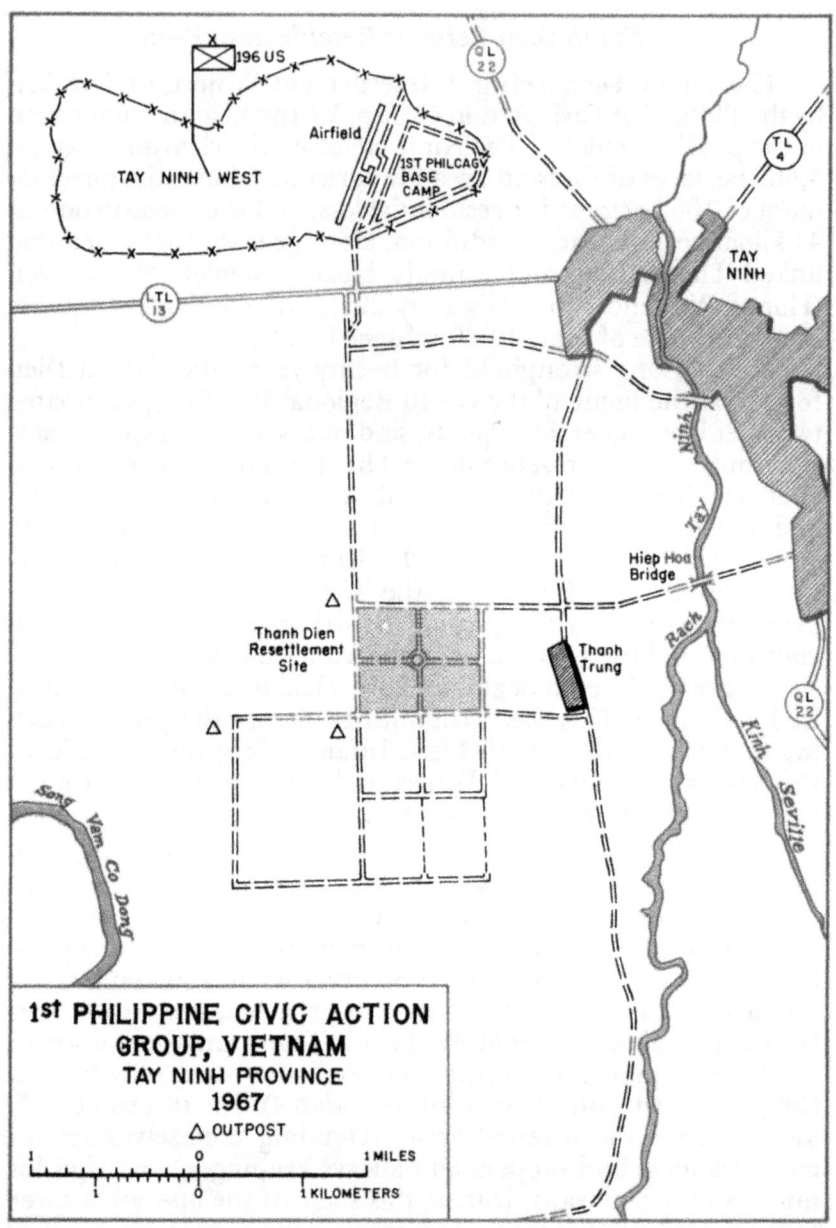

MAP 4

were killed and ten more wounded. In addition, two bulldozers and an armored personnel carrier were badly damaged, and a road grader and a tank were lightly damaged. With the degree of resistance increasing, it became obvious that the project was a threat to the Viet Cong hold on the area and the completion date of 30 July began to appear a little optimistic.

As the land was cleared Philippine engineers laid out the street pattern for the model village and began preparing farm plots. The Province Refugee Service then constructed refugee-type housing on the prepared sites. The Philippine group completed the engineering tasks that were beyond the means of the province. By the end of March the eastern half of the community subdivision was completed and on 4 April the first fifty refugee families were resettled by the province administration.

The province then formed a military and civil team composed of Regional Forces, Popular Forces, and Vietnamese government officials from the various provincial agencies. This team, working closely with a Philippine special civic action team, assisted the newly settled refugees to develop a viable community. CORDS, CARE (Co-operative for American Remittances to Everywhere), and Catholic Relief Service supplied commodities for distribution. Economic activities, tailored to the capabilities and skills of the villagers, were developed to assist them in becoming self-sufficient. For example, a carpentry shop started with donated tools made furniture for the Philippine enlisted men's club; a co-operative was begun for the manufacture of straw hats; small, short-term agricultural loans were made; vegetable seeds were distributed; piglets were given to selected families; and a pilot project was started to grow IR-8 rice developed by the Rockefeller International Rice Research Institute in the Philippines. As the clearing and the grading of the land proceeded, each new family received a half hectare of land for rice cultivation.

The development of the refugee resettlement site not only involved clearing and subdivision of the area, but the construction of community installations and facilities as well. Around the community center, the Philippine Civic Action Group constructed a hamlet office and information center, a dispensary and maternity clinic, and a ten-room schoolhouse. The province administration contributed to the project by constructing a public market and a powerhouse. Last, as an inspirational symbol, the Philippine group constructed a monument of "Hope" in the center of the community. (*Map 5*)

Economic improvements were not the only goals; efforts were also made to establish political institutions. A village chief was appointed by the province chief and the families were organized into residential blocks, each having a designated spokesman.

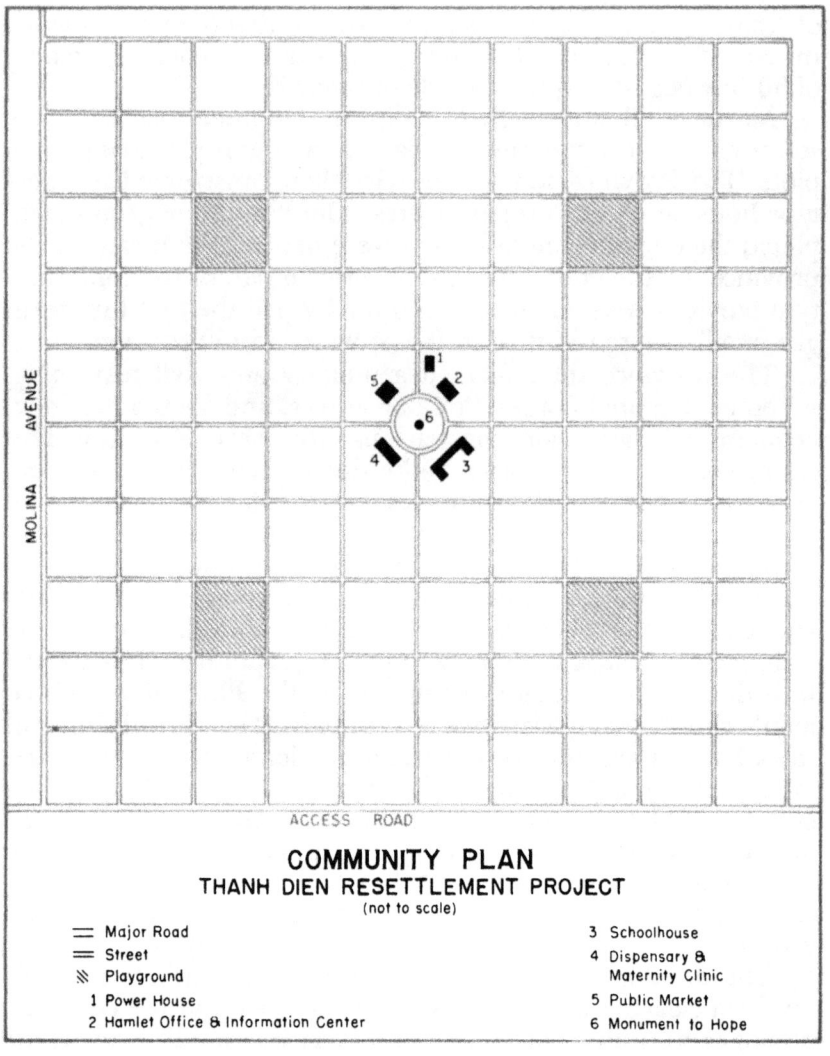

MAP 5

On 30 November 1967 the Thanh Dien Refugee Resettlement Project and the Hiep Hoa bridge were completed. Both projects were turned over to South Vietnamese authorities in a special ceremony on the following day. The bridge was opened with South Vietnamese Defense Minister Nguyen Van Vy as the guest of honor. At a parade staged in his honor, Minister Van Vy presented the Republic of Vietnam Presidential Unit Citation to the Philippine group for its civic action work. Philippine Ambassador Luis Moreno-Salcedo also presented the Philippine Presidential Unit Citation to the group in appreciation of its contributions in South Vietnam.

Unfortunately, this was not to be the last time the war touched Thanh Dien. On 16 December 1967 an estimated 200 Viet Cong guerrillas entered the hamlet. After holding a propaganda lecture and warning the new settlers to leave the community, they blew up the hamlet office, the powerhouse, and the brick home that had been built on a pilot basis. Similar, but less destructive incidents were to occur in other hamlets within the village but the Philippine Civic Action Group, Vietnam, was always quick to repair the damage.

CHAPTER IV

Australia and New Zealand

Long before President Johnson's "more flags" appeal, Australia had been providing assistance to South Vietnam. In 1962 Australia sent a thirty-man group of jungle warfare specialists as training advisers to the beleaguered nation. Located primarily in the northern provinces, they augmented U.S. advisory teams engaged in a similar mission. Two years later this first group was followed by an aviation detachment consisting of six Caribou aircraft with seventy-four men for maintenance and operations. Integrated into the Southeast Asia airlift, they provided valuable logistic support to dispersed Vietnamese military units. Over the years the Australian cargo aircraft unit was to maintain consistently higher averages in operational readiness and tons per sortie than did equivalent U.S. units.

Australia's support was not confined solely to military assistance. Beginning in July of 1964, a twelve-man engineer civic action team arrived to assist in rural development projects. Late in the same year Australia dispatched the first of several surgical teams, which was stationed in Long Xuyen Province. The second team arrived in January 1965 and was assigned to Bien Hoa.

From this rather modest beginning, Australia went on to provide an increasingly wide range of aid to South Vietnam under the Columbo Plan and by bilateral negotiations.[1] Unfortunately, not all of South Vietnam's ills could be cured by civic action, and as the situation became more desperate the Australian government planned to increase the size of its military contingent.

In 1965 the Australian Minister stated, in response to American overtures, that if the U.S. and South Vietnamese governments would request it, the Australian government would commit an infantry battalion to South Vietnam. Washington suggest-

---

[1] The Columbo Plan for Cooperative Development in South and Southeast Asia was drafted in 1951; with headquarters in Columbo on Ceylon, the co-operative had a membership of six donor countries—Australia, Canada, Great Britain, Japan, New Zealand, and the United States—and eighteen developing countries. Its purpose was to aid developing countries through bilateral member agreements for the provision of capital, technical experts, training, and equipment.

ed that Australia also take on the training mission for Vietnamese Regional Forces. On this proposition the minister expressed some doubt, but speculated that if an infantry battalion were sent to South Vietnam, some trainers—perhaps 100—might be attached to it. The American Ambassador in Saigon, General Taylor, then broached the subject with the South Vietnamese Prime Minister, Dr. Phan Huy Quat.

Talks continued at various levels and on 29 April 1965 Admiral Sharp conferred with the Australian Ambassador at the request of Ambassador Taylor. In the course of the discussions it was learned that the Australian government planned to dispatch to Saigon within fourteen days a small military planning staff to work out the logistic and administrative arrangements with U.S. Military Assistance Command, Vietnam, prior to the arrival of the Australian battalion. The battalion force would consist of 900 men, of which 100 were to be logistic and administrative troops; no integral support elements were planned for it. Moving both by sea and air, the unit was to reach South Vietnam by the first week of June. The Australian government agreed that the battalion should be under the operational control of General Westmoreland and that it should be used for the defense of base areas, for patrolling in the vicinity of base areas, and as a mobile reserve. However, the battalion was not to accept territorial responsibility for populated areas or to be involved in pacification operations.

By May when the plans were finalized they differed little from the earlier proposals. The Australian government was to send a task force composed of a headquarters element of the Australian Army, Far East, the 1st Battalion, Royal Australian Regiment, reinforced, the 79th Signal Troop, and a logistical support company. Also included in this total of approximately 1,400 troops were 100 additional jungle warfare advisers to be used in support of the original training detachments. The task force arrived in Vietnam during the early part of June 1965 and was attached to the U.S. 173d Airborne Brigade.

Operating from Bien Hoa, the 1st Battalion was limited to local security operations during the remainder of the year. This restriction was a result of the Australian government's insistence that Australian forces not be used in offensive or reaction operations except in conjunction with the defense of Bien Hoa air base. Although the interpretation of the restriction was fairly broad in that the battalion could participate in operations within approximately 30 to 35 kilometers of the base, General Westmoreland was not able to plan for its wider,use. For example, on

30 July, just shortly after their arrival, the troops of the Australian battalion were not permitted by the Australian chief of staff to participate in an operation with the 173d Airborne Brigade. Instead, in order to provide the airborne brigade with a third battalion to secure its artillery and fulfill the reserve role, a battalion from the U.S. 2d Brigade, 1st Infantry Division, was used. For all practical purposes this restriction was removed on 11 August 1965 when Brigadier O. D. Jackson, commander of the Australian Army Force, Vietnam, notified General Westmoreland that his superiors had expanded the Australian contingent's area of operations to encompass those provinces contiguous to Bien Hoa Province. A military working agreement had already been signed between Brigadier Jackson and General Westmoreland on 5 May that gave operational control of the Australian troops to the U.S. commander. The United States also agreed to provide complete administrative and logistical support. In a financial agreement concluded on 7 September, the Australian government agreed to repay the United States for this support. Additional combat and support troops became available on 30 September when a 105-mm. howitzer battery, a field engineer troop, an armored personnel carrier troop, a signal troop, and an air reconnaissance flight arrived to augment the battalion. At the end of 1965 the Australian strength in South Vietnam was 1,557.

The first contingent had hardly settled down before the Australian government began to consider increasing the size of its task force. Through their respective embassies in Saigon, the U.S. and Australian ambassadors held low key talks in December 1965 and again in January 1966, but the fear of public criticism initially kept the government of Australia from openly discussing plans to increase its military commitment to South Vietnam. On 8 March, however, the Australian government publicly announced that it would increase the one-battalion force to a two-battalion force with a headquarters, a special air service squadron, and armor, artillery, engineer, signal, supply and transport, field ambulance, and ordnance and shop units. At the same time the government suggested that the Australian Caribou flight, along with eight UH–1B helicopters, be given the primary mission of supporting the Australian task force. This commitment raised the Australian troop strength to slightly over 4,500.

General Westmoreland tentatively decided that the Australian task force would be based at Ba Ria, the capital of Phuoc Tuy Province, and placed under the control of the II Field Force

TROOPS OF ROYAL AUSTRALIAN REGIMENT *after arrival at Tan Son Nhut Airport.*

commander. He felt that this arrangement would place a large force in the area of Highway 15, a priority line of communication, and at the same time keep the Australian task force well away from the Cambodian border. Australia maintained diplomatic relations with Cambodia and for that reason had requested U.S. assurance that Australian units would not be used in operations along the Cambodian border. Additional artillery support, as needed, would be provided by the II Field Force. It was also decided that the eight UH–1B helicopters would come under the command of the task force; however, the request for task force control of the Australian Caribou units was denied because the Caribou units had a lift capacity in excess of the task force needs. It was agreed that reinforcing aircraft would be provided as needed.

During the first half of March 1966 the MACV staff and an Australian joint service planning team developed new military working arrangements and planned for the deployment of the task force. The agreement signed by both parties on 17 March superseded the previous agreement of 5 May 1965. The new agreement confirmed the mission of the Australian task force in

Living Quarters at an Australian Fire Support Base

Phuoc Tuy Province; the area of operations in the province was along Highway 15 and in the eastern portion of the Rung Sat Special Zone. Days later a financial arrangement was made by which Australia agreed to reimburse the U.S. government for support provided to Australian troops in South Vietnam.

The advance party for the 1st Australian Task Force left for South Vietnam on 12 April and the main body followed in several increments. After a brief training period, operational control of the task force passed from the Commander, Australian Force, Vietnam, to the Commanding General, II Field Force, Vietnam.

Discussions were meanwhile under way concerning a U.S. proposal that would bring an Australian squadron of twelve Caribou aircraft to South Vietnam to make up shortages in air sorties expected to result from U.S. deployment plans. General Westmoreland planned to employ the unit in support of South Vietnamese, South Korean, and U.S. ground operations as well as those conducted by the Australians. Operational control of the squadron would be given to the Seventh Air Force and, if politically acceptable to the Australian government, General Westmoreland planned to use the squadron against targets in Laos. On the sixth cf May Admiral Sharp took the proposal to the U.S. Joint Chiefs of Staff. The State Department concurred in the request and contacted the Australian Embassy in Washington to confirm that the squadron was available for deployment. The plan was never carried through.

With the arrival of reinforcements, the 1st Battalion, Royal Australian Regiment, left South Vietnam, having completed almost a full year of combat duty. In leaving, the "diggers"[2] could point with pride to a creditable performance during their stay, highlighted by participation in no fewer than nineteen major operations. Of particular note was an operation conducted in January 1966 which resulted in one of the biggest intelligence coups of the war up to that time. During a sweep of the so-called Iron Triangle, an area near Saigon heavily fortified and controlled by the Viet Cong, the Australian unit discovered a vast complex of tunnels, dug 60 feet deep in some places, which turned out to be a Viet Cong headquarters. In addition to capturing five new Chinese Communist antiaircraft guns, the Australians discovered 6,000 documents, many revealing names and locations of Viet Cong agents.

The effectiveness of the new Australian contingent was clearly demonstrated during the remainder of the year during which Australian troops killed more than 300 of the enemy, captured large stores of material, and helped secure Highway 15. Particularly successful was a battle conducted on 18 August 1966. Sweeping through a French rubber plantation called Binh Ba, 42 miles southeast of Saigon, Delta Company, 6th Battalion, Royal Australian Regiment, ran head on into a force estimated as 1,500 North Vietnamese and Viet Cong. In the initial exchange and at point-blank range the Aussies suffered most of their casualties. For three hours and in a blinding monsoon rain this company of approximately 108 men fought the enemy to a standstill. Taking advantage of their numbers, the enemy troops tightened the noose around the company, charged in human-wave attacks, but were beaten back continually. The fighting became so intense that the Australians ran low on ammunition and their helicopter pilots braved both the rain and heavy enemy fire to effect resupply. With the noise deadened by the downpour, a company of Australian reinforcements in armored personnel carriers moved unseen through the surrounding terrain and provided supporting fires with .50-caliber machine guns. At the same time Australian and other allied artillery units found the range to the targets. In the end, Delta Company routed the enemy troops from the battlefield, forcing them to leave behind 245 of their dead. During roughly four hours the Aussies killed

---

[2] A sobriquet variously ascribed to the prevalence of gold diggers in early Australian Army units and to the Australians' trench-digging activities in World War I.

AUSTRALIAN SOLDIER MANS MACHINE GUN POSITION

more of the enemy than they had in the entire preceding fourteen months.

Because of the forthcoming Australian elections, the Commander, Australian Force, Vietnam, did not expect to see any additional troops until after November. While Australian officials, both military and civilian, were aware of the task force's need for a third battalion, they did not wish at that time to add fuel to the fires of the critics of Australia's Vietnam policy. This course proved to be wise. Throughout the fall heated exchanges took place in the Australian House of Representatives over the troop question. Government officials continuously stated that no decision to increase Australian forces in South Vietnam had been taken, but at the same time they would not exclude the possibility of such a decision in the future. The Australian government gained additional maneuvering room when on 20 November 1966 the voters increased the ruling coalition's voting margin in the House of Representatives from nineteen to forty-one seats.

These events and the continuing controversy failed to interfere with other aid programs to South Vietnam and on 29 Nov-

MEMBERS OF AUSTRALIAN CIVIC ACTION TEAM *confer with village officials on plans for local improvements.*

ember a third Australian surgical team arrived in Saigon. This new group was assigned to the city of Vung Tau, and its thirteen members brought to thirty-seven the number of Australian medical personnel in South Vietnam.

From 1966 through 1968 Australian economic and technical assistance totaled more than $10.5 million and included the provision of technicians in the fields of water supply and road construction, experts in dairy and crop practices, and the training of 130 Vietnamese in Australian vocational and technical schools. In the area of refugee resettlement, Australia had provided over one and a fourth million textbooks, thousands of sets of hand tools, and over 3,000 tons of construction materials. Well recognizing the need and importance of an adequate communications system to allow the government to speak to the people, Australian technicians constructed a 50-kilowatt broadcasting station at Ban Me Thuot and distributed more than 400 radio receivers to civilian communities within range of the transmitter.

With a strong endorsement from the voters, the Australian government acted quickly to increase the size of the military contribution. The first step was to seek from the chairman of the Chief of Staff Committee, Australian Force, Vietnam, recommendation for the composition of additional forces which could be provided to South Vietnam on short notice. With little guidance and no knowledge of the ability of the U.S. and Vietnam governments to accommodate additional units, the chairman nonetheless made a recommendation. Cognizant of the desire of the Royal Australian Air Force and the Royal Australian Navy for action in South Vietnam and aware of the strong support given to a triservice contingent by the Australian Minister of Defense, he proposed an augmentation consisting of elements from all three services. Included in the offer was the H.M.A.S. *Hobart*, a guided missile destroyer; a Royal Navy diving team; a squadron of eight B-57 Canberra bombers, an 80-man civil affairs unit, and a 916-man increase to the existing Australian Army units in South Vietnam. Australia's three services and defense department supported the concept and were in accord with the idea that Australia should be the first nation, other than the United States, to support South Vietnam with a triservice contingent.

With regard to the ground forces, the 916 Australian Army reinforcements were provided for integration into units already in South Vietnam. Of that number, 466 were requested additions to the tables of organization and equipment of established units, and the remaining 450 constituted combat reinforcements to the 1st Australian Task Force.

The United States welcomed the idea of an increased Australian contingent and concurred with the request of the Australian government that H.M.A.S. *Hobart* and the Canberra squadron be deployed in conjunction with U.S. forces. It was expected that the *Hobart* would remain under Australian command but under operational control of the U.S. Navy. Until relieved by a like vessel, the ship would be available in all respects as an additional ship of the U.S. Navy force and without operational restrictions. Anticipated missions included shore bombardment of both North and South Vietnam, interdiction of coastal traffic, picket duties for carrier operations, and general operations in support of naval forces at sea. The command and control arrangements for the Canberra squadron would be similar to those for the *Hobart*, with the aircraft located where they could support Australian forces as part of their mission. The squadron would perform routine maintenance in Vietnam while relying on major maintenance from Butterworth, Malaysia, where two float aircraft would be retained. (While they were agreeable to the maintenance arrangements, the Malaysians stressed the fact that they did not care to publicize the matter.) The squadron was also to deploy with a 45-day stockage of 500-pound bombs. Other logistical support in the form of petroleum products, rations, accommodations, engineer stores, and common usage items would be provided by the United States on a reimbursable basis.

The initial conference between the Australian planning group, headed by Air Vice Marshal Brian A. Eaton, and the staff of U.S. Military Assistance Command, Vietnam, took place in Saigon during 3–7 January 1967. At this time logistical matters and command and control arrangements were firmed up as previously discussed. The Canberras would be based at Phan Rang and employed in the same manner as all other Seventh Air Force strike aircraft. Operational control was given to the Commander, Seventh Air Force, while the Commander, Australian Force, Vietnam, retained command and administrative control. Deployment of the Canberra squadron was thought ideal in view of the fact that the aircraft were considered obsolete and were due to be replaced in Australia by F–111 aircraft.

When the conference turned to naval matters, U.S. representatives asked for more details on the capabilities of the Australian diving team. The general concept of employment envisioned that the team would be integrated into operations of the Commander, U.S. Naval Forces, Vietnam, Rear Admiral Norvell

G. Ward. Australian and U.S. Navy representatives were meeting meanwhile in the Philippines to develop arrangements for the logistic and administrative support of H.M.A.S. *Hobart* while it operated with the Seventh Fleet. The Saigon conference agreed that MACV need not be involved in any arrangements pertaining to the *Hobart*.

The Australians returned home from South Vietnam seemingly pleased with the arrangements made and appreciative of U.S. assistance, especially since the government of Australia had allocated only limited time to get the operation moving. The Canberra squadron had been directed to be operationally ready by 1 April 1967. The Phan Rang facilities were crowded but the Australian squadron was only a small addition and the assurances given the Australians of their need and value made a lasting impression. In January and February the Australian 5th Airfield Construction Squadron left for South Vietnam to build the maintenance hangar and other facilities for the squadron. On 19 April eight of the ten Canberra bombers deployed to South Vietnam from Butterworth—the first such aircraft to enter the war. Personnel numbered approximately 40 officers, 90 noncommissioned officers, and 170 other enlisted men.

The H.M.A.S. *Hobart* was integrated into the war effort when she relieved a U.S. Navy destroyer off Chu Lai on 31 March. Operational employment, logistic support, command relations, and use of clubs, messes, and exchanges were arranged on a navy-to-navy basis.

In January 1967 the Australian government had indicated that ten navy antisubmarine warfare pilots qualified in the H–34 helicopter might be deployed to South Vietnam. MACV believed that after ten hours of transitional training in UH–1D aircraft the pilots could be integrated directly into U.S. Army aviation units. It was not until April, however, that the offer was formalized: eight pilots and some thirty men for maintenance and support were offered to relieve U.S. troops operating in support of the Australian task force. The pay and allowances of this contingent would be paid by Australia while the United States would provide the aircraft and logistical support. The men would be integrated into U.S. units and would relieve U.S. troops on an individual basis.

To facilitate administration, the U.S. Joint Chiefs of Staff had requested that the Australian pilots be stationed near a Royal Australian Air Force squadron. They further asked that, if practicable, the Australians be assigned to U.S. units that normally supported the Australian task force. General Westmoreland pointed out that U.S. Army helicopter units were not assigned to support specific organizations or task forces and that the assignment of the Australians would be dictated by the tactical situation. Later discussions revealed that while the Australian government wished to attach its troops to the Australian unit at Vung Tau for administrative support, there was no official requirement for Australian pilots to be assigned to U.S. units supporting the Australian task force. General Westmoreland replied that if the proposed Australian offer materialized, the Australians would be assigned to a helicopter company of the 12th Combat Aviation Group in the Bien Hoa-Bearcat area. From this location they would support units in the III Corps Tactical Zone where the Australian ground troops were stationed. Upon the arrival of the 135th Aviation Company in Vietnam, they would be reassigned to that unit. The 135th Aviation Company was to be stationed at Nui Dat, the location of an Australian Air Force helicopter squadron, only 35 kilometers northeast of Vung Tau. From Nui Dat the 135th Aviation Company would support the 1st Australian Task Force and others. Should the 135th arrive in Vietnam before the Australian helicopter contingent it would be assigned directly to that contingent. An Australian government request that the pilots be permitted to operate helicopter gunships was also honored.

In October 1967 the Prime Minister of Australia announced new plans to increase the Australian forces in South Vietnam by another 1,700 troops, thus raising the Australian contingent from about 6,300 to over 8,000 men. Increases in the ground forces were to consist of one infantry battalion, one medium-tank squadron with Centurian tanks (250 men), an engineer construction troop of 45 men, and an additional 125 men to augment the headquarters group. The infantry battalion, the 3d Battalion, Royal Australian Regiment, was to be deployed during November and December with the other units following as transportation became available. The additional air force contingent was to consist of eight Iroquois helicopters, ten helicopter pilots, twenty enlisted crew members, and 100 maintenance men. The helicopters and personnel were to be assigned to the Royal Australian Air Force No. 9 Helicopter (Utility) Squadron which had deployed the previous June. The Navy was to provide the small number of antisubmarine warfare helicopter pilots and maintenance personnel discussed earlier in the year.

The added force, deployed over an eight-month period beginning in November 1967, totaled 1,978, slightly over the proposed figure. The 3d Battalion, Royal Australian Regiment, with

Soldier of Royal Australian Regiment *pauses during sweep of cultivated area around a village.*

combat support and logistic elements closed in Vietnam in December 1967 and was attached to the 1st Australian Task Force in the III Corps Tactical Zone. The tank squadron with its logistical support elements arrived in late February and early March of 1968 with fifteen operational Centurian tanks. Eleven more tanks were added in September. The No. 9 Helicopter Squadron received its eight additional helicopters in July, giving that unit sixteen helicopters. A cavalry troop of thirty men was added in October 1968.

The type and degree of support provided the additional Australian forces was in accordance with a new military working arrangement signed on 30 November 1967. Under its terms the Australian government was to reimburse the U.S. government at a capitation rate for the support provided. U.S. support included base camp construction and cost of transportation within Vietnam for supplies of Australian Force, Vietnam, arriving by commercial means; billeting and messing facilities, but not family quarters for dependents (payment of meals and billeting service charges were paid for by the individual in the Saigon area);

some medical and dental care in Vietnam but not evacuation outside Vietnam except for emergency medical evacuation, which was provided on the same basis as that for U.S. troops; mortuary service, including preparation of the bodies for shipment, but not transportation outside Vietnam; transportation, including use of existing bus, sedan, taxi, and air service operated by the United States in Vietnam; delivery of official messages transmitted by radio or other electrical means through established channels; use of U.S. military postal facilities, including a closed pouch system for all personal and official mail (1st through 4th class); exchange and commissary service in Vietnam; special services, including established rest and recreation tours; necessary office space, equipment, and supplies; and spare parts, petroleum products, and maintenance facilities for vehicles and aircraft within the capabilities of U.S. facilities and units in Vietnam.

Agitation in Australia for troop withdrawals, noticeable in 1968, increased as the year 1969 came to a close, especially in view of U.S. redeployment plans. On 15 December 200 shop stewards and 32 labor union leaders representing over 1.5 million Australian voters passed a resolution protesting Australian participation in the war. Coupled with this was a second resolution calling upon Australian troops in South Vietnam to lay down their arms and refuse to fight. The next day the Secretary of the Trades Council criticized the resolution as being, " . . . a call for mutiny." On 16 December the Australian Prime Minister felt it necessary to outline the government position on South Vietnam. In a television address he stated:

> In my policy speech before the last election, I had this to say to the Australian people: "Should there be developments (in Vietnam) which result in plans for continuing reduction of United States Forces over a period, we would expect to be phased into that program." Since I spoke, developments have taken place, and you have today heard the announcement by the President of the United States that a further 50,000 troops are to be withdrawn over the next few months. . . . I have spoken directly with the President of the United States, in accordance with arrangements made on my last visit, and we were in complete accord in agreeing, in principle, that should the future situation permit a further substantial withdrawal of troops, then some Australian troops should be included in the numbers scheduled for such reduction. Such agreement in principle is all that has been reached, or all that can at present be reached. . . . So I wish to make it clear: That there is no firm timetable for further withdrawal of United States troops of which I know. . . . That there is no arrangement made as to how great any Australian reduction, which may take place in the future, will

be. . . . But these things are clear: We will not abandon the objects for which we entered the Vietnam War. We will participate in the next reduction of forces at some stage, when it comes. . . . We will remain to attain the objectives which we started to reach, but we are glad we are able to make reductions without endangering those objectives.

The first open talks with the Australians concerning troop redeployment were held on 28 January 1970 when the chief of staff of the Australian Force, Vietnam, met with the assistant chief of staff, J–3, of the U.S. Military Assistance Command, Vietnam, to discuss Australia's intentions on troop withdrawal. The Australian chief of staff could not confirm the existing rumors that Australian troops would be pulled out in April or May; he indicated that he had no knowledge of the subject other than the Prime Minister's announcement of 16 December. He went on to add that he believed only one battalion would be withdrawn initially and the pace of future moves would be keyed to moves by the United States.

On the second day of April the Military Assistance Command Training Directorate and the Central Training Command convened a conference to discuss an Australian proposal for in-

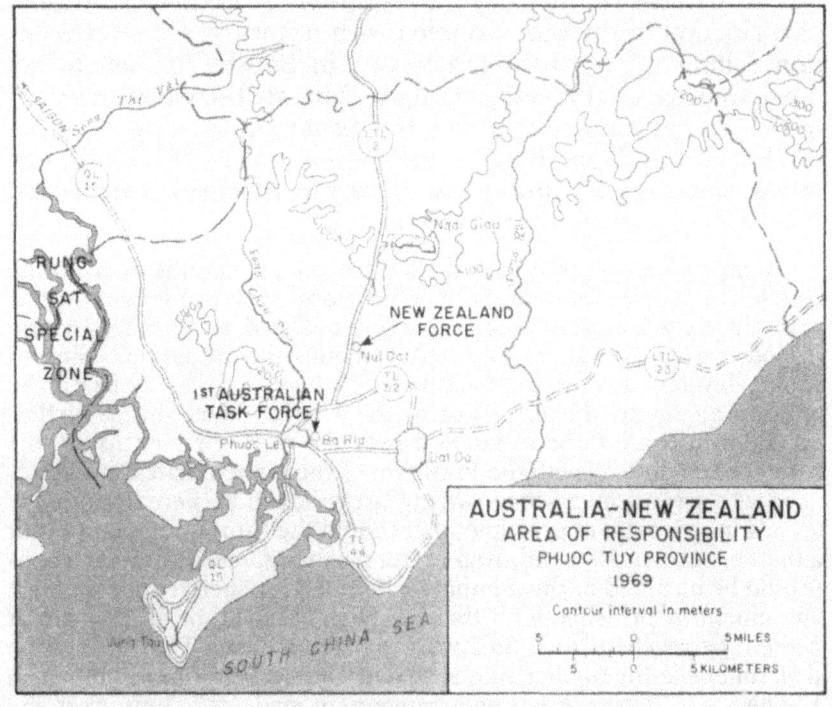

MAP 6

creased Australian support of Vietnamese training. The exact terms of this proposal had not yet been determined but the training would be supplied for the Regional and Popular Forces in Phuoc Tuy Province. (*Map 6*) Any increased training effort on the part of the Australians was to be linked to future withdrawals of Australian troops. No definite dates for withdrawals or specific numbers of men to be withdrawn had been decided upon.

The situation became clearer when the Australian government announced on 20 August the pending redeployment of the 8th Battalion, Royal Australian Regiment. This unit of approximately 900 men returned home about 12 November, leaving behind a force level of 6,062. The move was accompanied by an offer of approximately $3.6 million (U.S.) to South Vietnam as a direct grant for defense aid. This was the first phase of the Australian withdrawal; future reductions in troops were to be handled in much the same manner.

Almost one year later, 18 August 1971, the Australian government announced that it would withdraw its combat forces from South Vietnam in the next few months. Prime Minister William McMahon stated that the bulk of the force would be home by Christmas. To help offset the troop reduction the Australian government pledged $28 million in economic aid for civil projects in South Vietnam during the next three years. This placed the total monetary cost to Australia for active participation in the war in the neighborhood of $240 million.

The forces of discontent plaguing the Australian government's Vietnam policy were at work in New Zealand as well, but on a smaller scale. Just as New Zealand was prompted by the same rationale as Australia to enter the conflict in South Vietnam, it was prompted to leave for similar reasons. The Australian announcement of a troop reduction on 20 August 1970 was accompanied by a like announcement from New Zealand. On that date the Prime Minister stated his intention of reducing the New Zealand contingent by one rifle company of 144 men. Then in November 1970 New Zealand made plans to send a 25-man army training team to South Vietnam in early 1971. This announcement followed closely and was intended to offset the 12 November departure of the New Zealand rifle company. It was proposed that the training team serve as a contribution to a joint Vietnam-New Zealand training facility at the Chi Lang National Training Center in Chau Doc Province.

New Zealand again followed suit when on 18 August 1971 its government announced with Australia that New Zealand too would withdraw its combat forces from South Vietnam. In Wel-

MEMBERS OF ROYAL NEW ZEALAND ARTILLERY *carry out a fire mission.*

lington, New Zealand's Prime Minister, Sir Keith J. Holyoake, said that his country's combat forces would be withdrawn by "about the end of this year [1971]."

The New Zealand contingent in Vietnam served with the Australians. Both nations realized that their own vital interests were at stake. The decline of British power had made the security of New Zealand more dependent upon the United States and upon damming the flood of what Prime Minister Holyoake called in 1968 "terror and aggression." The fundamental issues, Holyoake said, were simple: "Whose will is to prevail in South Vietnam—the imposed will of the North Vietnamese communists and their agents, or the freely expressed will of the people of South Vietnam?"

Discussion surrounding the nature of New Zealand's aid to South Vietnam was conducted at various levels. The U.S. Military Assistance Command, Vietnam, became involved when Lieutenant Colonel Robert M. Gurr, a representative of New Zealand's Joint Chiefs of Staff, met with MACV representatives during the period 5–10 June 1963. The New Zealand government was interested in such categories of assistance as workshop teams, engineers, field medical elements, naval elements, and army combat elements. Information on the possible use of New Zealanders in each of these categories as well as other recommendations was provided. Colonel Gurr pointed out that while his government was reluctant to become deeply involved in combat operations for political reasons, the New Zealand military was interested in gaining knowledge of Vietnam and experience in combat operations.

New Zealand first contributed to the defense of South Vietnam on 20 July 1964 when an engineer platoon and surgical team arrived in Vietnam for use in local civic action projects. Then in May 1965 the government decided to replace the detachment with a combat force consisting of a 105-mm. howitzer battery. This unit, the 161st Battery, Royal New Zealand Artillery, arrived on 21 July, was put under the operational control of MACV, and was attached to the 173d Airborne Brigade with the primary mission of supporting the Australian task force in Phuoc Tuy Province. The following month a military working agreement was signed under which the United States agreed to furnish field administrative support. Although no financial working agreement had been signed by the end of the year, New Zealand was reimbursing the United States for the cost of support given. The contingent from New Zealand at this time numbered 119.

The year 1966 opened with discussions between General Westmoreland and the Ambassador of New Zealand over the possibility of increased military aid to South Vietnam. Specifically, General Westmoreland hoped that New Zealand could provide a battalion of infantry for a three-battalion Australian-New Zealand (ANZAC) brigade. While sympathetic to the proposal, the ambassador said there were political considerations governing the increase that were beyond his authority. In late February, a representative from the New Zealand Ministry of External Affairs met with General Westmoreland and indicated an interest in rounding out the 105-mm. howitzer battery from four to six guns. Despite election year pressure and subsequent political considerations tending to limit aid to nonmilitary areas, New Zealand announced on 26 March 1966 its decision to add two howitzers and twenty-seven men to its force in South Vietnam. In addition the surgical team in Qui Nhon was to be increased from seven to thirteen men.

During a visit to South Vietnam the Chief of the General Staff, New Zealand Army, told General Westmoreland that he believed New Zealand might respond to requests for additional military assistance, but not until after the November elections. Several possibilities were mentioned, including an infantry battalion of four companies and a Special Air Services company. Both units were in Malaysia, but could be redeployed to South Vietnam. Also under consideration was the use of an APC platoon and a truck company. The Army chief admitted that civilians and some military men in the New Zealand Defense Ministry did not share his views, hence there was little chance for the immediate implementation of the proposals.

The elections in the fall of 1966 seemed to define New Zealand's policy in regard to South Vietnam. With a solid voter mandate the New Zealand Prime Minister instructed his Defense Minister to review the entire situation and in doing so to consider the use of all or part of the New Zealand battalion of the 28th Commonwealth Brigade (Malaysia) for service in South Vietnam.

The New Zealand government then summarized the possibilities for military aid to Vietnam. The army possibilities for deployment were a 40-man Special Air Services company (squadron), or five 20-man troops to alternate 6-month periods of duty with an Australian counterpart organization. An armored personnel carrier troop of 30 men and 12 carriers was another possibility, but not for the immediate future. Also considered was an infantry rifle company from the battalion in Malaysia or the entire battalion. Last, small additional administrative and logistical support units were suggested by the Australians. Likely Air Force increases were from four to six Canberra (B–57) flight crews supported by forty to fifty ground personnel to be integrated into either U.S. or Australian Canberra squadrons. Because it was not practical to use the B–57's of the New Zealand Air Force with U.S. bombers, it was decided to leave them in New Zealand with a training mission. Other Air Force possibilities were a few fully qualified Canberra or Vampire pilots for a U.S. sponsored training program for F–4 aircraft and subsequent combat operations; the addition of a few operations, intelligence, and forward air controller personnel; several Bristol freighter transports with crews and necessary ground support personnel; and finally, air crews and ground-support personnel for Iroquois helicopters. Possible naval contributions ranged from the deployment of the frigate *Blackpool* from Singapore to a station with the Seventh Fleet off the coast of Vietnam to the man for man integration of from 20 to 40 men on U.S. patrol craft. Besides all this, the government of New Zealand had been considering the likelihood of substituting a medical team drawn

AUSTRALIAN CIVIL AFFAIRS TEAM MEMBER TREATS VILLAGE BOY

from the armed forces for the three civilian medical teams previously programmed for Binh Dinh Province.

The views of officials of the Military Assistance Command, Vietnam, and the office of the Commander in Chief, Pacific, on these proposals were passed to New Zealand in order of their preference. The United States preferred a full infantry battalion, an infantry rifle company, a Special Air Services company (special forces), and an armored personnel carrier troop, in that order. The infantry battalion from Malaysia could be used effectively in any corps tactical zone, but it would probably be most effective if attached to the Australian task force, thereby doubling the force's capacity to conduct search and clear operations. Moreover the move would enhance security in the Vung Tau area and aid the revolutionary development program. The existing two-battalion force had limited the size of the task force operations to one reinforced battalion, the other battalion being required for base camp security. If only an infantry rifle company were available, it would be employed as part of the Australian task force. The Special Air Services company (squadron) would help fill the need for long-range patrols and reconnaissance as the allied offensive gained momentum. The company could be used effectively in any corps area, but its use was preferred in the III Corps Tactical Zone under the operational control of II Field Force headquarters. The unit was to be employed alone, in a specified remote area, to observe and report on enemy dispositions, installations, and activities. The armored personnel carrier troop would be employed with the Australian task force, where its presence would increase the force's ability to safeguard roads as well as to conduct operations to open lines of communication.

With regard to New Zealand Air Force contributions, a Canberra squadron was believed to be the most desirable, followed by the Bristol freighter transports, support for Iroquois helicopters, F–4 pilots, intelligence specialists, and forward air controllers. The bombers would operate with the Australian squadron while the Bristol freighters would provide logistic support in Vietnam as well as lift for the Australian task force. Up to 25 officers and 25 enlisted men could be used in conjunction with the Iroquois helicopter company and it was hoped that the men would be available for a minimum of six months. Intelligence specialists and forward air controllers would be used to co-ordinate and direct tactical air and artillery support for ground forces. Augmenting the Seventh Fleet with a *Blackpool* type of destroyer would be especially desirable, as would the integration of a New Zealand contingent with U.S. crews on either MARKET TIME or GAME WARDEN patrol craft. No command and control problems were anticipated in any of these proposals.

The reviews and discussions surrounding increased New Zealand Air Force contributions finally resulted in some action. On 8 March 1967 the Australian government announced that it intended to send a sixteen-man triservice medical team to Binh Dinh Province in late May or early June to replace the U.S. team at Bong Son. At the same time a decision was made to double New Zealand military forces in South Vietnam through the deployment of a rifle company. Accompanied by support troops, this unit would be drawn from its parent battalion in Malaysia and rotated after each six-month tour of duty. The first element of V Company, Royal New Zealand Infantry Regiment, arrived in South Vietnam on 11 May 1967. In October General Westmoreland learned that the New Zealand government would add still another rifle company to its contingent some time before Christmas. This unit, W Company, Royal New Zealand Infantry Regiment, plus engineer and support troops arrived during the period 16–17 December 1967. Both rifle companies were integrated with an Australian unit to form an ANZAC battalion. A

SOLDIER OF ROYAL NEW ZEALAND ARMY COOKS HIS LUNCH

platoon of New Zealand Special Air Services also arrived in December and was integrated into a similar Australian unit. These deployments brought the New Zealand troop strength up to its authorized level for a total commitment of approximately 517 men.

Logistical support accorded the New Zealand forces was provided in a military working arrangement signed 10 May 1968. Under the terms of this arrangement, the New Zealand government was to reimburse the U.S. government at a capitation rate for the support provided. U.S. support included base camp construction and transportation costs within Vietnam for New Zealand force supplies arriving by commercial means; billeting and messing facilities (but not family quarters for dependents); some medical and dental care in Vietnam but not evacuation outside Vietnam except emergency medical evacuation, such as that provided for U.S. troops; use of U.S. operated bus, sedan, taxi, and air service; delivery of official messages transmitted by radio or other electrical means through established channels; use of U.S. military postal facilities, including a closed pouch system for all personal and official mail; exchange and commissary service in Vietnam; special services, including established rest and recreation tours; necessary office space, equipment, and supplies; spare parts, petroleum products, and maintenance facilities for vehicles and aircraft within the capabilities of U.S. facilities and units in Vietnam.

There was no significant change in strength or mission for the New Zealand forces in South Vietnam during the remainder of 1969. (*Table 2*)

TABLE 2—LOCATION, STRENGTH, AND MISSION OF NEW ZEALAND FORCES JUNE 1969

Unit	Location	Authorized Strength	Mission
Headquarters, New Zealand Force, Vietnam	Saigon, Gia Dinh	18	Comd and admin support
161st Battery, RNZIR	Nui Dat, Phuoc Tuy	131	Combat
RNZIR component; various appointments with 1st Australian Task Force	Nui Dat, Phuoc Tuy	18	Combat
V Company, RNZIR	Nui Dat, Phuoc Tuy	150	Combat
W Company, RNZIR	Nui Dat, Phuoc Tuy	150	Combat
Administrative Cell	Nui Dat, Phuoc Tuy	9	Admin support
No. 4 Troop, NZ SAS	Nui Dat, Phuoc Tuy	26	Combat
Logistical support element	Nui Dat, Vung Tau, Phuoc Tuy	27	Logistical support
1 NZ Svcs Med Team	Dong Son, Binh Dinh	16	Asst to GVN

While there appeared to be some hesitancy over the type and amount of New Zealand's military aid, the country's financial assistance to South Vietnam continued unabated. Commencing in 1966, financial aid averaged approximately $350,000 (U.S.) annually. This sum financed several mobile health teams to support refugee camps, the training of village vocational experts, and the establishment of the fifteen-man surgical team deployed to the Qui Nhon–Bong Son area. Other appropriated support funded the cost of medical and instructional material for Hue University and the expansion of Saigon University. During the 1967–68 period nearly $500,000 (U.S.) of private civilian funds were donated for Vietnamese student scholarships in New Zealand and increased medical and refugee aid.

For a number of years the Australian and New Zealand troops, distinctive in their bush hats, operated in their own area of responsibility in Phuoc Tuy Province. Their job was essentially to conduct offensive operations against the enemy through

AUSTRALIAN SOLDIER SEARCHES FOR ENEMY IN HOA LONG VILLAGE

"clear and hold" actions. Related and equally important tasks included the protection of the rice harvest and a civic action program. When the Australian task force was introduced into Phuoc Tuy Province in 1965, its commanding general, recognizing the need to develop rapport with civilians, directed the task force to develop an effective modus operandi for civic action operations. After several months and considerable co-ordination with other agencies a concept of operations was developed. In July 1966 the program went into effect.

In the first stage, civic action teams composed of four men each were sent to hamlets in the area surrounding the task force command post in Long Le District. At this time the objective was simply to develop rapport with the local population; the teams made no promises and distributed no gifts. The Long Le area had been largely under Viet Cong domination since the early fifties and the people therefore were at first somewhat reluctant to accept the Australians, who looked and spoke like Americans, but yet were different. This reluctance was gradually overcome.

The first stage lasted for approximately two weeks and was followed by the preparation of a hamlet study that outlined the

Soldier of Royal Australian Regiment With M60

type of projects to be undertaken. Some material support was solicited from U.S. Agency for International Development, Joint U.S. Public Affairs Office, and Military Assistance Command, Vietnam. In addition, the Australians had a sizable fund at their disposal for the purchase of materials and payment of labor. In executing the plan, priorities for project construction were set and forwarded to the province chief for his approval. After approval, construction commenced. The results were impressive. In a one-year period in the district town alone, eight classrooms, a Vietnamese information service headquarters, a district market, a maternity ward, a three-room dispensary, a town meeting hall, large warehouses, a dozen capped wells, a district headquarters building, a police checkpoint, and several other hard structure projects were completed.

In the execution of this program the Australians initially commited one basic error which is worth noting. They did not recognize sufficiently the critical importance of the hamlet, village, and district governments and the imperative need to consult, work with, and co-ordinate all projects with local Vietnamese officials. This lack of co-ordination resulted in some problems. For example, maintenance on projects was not performed because no one felt responsible and no prior commitment had been made. And while the projects were thought to be in the best interests of the local population by Vietnamese officials, their precise location and design did not necessarily match the people's desires.

The people respected the Australians for their fine soldiering and discipline. In a study of Phuoc Tuy Province the respondents remarked that Australians never went over the 10 miles per hour limit in populated areas, individually helped the Vietnamese, and paid fair wages for skilled and unskilled labor.

One reason for the success of the Australians in Vietnam was their experience of over a generation in fighting guerrilla wars. The Australian Army, before going to Vietnam, saw action in the jungles of Borneo against the Japanese and then spent twelve years helping the British put down a Communist insurgency in Malaya. Another reason for the effectiveness of the Australian soldiers could be attributed to their training. Because of its small size the Australian Army trained exclusively for the one kind of war it was most likely to face—guerrilla war in the jungles and swamps of Asia. Furthermore the army, composed largely of volunteers, is a highly specialized organization. One ranking Australian officer who advised the South Vietnamese security forces compared his country's army to the Versailles-

Royal Australian Air Force Civic Action Team *moves out past Vietnamese temples to Mung Duc.*

restricted German Army after World War I which became so "cadre-ized" that even the lowest ranking private could perform the duties of a captain.

CHAPTER V

The Republic of China

Nationalist Chinese contributions to the war in Vietnam were limited by extremely sensitive considerations involving the possible reactions of Peking and Saigon to the presence in South Vietnam of Chinese in military uniform. Offers of combat troops from the Republic of China for Vietnam were made early in the war by President Chiang Kai-shek to President Johnson. Later, on 24 February 1964, Chiang Kai-shek again stressed to Admiral Jerauld Wright, Ambassador to the Republic of China, and Admiral Harry D. Felt, Commander in Chief, Pacific, that the United States should plan with the government of the Republic of China for possible use of the republic's armed forces against North Vietnam. Dr. Yu Ta-Wei, Minister of Defense, also pursued the subject of troop contributions with Admiral Felt, including discussion of a possible Chinese Nationalist attack on the island of Hainan. The United States was wary, however, of military assistance from the Chinese Nationalists and excluded their government when soliciting the Republic of Korea, the Philippines, and other countries for contributions of noncombat units in uniform. There was some concern on the one hand that the Republic of China would feel offended if left out, but on the other hand the United States was aware of the Chinese Communist view of Nationalist Chinese intervention and decided not to risk provoking Communist China. The United States decided that the dispatch of Nationalist engineer units would not provoke overt Chinese Communist retaliation, even though the move could provide a pretext for intervention at a later date. To preclude the possibility of Chinese Communist interference in the Formosa Strait, or elsewhere for that matter, the United States tried to play down the role of Republic of China military assistance and direct the aid of the republic primarily to the field of civic action.

Assistance from the Republic of China arrived in South Vietnam in the form of an advisory group on 8 October 1964. The mission of this Republic of China Military Assistance Advisory Group, Vietnam, was to furnish political warfare advisers and medical men and to help with the problem of refugees. Three LST crews were also to assist in the waterborne logistical effort. The LST's belonged to the U.S. Navy port, Keelung, on Taiwan.

Two political warfare advisers were stationed in each of the four corps tactical zones, three advisers at the Republic of Vietnam Armed Forces Political Warfare College in Dalat, and the other three with the Armed Forces General Political Warfare Directorate in Saigon. Sponsored and supported by the U.S. Agency for International Development, the seven-member provincial health assistance team worked in the provincial hospital at Phan Thiet. The Republic of China also provided two C-46 aircraft and crews for refugee relief missions in South Vietnam. By the end of 1965 assistance from the Republic of China had been increased to include eighty-six agricultural experts and a nine-man mission to supervise construction and operation of the 33,000-kilowatt power plant located at Thu Duc.

Additional aid was sought from the republic early in 1966 when the United States requested six LST's for service in South Vietnam. Originally given to the Nationalists under the U.S. Military Assistance Program, the ships were to be manned by Chinese crews in civilian clothing and fly U.S. flags. The United States would bear the cost of crew wages and ship maintenance. The mission of the ships was to fill the need for shallow-draft coastal vessels and help ease harbor congestion. The Republic of China was able to provide only two ships; their transfer took place in April in a low key atmosphere without publicity.

In June General Westmoreland was asked to comment on the possibility of having Chinese Nationalist troops in South Vietnam. Since other Free World forces had been introduced, the prospect could possibly now be viewed in a different light. From a purely military point of view, General Westmoreland believed the use of Chinese Nationalist troops would be highly desirable. Military Assistance Command, Vietnam, would welcome the addition of a well-trained, motivated, and disciplined marine brigade as early as it could be deployed; but from a political point of view, there were still many reservations concerning the introduction of Chinese Nationalist troops into the Vietnamese War. The U.S. Embassy at Saigon declined to make any specific comments or recommendations without first consulting the government of South Vietnam; however, the classification given to the subject made consultation impossible. It was the U.S. Embassy's belief that while some key figures in the government of South Vietnam would see the advantages of using troops from the Republic of China there was sufficient cause to believe that a

Chinese Nationalist involvement might be counterproductive. The embassy thought that while the introduction of Chinese Nationalist troops in South Vietnam probably would cause no change in Chinese Communist strategy, the rest of the world might view the act as a prelude to another war. In addition, the traditional anti-Chinese attitude of the Vietnamese had to be taken into account because it could have a strong bearing on the acceptability of Chinese Nationalist troops to the government of South Vietnam. Weighing both the military and political aspects of the question, General Westmoreland recommended that Republic of China troops be deployed only when the political questions had been resolved.

During 1967 the team of Chinese advisers on electric power was increased to thirty-four and a sixteen-man surgical team was introduced into Vietnam to assist in expanding public health programs. In mid-June 1967, having already obtained Vietnam government approval, the Republic of China military attaché in Saigon wrote General Westmoreland for permission to send four groups of officers to South Vietnam for one month's on-the-job training. The groups would consist of from eight to ten officers each in the branches of intelligence, artillery, armor, ordnance, and engineering and would be assigned to a compatible U.S. unit. General Westmoreland, with concurrence from the U.S. Embassy, opposed the project for several reasons. First, the military working agreement signed by General Westmoreland and the commanding general of the Republic of China Military Assistance Advisory Group, Vietnam, provided only for essentially political and psychological warfare advisory personnel and prohibited their engagement in combat missions. Second, this new proposal would expose Chinese officers to combat, with the risk of their death or capture, and provide a ready-made situation for Chinese Communist charges of Nationalist Chinese military intervention. Of lesser importance was the fact that the officers' association with U.S. units would disclose their presence to news correspondents. Approval of such a request would also establish a precedent likely to encourage additional Chinese requests for a long-term commitment of more contingents, and might also tempt others to follow Nationalist China's example. The proposal clearly posed serious political risk and military burden to the United States without any tangible benefits.

The State Department agreed with General Westmoreland's appraisal and hoped that the U.S. Military Assistance Advisory Group, Republic of China, and the U.S. Embassy at Taipei would let the matter drop before the State Department had to

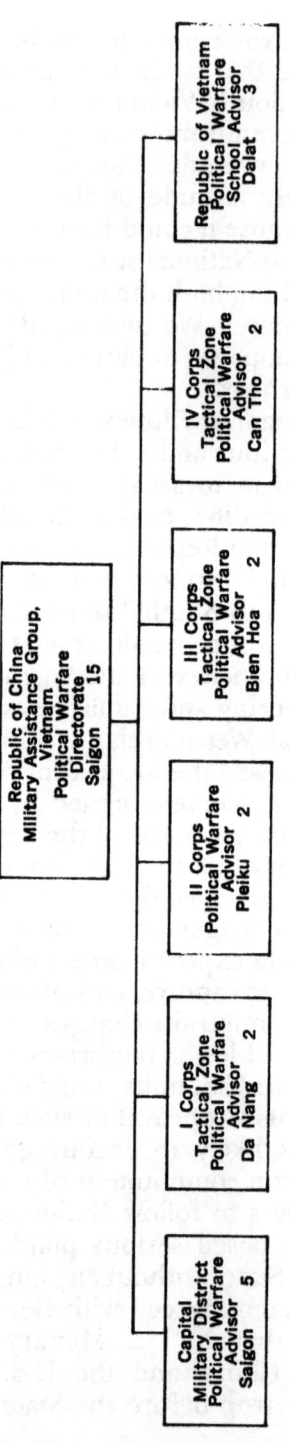

CHART 5—REPUBLIC OF CHINA MILITARY ASSISTANCE GROUP, VIETNAM

reply officially. The Minister of Defense of the Nationalist government explained that the purpose behind the request was to reinforce the combat experience of the armed forces. When the chief of the U.S. Military Assistance Advisory Group, Taipei, presented the reasons behind the U.S. intent to refuse the request, the minister withdrew the proposal.

Arrangements between the governments of the United States and the Republic of China were formalized when USMACV signed a military working arrangement on 19 December 1968 with the Republic of China Military Assistance Advisory Group, Vietnam. Under the agreement Republic of China Military Assistance Advisory Group, Vietnam, was controlled and co-ordinated by the Free World Military Assistance Policy Council and command of the group was vested in the military commander designated by the government of the Republic of China. The United States would provide quarters, office space, and transportation within Vietnam.

During the period 1969–1970 the Republic of China assistance group continued to function as before with no significant changes in personnel strength. (*Chart 5*) After mid-1964, the Chinese group also provided $3 million in economic and technical assistance to Vietnam. As previously mentioned, Chinese technical personnel in the fields of agriculture, electrical power, and medicine were sent to Vietnam, while almost 300 Vietnamese technicians received training on Taiwan. During the *Tet* offensive of 1968, the Republic of China was one of the first countries to offer assistance, in the form of a gift of 5,000 tons of rice, to meet that emergency situation. In the way of other goods and materials, it provided aluminum prefabricated warehouses, agricultural tools, seeds, fertilizers, and 500,000 copies of mathematics textbooks.

CHAPTER VI

The Republic of Korea

In the spring of 1965 when the American Army first sent combat units to Vietnam, the principal threat to the country from the North Vietnamese was in the border areas of the Central Highlands. By July 1965 the North Vietnamese had shown that their main thrust was to come through the highlands, eastward by means of Highway 19, and out to Qui Nhon to split the country into two parts; they would then work from a central area to broaden their control in both northerly and southerly directions.

The critical highlands terrain in II Corps was primarily in Pleiku and Binh Dinh Provinces. Except for major towns, Binh Dinh was completely controlled by the North Vietnamese and Viet Cong. The most populated coastal province in the II Corps area, with roughly 800,000 people, Binh Dinh had been dominated by the Viet Cong for many years.

In August 1965, when American troops arrived, Qui Nhon was the only secure town in the province of Binh Dinh. All the highways leading out from Qui Nhon were controlled by the enemy. In Pleiku Province the roads out of Pleiku City were also controlled by the North Vietnamese or the Viet Cong. With the exception of the main towns in II Corps area, all the other communities were threatened and harassed because the enemy controlled routes of travel and communication. Thus, in August 1965 when the Americans began bringing their forces into the II Corps area, the situation was serious in the three major populated areas—the Central Highlands, Binh Dinh, and the Tuy Hoa area to the south of Qui Nhon. A demoralized South Vietnam Army compounded the need for quick, extensive military assistance. This assistance was provided by the United States and Free World countries such as Korea.

The Korean Commitment

In early 1954 the Republic of Korea's President Syngman Rhee offered, without solicitation, to send a Korean Army element to Vietnam to assist in the war against the Communists.

This proposal was made to Lieutenant General Bruce C. Clarke, ranking U.S. officer in Korea at the time, who relayed it to the Department of State where it was promptly turned down. Korean forces were not sent, nor was there any further action.

Ten years later, in May 1964, Major General Norman B. Edwards, Chief, U.S. Joint Military Advisory Group, Korea, began preliminary planning to send a Korean Mobile Army Surgical Hospital to Vietnam. On 10 July 1964 the Korean Minister of National Defense, Kim Sumg Eun, confirmed this planning in a letter to General Hamilton H. Howze, then Commander in Chief, United Nations Command, stating that the government of the Republic of Korea was prepared to send one reinforced Mobile Army Surgical Hospital and ten Taekwondo (karate) instructors to the Republic of Vietnam upon the request of that government. On 16 July 1964, General Howze wrote Minister Kim that in his capacity as chief of the United Nations Command he would concur in the release of such personnel as would be required to staff the mobile hospital and provide the Taekwondo instructors. He further noted that the U.S. Department of Defense would provide logistical support for the movement and continued operation of these deploying forces. The support was to be provided through Military Assistance Program channels in accordance with the applicable procedures of that program. Equipment, supplies, and services to be provided were to include organizational equipment listed in the mobile hospital table of distribution and allowances as approved by Headquarters, Provisional Military Assistance Advisory Group, Korea, beyond the capabilities of the Republic of Korea to provide, and subsistence and clothing for military personnel. Pay, travel, and per diem costs or other allowances for the personnel involved were not to be provided by the United States.

Following these discussions the Republic of Korea Survey (Liaison) Team, which included six Korean and five U.S. officers, departed on 19 August 1964 for Vietnam. After a series of meetings with officials of both the Vietnamese Ministry of Defense and the U.S. Military Assistance Command, Vietnam, working agreements were signed on 5 September 1964 at Saigon between the Korean and Vietnamese representatives. In essence, the agreements provided that the Republic of Vietnam would build and maintain the hospital and provide quarters; the Korean Army mobile hospital unit would operate the hospital; Korea would provide Taekwondo instructors, and the United States would support the thirty-four officers and ninety-six enlisted men of the hospital unit and the ten instructors through the Military Assistance Program in accordance with Howze's letter to Minister Kim. Accordingly, on 13 September 1964, at the request of the Republic of Vietnam, the Republic of Korea deployed the Mobile Army Surgical Hospital and instructors.

In late December 1964, after a request from the Republic of Vietnam, the Korean government organized an engineer construction support group to assist the Vietnamese armed forces in restoring war-damaged areas in furtherance of Vietnamese pacification efforts. During the period February to June 1965, a Korean construction support group, a Korean Marine Corps engineer company, Korean Navy LST's and LSM's, and a Korean Army security company were dispatched. These elements, totaling 2,416 men, designated the Republic of Korea Military Assistance Group, Vietnam, were better known by their nickname, Dove Unit.

In early 1965, the government of Vietnam, aware that additional assistance was needed to combat the growing Viet Cong pressure, officially asked the Republic of Korea to provide additional noncombatants. The immediate reason for this request was that Vietnamese troops had been diverted to civic action projects related to the heavy flooding during the fall monsoon in 1964. The Korean government agreed that more support could be provided and undertook to supply a task force composed of the commander of the Republic of Korea Military Assistance Group, Vietnam; an Army engineer battalion; an Army transport company; a Marine engineer company; one LST with crew; a security battalion; a service unit; a liaison group, and a mobile hospital (already in Vietnam).

Arrangements for arrival of the Dove Unit were completed by the Free World Military Assistance Policy Council on 6 February. In September a revised military working agreement was signed between the Korean Military Assistance Group and the Vietnam Air Force and on 8 February an arrangement between the commander of the Korean group and General Rosson. The arrangement between the Korean and Vietnamese governments included several unusual features. The Koreans were not to fire unless attacked, but in any event, could not fire on or pursue the enemy outside the area delineated for Korean operations. In case of a Viet Cong attack, the senior Vietnam Army commander in the area would provide assistance. Koreans were not to act against civil demonstrations unless forced to by circumstances and authorized by a Vietnam Army liaison officer. Operational control was not mentioned in these arrangements, although it was implied that in combat action the senior Vietnam Army officer would exercise control. The arrangements provided that both MACV and the Vietnam armed forces would provide logistical support for the Korean force. Equipment specified in tables of equipment would be provided through the Military Assistance Program and issued by the Vietnam Army. Maintenance services would be provided by the Vietnam Army. Basic Class I supplies, including rice, salt, tea, sugar, and shortening would be provided by the Vietnam government; supplemental rations and other necessary equipment not available through the Military Assistance Program would be supplied by MACV.

Command and control posed a problem for the three nations involved. At one point, the government of Vietnam stated that it desired full operational control by the appropriate corps commander over all Free World military assistance forces employed in Vietnam. In January 1965 Major General Lee Sae Ho, Senior Korean officer in Vietnam, declared that his government could not accept control by any national authority other than the United States. Using as a precedent the fact that the initial Korean element had been placed under the operational control of General Westmoreland, an agreement was reached whereby the Free World Military Assistance Policy Council was utilized as a combined staff to determine the general operational functions of the Korean force. This council was composed initially of the chief of staff of the U.S. Military Assistance Command, Vietnam, the senior Korean officer in Vietnam, and the chief of the Vietnamese Joint General Staff. Later General Westmoreland took the place of his chief of staff. Various subordinate staffs handled day-to-day operations. Evidently, the three nations involved found these arrangements to be satisfactory. The military working arrangement between General Rosson and General Lee, signed on 8 February and revised in September, contained provisions which the council used to establish operating limits for the Dove Unit: command would be retained by General Lee, operational control would belong to General Westmoreland, and the force would be responsible to the senior commander in any given area of operations.

On 25 February 1965 the advance element of the Dove Unit arrived, followed on 16 March by the main party. The group was located at a base camp in Bien Hoa and during 1965 constructed three bridges, four schools, two dispensaries, and two hamlet offices, as well as accomplishing numerous other minor projects. Medical elements of the Dove Unit treated some 30,000 patients. In line with recommendations by Westmoreland, the Korean group was increased by 272 officers and men on 27 June and by two LSM's (landing ships, mechanized) on 9 July.

Further discussions between the U.S. and Korean authorities on this dispatch of troops soon followed. At a meeting between the Korean Minister of National Defense and the Commander in Chief, United Nations Command, on 2 June 1965, the Korean Minister disclosed that as a result of high-level talks between President Johnson and President Park during the latter's visit to Washington in May 1965 the Korean government had decided to send an Army division to Vietnam. The division, minus one Army regiment but including a Korean Marine regiment, was to be commanded by a Korean Army general. Subsequently, Korea also proposed to send an F−86 fighter squadron to provide combat support for Korean ground elements.

Korean Defense Minister Kim also disclosed that a pay raise for Korean troops had been discussed, and although no firm commitment had been made, the inference was that the United States would help. Because Korea would have one of its divisions in Vietnam, Defense Minister Kim felt that the United States should not continue to entertain proposals to reduce U.S. troop strength in Korea, and instead of suspending the Military Assistance Program transfer project should increase the monetary level of the assistance to Korea. Finally, the minister requested that the United States establish an "unofficial" fund to be administered by Korean officials and used in pension payments to the families of soldiers killed or wounded in Vietnam.

On 23 June 1965 Defense Minister Kim again met with Commander in Chief, United Nations Command, this time in the latter's capacity as Commander, U.S. Forces, Korea, to discuss the problems connected with the deployment of the Korean division to Vietnam. Before concrete plans could be drawn up, however, the Korean Army needed to obtain the approval of the National Assembly. Although approval was not necessarily automatic, the minister expected early approval and tentatively established the date of deployment as either late July or early August 1965.

The minister desired U.S. agreement to and support of the following items before submitting the deployment proposal to the National Assembly:

1. Maintenance of current U.S. and Korean force ceilings in Korea.

2. Equipment of the three combat-ready reserve divisions to 100 percent of the table of equipment allowance and the seventeen regular divisions, including the Marine division, with major items affecting firepower, maneuver, and signal capabilities to avoid weakening the Korean defense posture.

3. Maintenance of the same level of Military Assistance Program funding for Korea as before the deployment of the division.

4. Early confirmation of mission, bivouac area, command channels, and logistical support for Korean combat units destined for service in Vietnam.

5. Establishment of a small planning group to determine the organization of the Korean division.

6. Provision of signal equipment for a direct and exclusive communication net between Korea and Korean forces headquarters in Vietnam.

7. Provision of transportation for the movement of the Korean division and for subsequent requirements such as rotation and replacement of personnel and supplies.

8. Provision of financial support to Korean units and individuals in Vietnam, including combat duty pay at the same rate as paid to U.S. personnel, gratuities and compensations for line-of-duty deaths or disability, and salaries of Vietnamese indigenous personnel hired by Korean units.

9. Provision of four C-123 aircraft for medical evacuation and liaison between Korea and Vietnam.

10. Provision of a field broadcasting installation to enable the Korean division to conduct anti-Communist broadcasts, psychological warfare, and jamming operations and to provide Korean home news, war news, and entertainment programs.

Some years later, in January 1971, General Dwight E. Beach, who had succeeded General Howze as Commander in Chief, United Nations Command, on 1 July 1965, commented on the list.

> The initial Korean bill (wish-list) was fantastic. Basically, the ROK wanted their troops to receive the same pay as the Americans, all new U.S. equipment for deploying troops and modernization of the entire ROK Army, Navy and Air Force. I told them with the Ambassador's concurrence that their bill was completely unreasonable and there was no chance whatever of the U.S. agreeing to it. The final compromise included a very substantial increase in pay for the troops deployed, as much good equipment as we could then furnish and a U.S. commitment that no U.S. troops would be withdrawn from Korea without prior consultation with the ROK. The latter, to the Koreans, meant that no U.S. troops would be withdrawn without ROK approval. Obviously, the latter was not the case as is now evident with the withdrawal of the 7th U.S. Division from Korea.

The U.S. Department of State and Department of Defense ultimately resolved the matter of the Korean requirements.

The request that three combat-ready reserve divisions be equipped to 100 percent of their authorized table of organization and equipment was, the commander of U.S. forces in Korea stated, heavily dependent upon the availability of Military Assistance Program funds. The dispatch of the Korean division to Vietnam might affect Military Assistance Program funds, but whether adversely or not could not be predicted. Under consideration was the possibility of using Korean Military Assistance Program funds to finance the readying and dispatch of the division and for the divison's support while it was in Vietnam. Early confirmation of mission, bivouac areas, and other routine requirements was dependent upon information from the Commander in Chief, Pacific. The requirement to provide men for a small planning group to determine the organization of the Korean division met with immediate approval.

The request for signal equipment for direct communication between Korea and the Korean division in Vietnam was not approved. Although high-frequency radio equipment was available, the commander of U.S. forces in Korea, General Beach, felt that a better solution was for the Koreans to use the current U.S. communication system on a common-user basis. The commander agreed that the United States should provide transportation for the division but, depending upon the availability of U.S. shipping, certain Korean vessels might have to be used.

The request for financial support to Korean units and individuals in Vietnam met with disapproval. The U.S. commander in Korea did not favor combat duty pay—especially at the same rate paid to U.S. troops—but was in agreement with the payment of an overseas allowance. If the United States had to pay death benefits or make disability payments, the rates should be those presently established under Korean law on a one-time basis only. The United States would not pay directly for the employment of Vietnamese nationals by Korean forces but was in favor of including such expenses in the agreements between the Republic of Korea and the Republic of Vietnam. Since the request for four C–123 aircraft appeared to overlap a previous transportation request, the commander felt that the United States should provide only scheduled flights to Korea or reserve spaces on other U.S. scheduled flights for Korean use.

At first glance, the request for a field broadcasting installation appeared to conflict with the psychological warfare programs already in operation in Vietnam, but final resolution of the matter would have to await an on-the-ground opinion.

On 13 July 1965 the U.S. State Department authorized the

U.S. Ambassador to Korea to offer a number of concessions to the Korean government to insure the prompt deployment of the Korean division to Vietnam. The United States agreed to suspend the Military Assistance Program transfer project for as long as the Korean government maintained substantial forces in Vietnam. The United States also agreed to offshore procurement from Korea for transfer items such as petroleum, oil, lubricants, and construction materials listed in the fiscal year 1966 Military Assistance Program. Subsequently, and during the period of the transfer program, the United States would determine offshore procurement from Korea on the basis of individual items and under normal offshore procurement procedures.

These concessions to the Korean government were made, however, with the understanding that the budgetary savings accruing to Korea from the actions taken would contribute to a substantial military and civil service pay-raise for Koreans. Actually, the Korean government would not incur any additional costs in deploying the division to Vietnam but would secure a number of economic benefits. On the other hand, the cost to the United States for Koreans already in Vietnam approximated $2,000,000 annually, and first year costs for the operation of the Korean division in Vietnam were estimated at $43,000,000.

In a later communication on 16 July 1965, the Commander, U.S. Forces, Korea, informed the Commander in Chief, Pacific, of other decisions that had been made in resolving the Korean requests. With respect to the reduction of U.S. force levels in Korea, the U.S. Commander in Korea and the American Ambassador to Korea, Winthrop D. Brown, prepared a letter assuring the Korean government that President Johnson's earlier decision that there would be no reduction in U.S. force levels remained unchanged, and that any further redeployment of U.S. forces from Korea would be discussed with the Korean government officials beforehand.

By August agreement had been reached with the Korean government on the force structure of the divison and support troop augmentation, but the military aspects of control and command and the proposed unified Korean headquarters were still under discussion. Consolidated equipment lists for the Korean division, understrength, and the Marine force, as well as the table of allowances for a Korean field support command had been developed and were to be forwarded to General Westmoreland. In logistics, initial and follow-up support of Class II, IV, and V supplies had been settled, but the matter of Class III supplies could not be resolved until information had been received from MACV on the availability and receipt of storage for bulk petroleum products. Class I supplies were still under study. A maintenance policy had been worked out for the evacuation of equipment for rebuild and overhaul. All transportation problems had been solved and, finally, training plans had been completed and disseminated.

Because of the unpredictable outcome of Korean plans to deploy a division to Vietnam and the urgent need to have another division there, the Military Assistance Command, Vietnam, informed the Commander in Chief, Pacific, through U.S. Army, Pacific, that if deployment of the Korean division did not take place by 1 November 1965, a U.S. Army division would have to be sent to Vietnam instead. Since planning actions for the movement of a division from either the Pacific command or the continental command would have to be initiated at once, the Joint Chiefs of Staff asked Admiral Sharp's opinion on the best means of getting a substitute for the Korean division if the need arose.

Admiral Sharp's view was that the two U.S. divisions then in Korea constituted an essential forward deployment force that should not be reduced. Commitment of the 25th Infantry Division to Vietnam—except for the one-brigade task force requested in the event of an emergency—would deplete Pacific command reserve strength at a critical time. Moreover, the 25th Infantry Division was oriented for deployment to Thailand, and if moved to Vietnam should be replaced immediately with another U.S. division. With deployment of the Korean division to Vietnam, the 25th Infantry Division would be available as a substitute for the Korean division in Korea.

On 19 August 1965 the Korean National Assembly finally passed a bill authorizing the dispatch of the Korean division. The division was to deploy in three increments: the first on 29 September 1965; the second on 14 October 1965; and the third on 29 October 1965. Initial equipment shortages were not expected to reduce the combat readiness of the division.

Definitive discussion between U.S. and Korean authorities on the dispatch of troops began immediately. As a result, the first combat units, the Republic of Korea's Capital (Tiger) Infantry Division, less one regimental combat team, and the 2d Marine Corps Brigade (Blue Dragon) and supporting elements, totaling 18,212 men, were sent during the period September through November 1965.

The Korean government then sought reassurance that sending troops to Vietnam would neither impair Korean defense nor adversely affect the level of U.S. military assistance to Korea. It also sought agreements on the terms of U.S. support for Korean troops in Vietnam. Resulting arrangements between the United States and Korea provided substantially the following terms.

1. No U.S. or Korean force reductions were to take place in Korea without prior consultation.

2. The Korean Military Assistance Program for 1966 was to include an additional $7 million to provide active division equipment for the three Korean Army ready-reserve divisions.

3. Korean forces in Korea were to be modernized in firepower, communications, and mobility.

4. For Korean forces deployed to Vietnam, the United States was to provide equipment, logistical support, construction, training, transportation, subsistence, overseas allowances, funds for any legitimate noncombat claim brought against Republic of Korea Forces, Vietnam, in Vietnam, and restitution of losses of the Korean force not resulting from the force's negligence.

General Westmoreland also agreed to provide the Korean force with facilities and services comparable to those furnished U.S. and other allied forces in Vietnam. Korean forces in Vietnam had custody of the equipment funded by the Military Assistance Program brought into Vietnam and equipment funded by the Military Assistance Service and provided by General Westmoreland. Equipment funded by the Military Assistance Program that was battle damaged or otherwise attrited was replaced and title retained by the Republic of Korea. In an emergency redeployment to Korea, the Koreans would take with them all equipment on hand. In a slower deployment or rotation, equipment would be negotiated, particularly that held by Koreans in Vietnam but not compatible with similar equipment held by Korean forces in Korea and items extraneous to the Military Assistance Program.

Prior to the arrival of the Korean division, considerable study of possible locations for its deployment took place. The first plan was to employ the division in the I Corps Tactical Zone, with major elements at Chu Lai, Tam Ky, and Quang Ngai; Korean troops would join with the III Marine Amphibious Force, and perhaps other Free World units to form an international Free World force. Subsequently, this idea was dropped for several reasons. First of all, support of another full division in that area would be difficult logistically because over-the-beach supply would be necessary. Deployment of the division in the I Corps Tactical Zone would also necessitate offensive operations since the enclaves were already adequately secured by elements of the III Marine Amphibious Force. Offensive operations might, in turn, provoke problems of "face" between the two Asian republics, Vietnam and Korea, especially if the Korean forces turned out to be more successful during encounters with the Viet Cong and the North Vietnamese. There were still several other possible locations at which Korean troops could be stationed. Affecting each of the possibilities were overriding tactical considerations.

The 2d Korean Marine Brigade (the Blue Dragon Brigade) was initially assigned to the Cam Ranh Bay area but did not remain there very long because the security requirements were greater elsewhere. Hence shortly after its arrival the 2d Brigade was moved up to the Tuy Hoa area where the enemy, the 95th Regiment of the North Vietnam Army, had been deployed for several weeks. This enemy unit had been pressing more and more on the population in and around Tuy Hoa and was threatening the government as well as the agriculture of that area.

The Capital Division, affectionately called by the Americans the Tiger Division, arrived at its station about six miles west of Qui Nhon during November 1965, initially with two regiments. The area was chosen, among other reasons, because it was not populated and would therefore not take agricultural land away from the local inhabitants. It was, moreover, high ground that would not be adversely affected by the rains. These circumstances would give the Koreans an opportunity to spread out their command post as much as they wished and allow the first troop units some training in operating against the enemy.

Another reason for not stationing the Capital Division nearer Qui Nhon was that Qui Nhon was to become a major logistic support area, eventually providing the base support for both Korean divisions as well as for the U.S. 1st Cavalry Division (Airmobile) and the 4th Infantry Division. All the land immediately surrounding Qui Nhon, therefore, was to be used for logistical purposes.

Placed as it was in the Qui Nhon area, the Capital Division would be able to move in several critical directions: it could keep Highway 19 open as far as An Khe; it would be close enough to protect the outskirts of Qui Nhon; it could move northward to help clean out the rice-growing area as well as the foothills to the northwest; and it could move southward on Highway 1 toward Tuy Hoa and assist in clearing out the enemy from the populated areas along both sides of the highway.

The 1st Brigade, 101st Airborne Division, was sent to the Qui Nhon area prior to the arrival of the Capital Division to insure that the area was protected while the initial Korean units settled down and established camp.

In early 1966 additional Korean troops were again formally requested by the Republic of Vietnam. Negotiations between the U.S. and Korean governments on this request were conducted between January and March 1966. The Korean National Assembly approved the dispatch of new troops on 30 March 1966, and the Commander in Chief, United Nations Command, concurred in the release of the 9th Infantry Division—the White Horse Division. This unit, which began to deploy in April 1966, brought the strength of the Korean forces in Vietnam to 44,897.

The 9th Korean Division arrived in Vietnam during the period 5 September–8 October 1966 and was positioned in the Ninh Hoa area at the junction of Highways 1 and 21. Division headquarters was situated in good open terrain, permitting deployment of the units to best advantage.

Of the Korean 9th Division the 28th Regiment was stationed in the Tuy Hoa area, the 29th Regiment in and around Ninh Hoa, adjacent to division headquarters, and the 30th Regiment on the mainland side to protect Cam Ranh Bay. With these three areas under control, the 9th Division could control Highway 1 and the population along that main road all the way from Tuy Hoa down to Phan Rang, from Tuy Hoa north to Qui Nhon, and as far north of that city as the foothills of the mountains in southern Binh Dinh Province. (*Map 7*) A Korean Marine battalion and additional support forces arrived in Vietnam in 1967. In all, the Republic of Korea deployed 47,872 military personnel to Vietnam in four major increments.

Time Dispatched	Organization	Strength
1964–1965	Medical and engineer groups (Dove)	2,128
1965	Capital Division (–RCT) with support forces and Marine brigade	18,904
1966	9th Division with RCT and support forces	23,865
1967	Marine battalion (–) and other support forces	2,963
1969	C–46 crews, authorized increase	12

Logistically, the United States had agreed to support fully the Korean operations in South Vietnam; there never was any doubt that the Koreans would get all the requisite support—the transportation, artillery support, extra engineer support, hospital supplies, food, aviation support, communications support—from the U.S. bases in Vietnam.

Operational Control of Korean Troops

When the Korean Army arrived in South Vietnam, Major General Chae Myung Shin assured General Westmoreland that

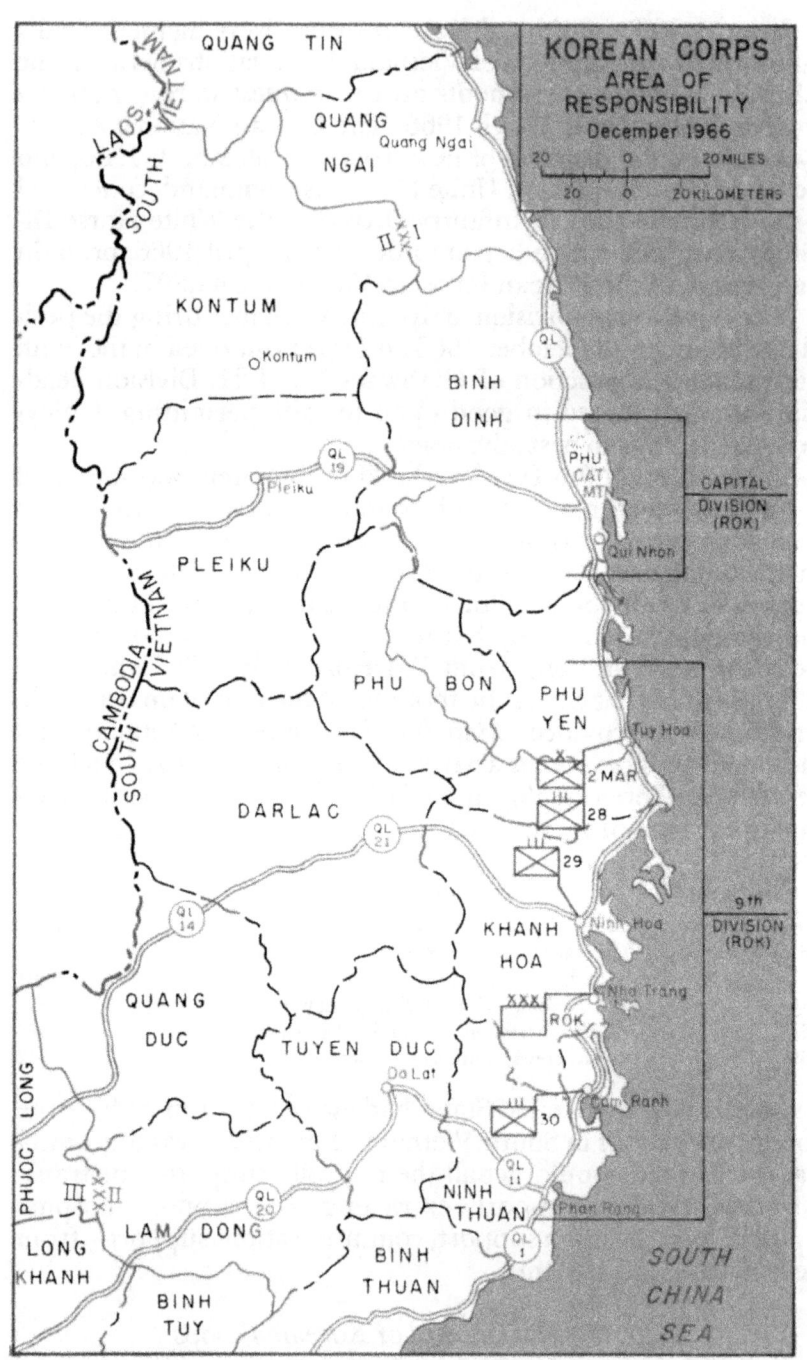

MAP 7

whatever mission General Westmoreland gave him he would execute it as if he were directly under Westmoreland's operational control. There was a certain amount of confusion, nonetheless, as to whether the Korean force in South Vietnam would actually come directly under U.S. operational control or whether it would be a distinct fighting force working in close co-ordination with the other allies but under separate control. The confusion was perhaps based on misunderstanding since there never had been a clear-cut agreement between the Korean government and the U.S. government concerning operational control.

On 2 July 1965 General Westmoreland had submitted to Admiral Sharp his views on the command and control organization to be used when a Korean division arrived in Vietnam. If a Korean regiment deployed to Vietnam before the establishment of a field force headquarters, MACV would exercise operational control of both Korean and U.S. units through a task force headquarters located in the II Corps Tactical Zone. When the full Korean division arrived, the division would assume command of the Korean regiment and would come under the direct operational command of the field force headquarters.

General Westmoreland had no objections to a unified Korean command, provided the command was under his operational control and he retained the authority to place the Korean regiment, brigade, or division under the operational control of a U.S. task force headquarters or U.S. field force headquarters. Such an arrangement was necessary so that the U.S. commander would have the authority to maneuver the Korean division or any of its elements to meet a changing tactical situation.

Under this arrangement, noncombatant Korean forces would continue to be under General Westmoreland's operational control through the provisions of the International Military Assistance Policy Council, later designated the Free World Military Assistance Policy Council. Inasmuch as General Westmoreland wanted the commanding general of the Korean division to be free to devote all his energies to tactical matters, he recommended that the Republic of Korea Military Assistance Group, Vietnam, be augmented so that it could assume the responsibilities of a Korean unified command.

After the arrival in Vietnam of the advance planning group for the Korean division and after a series of conferences, new working arrangements were signed between the Vietnamese armed forces and the Commander, Republic of Korea Forces, Vietnam, on 5 September and between General Westmoreland and the Commander of the Korean forces on 6 September. The new arrangements contained several interesting features. There was no reference to operational control. The only formally recognized control agency was the Free World Military Assistance Policy Council that continued in its policy-making role. Command, of course, remained with the senior Korean officer.

Since there was no provision for command and control in the military working arrangement signed between General Westmoreland and the commander of the Korean force, General Chae, on 6 September 1965, the policy council prepared a draft joint memorandum indicating that General Westmoreland would exercise operational control over all Korean forces in Vietnam. General Westmoreland presented this proposed arrangement to General Chae and Brigadier General Cao Van Vien, chief of the Joint General Staff, on 23 October. At that time, General Chae declared that he could not sign the arrangement without first checking with his government; however, in the interim, he would follow the outlined procedures. The Koreans submitted a revised draft of the command and control arrangement which, after study, General Westmoreland determined to be too restrictive. On 20 November the draft was returned to General Chae, who was reminded that the verbal agreement made on 23 October would continue to be followed.

After additional discussion with General Chae, General Westmoreland reported to Admiral Sharp that a formal signed arrangement could be politically embarrassing to the Koreans because it might connote that they were subordinate to, and acting as mercenaries for, the United States. General Westmoreland felt that a formal arrangement was no longer necessary since General Chae had agreed to *de facto* operational control by U.S. commanders. Lieutenant General Stanley R. Larsen, Commanding General, I Field Force, Vietnam, and General Chae understood that although directives to Korean units would be in the form of requests they would be honored as orders. It was also thought appropriate that Korean officers be assigned to the field force staff to assist in matters relating to Korean elements. This would not constitute a combined staff as the Korean officers would serve as liaison officers.

There were several logical reasons for the Korean Army in South Vietnam to be constituted as a separate and distinct force. To begin with this was one of the few times in Asian history that a Far Eastern nation had gone to the assistance of another nation with so many forces. It was of great political significance for the Korean government to be able to send its army as an independent force. Many observers felt that the eyes of the world would be upon the Koreans and that, as a nation, the Koreans must succeed for the sake of their home country. The Koreans felt much attention would be focused on them to see how well they were operating in conjunction with U.S. forces. If they were working independently, it would show the other countries that not only were the Koreans in a position to act on their own, but they were also freely assisting the United States. The United States could then point out that countries such as Korea, which they had helped for many years, were now operating freely and independently, and not as involuntary props of American policy. Korea's entry into the war in Vietnam showed the world that while Korea was not directly affected by the war it was, nevertheless, willing to go to its neighbor's assistance.

Another reason that the Koreans did not wish to come under *de jure* U.S. operational control had to do with their national pride. Since Korea had received U.S. assistance for so many years after the Korean War and had followed American tutelage on the organization and leadership of a large armed force, the Vietnam War was an opportunity to show that Koreans could operate on their own without American forces or advisers looking over their shoulders. In effect, the Koreans desired to put into play the military art the United States had taught them.

Initial Developments

Assigned to the Qui Nhon area, the Capital Division initially was given the mission of close-in patrolling and spent its first days in South Vietnam getting accustomed to the surrounding terrain and to the ways of the Vietnamese. Though the Koreans and Vietnamese were both Orientals, their languages were completely foreign to each other. They handled people differently; the Koreans were much more authoritative. General Chae attempted to overcome the differences by working with government representatives to establish methods of bringing the Koreans and the Vietnamese together. For instance, the Korean soldiers attended the local Buddhist churches and also repaired facilities which had been either destroyed by enemy operations or suffered from neglect.

The first major operation in the fall of 1965 involving the Capital Division was an effort to protect Highway 19 up to An Khe from just outside Qui Nhon. The 1st Brigade, 101st Airborne Division, then stationed in the area, remained in place for about one month and gradually turned over its area of responsibility to the Korean division. Little by little, the Koreans moved into the river paddy area north of Qui Nhon where they engaged in small patrolling actions and developed their own techniques of ferreting out enemy night patrols.

The Viet Cong quickly learned that the Capital Division was not an easy target for their guerrilla small-unit tactics. Within two months following the Capital Divisions's entrance into Vietnam, tactical units of the two regiments and the division initially deployed to Vietnam had reached a position nearly halfway between Qui Nhon and Muy Ba Mountain, nicknamed Phu Cat Mountain after the large town to the west of it. The people in that area had been dominated by the Viet Cong for many years. In the process of mopping up the small enemy pockets in the lowlands and rice paddies, military action caused many hardships for the local populace, making it so difficult for them to live that the women and children—and eventually all the pro-government segment of the population—gradually moved out of the area.

By June of 1966 the Capital Division controlled all the area north of Qui Nhon to the east of Highway 1 and up to the base of Phu Cat Mountain. It extended its control also to the north and south of Highway 19 up to the pass leading into An Khe. Working south along Highway 1 down toward Tuy Hoa and within the province of Binh Dinh, the Capital Division sent out reconnaissance parties and carried out small operations as far south as the border between Binh Dinh and Phu Yen.

The Korean Marine brigade, assigned at first to the Cam Ranh Bay area in September and October 1965, was moved to the Tuy Hoa area in December of that year. The reason for the shift was the presence of the 95th Regiment near Tuy Hoa. This regiment, a North Vietnam divisional unit, had disappeared from the western area of South Vietnam and its whereabouts remained unknown for several weeks. It finally showed up in midsummer 1965 in the Tuy Hoa area where it began operations, threatening and dominating the outer regions of the Tuy Hoa area.

Tuy Hoa was a well-populated region, harvesting 60,000 to 70,000 tons of rice a year. The rice paddy land was poorly protected, wide open to control by the Viet Cong and North Vietnam's 95th Regiment. Since the Viet Cong and North Vietnamese utilized the area to supply rice to their own troops all the way up to the Central Highlands, the rice land had become a strategic necessity for the enemy. During the summer of 1965 the North Vietnamese 95th Regiment gained control of more and more of the rice production and by the middle of the wet season, October and November, a crisis had developed. The morale of

KOREAN MARINES PREPARE DEFENSIVE POSITIONS NEAR TUY HOA

the people had sunk to a dangerous low; something had to be done soon, not only to protect the local inhabitants but also to assure them that protection would continue. The Korean Marine brigade therefore was moved from Cam Ranh Bay to the Tuy Hoa area.

The 1st Brigade, 101st Airborne Division, meanwhile having completed its assignment to protect the higher perimeter around Qui Nhon until the Capital Division was settled, moved down to the Tuy Hoa area and began probing for the enemy. When the Korean brigade moved to the Tuy Hoa area, the two brigades, U.S. and Korean, worked side by side for several weeks, but at Christmas 1965 the 1st Brigade of the 101st Division moved south to Phan Rang, its home base, leaving the entire Tuy Hoa area to the Korean brigade.

After the 9th Korean Division arrived in South Vietnam, General Westmoreland recommended that General Chae develop a corps headquarters in Nha Trang adjacent to that of the U.S. I Field Force. When the Korean corps headquarters was established and became operational in Nha Trang during August 1966, General Chae decided that he should also establish a headquarters in Saigon and wear a second hat as commander of all Korean troops in Vietnam, representing the Korean government on an equal basis with the U.S. Military Assistance Command, Vietnam.

There were obvious command and control reasons for establishing the Korean corps headquarters in Nha Trang close to I Field Force. Inasmuch as the Koreans now had more than 50,000 troops in the area, the South Vietnamese two and one-half divisions in II Corps, and the Americans two full divisions and a brigade in Vietnam, the Korean corps headquarters facilitated liaison between allied forces. Since there had to be close co-ordination with the Koreans in logistical as well as tactical matters, there had to be close understanding between the two corps headquarters on planning new missions and guaranteeing the kind of support, both tactical and logistical, required to sustain the Korean fighting forces wherever they were conducting operations.

The operation and co-ordination of the Korean corps alongside I Field Force in Nha Trang tied in very closely with the operations of the Americans. By mutual agreement the two staffs were in continuous contact with one another. The operations officers of the I Field Force and the Korean corps met four or five times a week, and intelligence officers from both commands interchanged information. There was no requirement to effect

THE REPUBLIC OF KOREA

FIELD COMMAND HEADQUARTERS *of Republic of Korea Force, Vietnam, at Nha Trang.*

any administrative co-ordination. Logistically, however, the Koreans had close liaison with the I Field Force logistics staff officers by whom logistics support requirements for impending operations were verified.

One of the more important relationships developed by the U.S., Korean, and South Vietnam corps commanders in the II Corps area was in planning future operations. These had to be worked out weeks in advance with General Vinh Loc, commander of the Vietnam II Corps; General Larsen, commander of the U.S. I Field Force; and General Chae, commander of the Korean corps. Every six months the three commanders, with their staffs, co-ordinated the next six months of operations and campaign strategy. There was never any conflict with respect to areas of major responsibility. Only the timing and kind of support, both in weaponry and in helicopters, for the planned operations had to be worked out.

It was through this working arrangement that one of the major campaigns of the war took place in Binh Dinh Province in September 1966. The Capital Division, commanded by the young and extremely capable General Lew Byong Hion, worked out the details with the commanding general of the 1st Cavalry Division, Major General John Norton, and General Nguyen Van Hieu of the 22d Vietnam Division, with headquarters in Qui Nhon.

The tactical agreement among the three division commanders was that at a given time the 1st Cavalry Division would move north out of An Khe and then, in a southerly sweep of the area north of Phu Cat Mountain, pin down the area and search it for any enemy activity involving the 2d Viet Cong Regiment, the 18th North Vietnamese Regiment, and portions of the 22d North Vietnamese Regiment, all under the command of the North Vietnam 3d Division with headquarters north of Bong Son. The Koreans would move north, sweeping all of Phu Cat Mountain, and occupy the strip along the ocean north of the mountain while elements of the 22d Vietnamese Division would move between the Koreans and U.S. troops from Highway 1 toward the sea.

In a succession of rapid movements up Phu Cat Mountain, the Koreans rapidly occupied key points of the terrain and in a matter of a few days had completely dominated an area occupied by at least two North Vietnamese battalions. The drive on Phu Cat Mountain by the Korean forces was extraordinarily thorough and effective. The count of captured weapons alone amounted to more than 600 rifles.

By the end of 1965 the Korean corps under General Chae, who had been promoted from commanding general of the Capital Division to commander of the corps, had assumed responsibility all the way from Phu Cat Mountain down to Phan Rang. The tactical area of operations included the mission of protecting all the populated area on each side of Highway 1. With the exception of the northern third of Phu Yen Province between the northernmost brigade of the Korean 9th Division in Tuy Hoa and the Capital Division in Binh Dinh Province, where the 1st Brigade of the U.S. 101st and elements of the U.S. 4th Division were brought in to fill the gap in early and mid-1966, the entire area had become the responsibility of the Koreans, working in conjunction with the South Vietnamese Army whenever they were in the same area.

Another example of the Koreans' capability in small unit tactics was the co-ordination between I Field Force headquarters and General Chae that provided a Korean battalion in the Central Highlands to work with the U.S. 4th Infantry Division south of Highway 19, just east of the Cambodian border. When the battalion arrived it was divided into three separate company outposts and embarked on operations involving small unit patrols in all directions from each of the base camps.

On the sixth night after arrival of the Koreans in the highlands, a battalion of North Vietnamese (believed to be a battalion of the 101st North Vietnamese Regiment) attacked the northernmost company at night. In a succession of close combat actions the North Vietnamese tried for several hours to break into the company area, but they were repulsed at each attempt. When the next morning dawned, the Koreans had lost only seven men and had killed, by actual count, 182 of the enemy, exclusive of the number of bodies and other casualties dragged away. The Korean company was assisted by three U.S. Army tanks, and the American tankers had endless praise for the Koreans in this action.

The Korean contribution to the war in Vietnam may, in a large measure, be summed up by a description of the type of soldier sent from the Land of the Morning Calm. President Park insisted that only volunteers be sent to Vietnam. Since a vast number of soldiers volunteered to go with their Army to South Vietnam, commanders were able to handpick the men they wished to accompany their units. The tour of duty was one year, but if the soldiers did not live up to the high standards established by the Korean Army, they were to be sent home from the combat area immediately.

The units selected had the longest service and the best records in the Korean War. According to the Korean Army military historians, these units were selected on the basis of their heritage (decorations and campaigns), mission, and location. The Korean Capital (Tiger) Division was ideal since it was one of the Korean Army's most famous divisions. It was also a Korean Army first reserve division, and its removal therefore had less effect on the frontline tactical situation in Korea than would the withdrawal of divisions in the lines. Furthermore the terrain in the division's former area approximated the terrain in Vietnam. The 9th (White Horse) Division was chosen because it, too, was a renowned fighting unit and did not occupy a critical frontline position at the time of its selection. The United States had no direct veto on the units selected. Although concurrence of the Commander in Chief, United Nation's Command, was solicited and received, the units were selected unilaterally by the Korean Ministry of National Defense.

Since this was the first time in modern history that Korean soldiers would serve abroad, Korean military leaders wanted to put their best foot forward. This national position produced a soldier who was highly motivated, well trained, and well disciplined; each individual Korean trooper appeared to speak well for the ambitions and discipline of the Korean Army by his tactical ability and his conduct as a personal representative of his country in a foreign combat zone.

The entire Korean Army was screened and many of its finest officers and men were assigned to the Korean Capital Division. Almost all of the combat arms' junior officers were graduates of the Korean Military Academy. Each officer was handpicked by senior Capital Division officers. A complete replacement of the division staff was accomplished within the first few days of activation. An after action report of 26 November 1965 gave the method used.

Since the Capital Division was a reserve division within a reserve corps and therefore had a very low priority with respect to all personnel actions, more than ninety percent of the personnel had to be replaced to comply with the high standards for assignment. The result was that a large number of highly skilled personnel were transferred from units within First ROK Army to fulfill the requirement. In order to insure that an imbalance among levied units did not occur as a result of this action, a directive was sent to each combat division which equitably distributed the levy of critical MOS's. Approximately 500 personnel were obtained from each division. Unit replacement into the receiving unit, at squad and platoon level, was accomplished by this action.

Enlisted men were given inducements to serve in the division. They would receive credit for three years of military duty for each year served in Vietnam as well as additional monetary entitlements; further, combat duty would enhance their future Army careers. Similar procedures and benefits applied to the 9th (White Horse) Division as well.

President Park Chung Hee personally selected such senior officers as General Chae. Chae was a good man in Korea and, considering his instructions from his president, did as well if not better than anyone else the Korean government could have sent. It is believed that if General Chae had been under U.S. operational control, all Americans who had official contact with him would have sung his praises. As it was, he had the difficult job of pleasing his government at home and staying on somewhat good terms with the Americans as well.

It is of considerable interest to compare the Koreans as the Americans had known them in the Korean War with the Koreans as they operated in combat in South Vietnam. In Korea they had leaned heavily upon the Americans for competent advice in most fields of tactical support. In Vietnam, it may be unequivocally stated, the Korean forces handled themselves with proven competence in both tactical and tactical-support operations as well as in logistics, including engineering and medical administration. It was a source of pride to those Americans who had been dealing with the Koreans over the years to observe the independence and self-confidence displayed at every turn by the Korean commanders and troops in Vietnam. The Koreans had been primarily taught to act defensively, that is to fight in the defense of their own country. It was assumed they would fight defensively in South Vietnam. The Korean actually is an aggressive soldier when provided the opportunity to prove his mettle. While many Korean missions were undertaken to protect the indigenous population, the Korean soldier and his immediate leader—his sergeant, his lieutenant, his company commander— were extremely aggressive in their pursuit of the enemy. Some differences between American and Korean troops were probably due to the fact that early in the Vietnam War U.S. troops had been taught to make full use of the helicopter. The Americans had extensive logistical support and, in addition, had a much larger area of tactical operations. There was a derivative requirement that American troops be able to move from one area to another quickly in order to meet the enemy wherever it was suspected he might be located. The Koreans, on the other hand, had a set area more or less tied to the local population, a circumstance that required the Koreans to be more careful of the manner in which they handled themselves tactically in searching out the enemy. The Koreans had slightly different missions, too, one of which was to keep the roads and Highway 1 open and to protect the local people at whichever point they made contact with them.

The Koreans were thorough in their planning and deliberate in their execution of a plan. They usually surrounded an area by stealth and quick movement. While the count of enemy killed was probably no greater proportionately then that of similar U.S. combat units, the thoroughness with which the Koreans searched any area they fought in was attested to by the fact that the Koreans usually came out with a much higher weaponry count than U.S. troops engaged in similar actions.

Since all of the senior Korean officers and many of the junior officers spoke excellent English, they had no difficulty in communicating with the Americans, and their understanding of U.S. ground tactics made it easy for the forces of the two nations to work together.

Although support was available to them, the Koreans showed

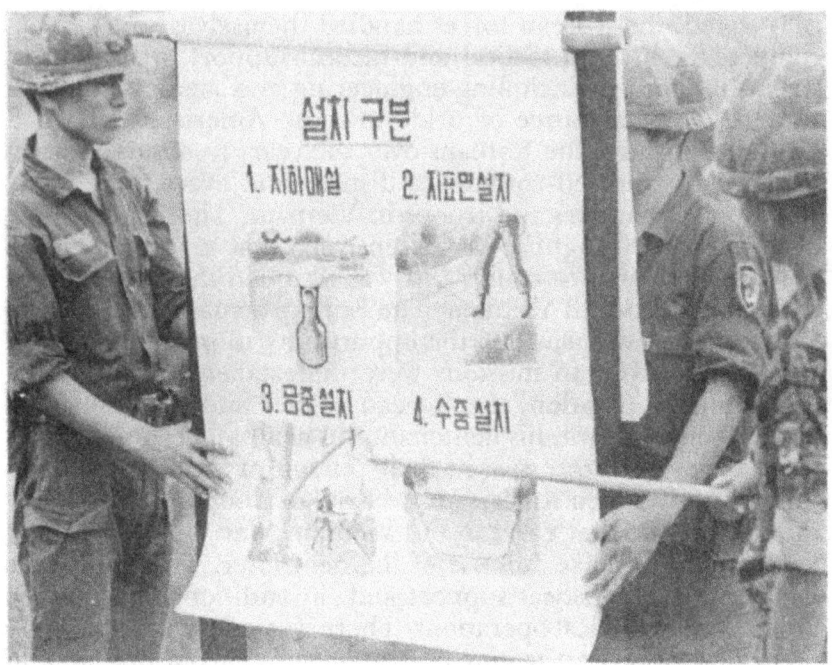

Korean Troops Use Chart *to show villagers types of Viet Cong booby traps.*

remarkable ingenuity in handling many of their requirements with a minimum of equipment. With the Koreans the overriding premise that things should get done precisely when they were needed required the individual to use substitute methods when necessary, whether the job be building bridges, building houses and covering them with watertight roofs, or creating comforts for themselves out of materials their American brothers could not imagine using productively. For example, the Koreans used ammunition boxes to build windows, doors, and even frame houses. Cardboard ration boxes were overlapped and used as roof shingles. These shingles would last for many months and during monsoon weather when they wore out there always seemed to be a good supply of replacements on hand. When new bases were established, in no time at all the Koreans would have two, three, or four men to a hut, enjoying as much if not more comfort than their American counterparts. It was quite obvious to any visitor arriving in a Korean bivouac area that the Korean soldier took pride in his job and in handling his personal needs and wants.

One of the most noteworthy assets of the Korean troops was their discipline; it was immediately clear that Korean soldiers were well prepared, trained, and dedicated. Each regiment arrived, established base camps, and immediately went out on training missions which, in turn, led to combat missions under its capable officers. Korean discipline is a self-discipline, an inner disicipline; a sense for self-preservation serves as a spark to generate initiative to get out of any predicament the Korean soldier may find himself in when his leaders are not around. Another indication of his discipline, and his fierce pride, is his personal appearance. Rarely could one find a Korean soldier who did not appear immaculate, whether he was assigned to an administrative or a combat area.

In any assessment of the Koreans' contributions in South Vietnam it must be underlined that they provided the man-to-man equivalent of the Americans in that Southeast Asian country. In other words, every Korean soldier sent to South Vietnam saved sending an American or other allied soldier. The Koreans, who asked for very little credit, have received almost no recognition in the U.S. press and it is doubtful if many Americans fully appreciate their contributions in South Vietnam. In addition to saving roughly 50,000 U.S. troops from being deployed to South Vietnam, the Koreans provided protection to the South Vietnamese for a distance of several hundred miles up and down the coast, preventing a renewal of North Vietnamese and Viet Cong harassment and domination.

In mid-January 1966 when General Westmoreland was asked to evaluate the Korean forces then in Vietnam, he indicated that for the first two or three months after their arrival Korean senior commanders had closely controlled the offensive operations of their forces in order to train their troops for combat in their new environment. This policy had given the impression that the Koreans lacked aggressiveness and were reluctant to take casualties. In Operation FLYING TIGER in early January of 1966, the Koreans accounted for 192 Viet Cong killed as against only eleven Koreans. This feat, coupled with Korean success in Operation JEFFERSON, constituted a valid indication of the Koreans' combat effectiveness.

The Koreans had an initial period of difficulty in their relations with the Vietnamese military forces because they were better equipped than the troops of the Vietnamese Army and those of the Regional Forces and Popular Forces, because of language barriers, and because of the Oriental "face" problem. The attitude of the Vietnamese Army quickly changed, however, and its appraisal of the Korean forces appears to be essentially the same as the U.S. evaluation. The Koreans had much in common with the Vietnamese public in areas where they were stationed because of the common village origin of the Korean soldier and the Vietnamese peasant, the common rice economy of the two countries, and their similarities in religion and rural culture.

The Koreans remained independent and administratively autonomous. In handling disciplinary matters arising with Vietnamese citizens and the Vietnam government, for example, the Koreans used their own military police and accepted full responsibility for their troops. They handled untoward incidents independently. Military police courtesy patrols in areas of overlapping American, Vietnamese, and Korean responsibility were formed with representatives of each of the three countries.

The size of the Korean force was determined piecemeal and was based solely on what the United States thought was possible from the Korean point of view and on what the United States was willing to pay. Military requirements had very little to do with it. The United States negotiated first for a one-division force. After it was in Vietnam, completely new negotiations to increase the force to a two-division-plus corps were begun. With the second negotiations, the cost to the United States went up, with the Koreans trying to get the maximum out of the Americans. Each major unit was considered separately.

In summary, a formal agreement on the use and employment of the Koreans did not exist. At first General Westmoreland told the I Field Force commander the Koreans would be under his control. The Capital Division commander, General Chae, on his first visit to I Field Force made clear that he did not consider himself under U.S. control. After the second Korean division and the Marine brigade arrived and a Korean corps took over, with General Chae commanding, the Koreans were independent of I Field Force. Operations, however, were co-ordinated in an amiable spirit. The Koreans had specified their desire to be deployed in a significant, prestigious area, on the densely populated coast, where the Korean presence would have the greatest impact at home and abroad. The Koreans were also under instructions to avoid heavy casualties.

President Park, during his visit to the Republic of Vietnam, had told General Westmoreland that he was proud to have Koreans fight under Westmoreland's command. This verbal statement was as far as any admission of subordination of Korean forces to U.S. command ever went. General Westmoreland told the commander of I Field Force to work out an arrangement on

THE REPUBLIC OF KOREA

KOREAN SOLDIERS SEARCH THE JUNGLE NEAR QUI NHON FOR VIET CONG

the basis of letting "water seek its own level." Relationships and co-operation were good, but required diplomacy and tact. The Koreans gradually spread out over large coastal areas and pacified the people. Persuasion to follow U.S. suggestions appears to have been necessary at times. The Koreans believed they were specially qualified to work with the indigenous population because of their common background as Asians.

Results of Korean Combat Operations

The success of the Korean Army and Marine forces in Vietnam was exemplified by the numerous casualties inflicted on the enemy and the very high kill ratio enjoyed by the Korean forces. In addition the large number of weapons and the amount of matériel captured as well as the serious disruptions of the Viet Cong organization in the Koreans' tactical area of responsibility attest to, in the words of General Westmoreland, "the high morale, professional competence, and aggressiveness of the ROK soldier." He went on to say that reports were "continually received on the courage and effectiveness of all ROK forces in South Vietnam."

Following Operation OH JAC KYO in July 1967 the Korean 9th and Capital Divisions thwarted enemy intentions to go on the offensive in Phu Yen Province by inflicting large troop and equipment losses primarily on the North Vietnamese 95th Regiment. Operation HONG KIL DONG alone accounted for 408 enemy killed and a kill ratio of 15 to 1 between 9 and 31 July. By the time the operation was terminated on 28 August, in order to provide security for the coming elections, the total enemy killed had reached 638 and the kill ratio was 24 to 1. In addition, some 98 crew-served and 359 individual weapons had been captured.

In the last four months of 1967, however, no major Korean Army operations were undertaken. This was due partly to the need to provide security for the South Vietnamese elections of September in the face of increased enemy attempts to thwart those elections and partly to the need to keep more than 350 kilometers of Highways 1 and 19 "green." Small unit actions continued to be numerous.

During 1968 the pattern of Korean operations did not change materially from that of previous years; the Korean troops continued to engage in extensive small unit actions, ambushes, and battalion and multibattalion search and destroy operations within or close to their tactical areas of responsibility. Over-all these operations were quite successful. An analysis of an action by Korean Capital Division forces during the period 23–29 January 1968 clearly illustrates the Korean technique. After contact with an enemy force near Phu Cat, the Koreans "reacting swiftly . . . deployed six companies in an encircling maneuver and trapped the enemy force in their cordon. The Korean troops gradually tightened the circle, fighting the enemy during the day and maintaining their tight cordon at night, thus preventing the enemy's escape. At the conclusion of the sixth day of fighting, 278 NVA had been KIA with the loss of just 11 Koreans, a kill ratio of 25.3 to 1."

Later in 1968 a Korean 9th Division operation titled BAEK MA 9 commenced on 11 October and ended on 4 November with 382 enemy soldiers killed and the North Vietnamese 7th Battalion, 18th Regiment, rendered ineffective. During this operation, on 25 October, the eighteenth anniversary of the division, 204 of the enemy were killed without the loss of a single Korean soldier.

By and large, however, the Korean Army continued to stress small unit operations. In its operational assessment for the final quarter of calendar year 1968, the U.S. Military Assistance Command, Vietnam, Quarterly Evaluation states:

As the quarter ended Allied forces in II CTZ were conducting ex-

THE REPUBLIC OF KOREA

tensive operations throughout the CTZ to destroy enemy forces and to provide maximum possible support to the Accelerated Pacification Campaign. The prime ingredient in the overall operation was small unit tactical operations. For example, as the Quarter ended . . . ROK forces were conducting some 195 small unit operations.

This Korean emphasis was in keeping with the policy in the II Corps Tactical Zone of economy of force in the first quarter of calendar year 1968 and the greater stress on effective defense of cities and installations.

The primary effort in the II Corps Tactical Zone during the first three months of 1969 was directed toward pacification and improvement of the effectiveness of the armed forces of the republic. The Koreans continued to maintain effective control of the central coastal area from Phan Rang in Ninh Thuan Province to the north of Qui Nhon in Binh Dinh Province. All allied forces found enemy base areas and supply caches with increasing frequency. Binh Dinh Province continued to lead all other provinces in number of enemy incidents; however, the majority of reported actions were small unit contacts with generally minor results. Allied units, particularly the Korean force, continued to place great emphasis on small unit operations. The enemy continued to avoid decisive engagements and directed his activity mainly against territorial forces and civilian population centers.

An analysis of Korean cordon and search operations was provided by Lieutenant General William R. Peers, who considered the Koreans to have more expertise in this kind of operation than any of the other forces he had seen in South Vietnam:

> There were several key elements in their conduct of this type of operation. First, they are thorough in every detail in their planning. Secondly, their cordon involves a comparatively small area, probably not in excess of 9 to 10 square kilometers for a regimental size force. Third, the maximum force is employed, generally consisting of a regiment up to something in excess of a division. And finally, the operation is rehearsed and critiqued before it is begun. Units are moved into locations around the periphery of the cordon by a variety of means, including helicopters, trucks and by foot, but so timed that all arrive in position simultaneously to complete the encirclement. The density of the troops is such that the distance between individuals on the cordon is less than 10 meters. They leave little opportunity for the enemy to exfiltrate in small numbers. Areas, such as streams and gulleys, are barricaded with barbed wire and other barrier materials, reinforced by troops who may remain in water chest deep over night. The closing of the cordon is very slow and deliberate, not a rock is left unturned or piece of ground not probed. When the area has been cleared, they will surge back and forth through it to flush out any of the remnants. An-

other critical feature of their operation is the availability of reaction forces. The enemy soon knows when such a cordon is put around him. If he cannot exfiltrate by individuals or in small numbers, he may attempt to mass his forces and break out at one point. Against such contingencies the ROK's utilize several reaction forces to reinforce critical areas. They have found that the enemy may make one or even several feints at various points around the cordon prior to making the main effort to breach the encirclement. Hence, the ROK deployment of reaction forces is by small incremental elements until such time as the main effort is located, and then the action becomes rapid and positive. Through the use of these tactics, the ROK's have developed the cordon and search operation to a fine state of art. The ratio of enemy to friendly casualties has been phenomenal—on one occasion in excess of 100 to 1.

Generally Korean large-scale operations during 1969 were of regimental size or less, of brief duration, and with a specific target. One significant operation of this kind was DONG BO 7, carried out near Cam Ranh from 9 to 11 May 1969. Soldiers of the 2d Battalion, 30th Regiment, 9th (White Horse) Division were airlifted onto Tao Mountain, a base for units of the 5th North Vietnam Army Division, and searched the caves and trenches on the mountain. When the operation ended, 155 enemy soldiers had been killed while the Koreans had three killed and one wounded.

Throughout 1970 the Koreans continued to conduct many operations of short duration aimed at supporting the over-all pacification program and the general campaign goals. The Korean Army division conducted an average of 150 small unit actions each day, including ambushes, search and clear operations, and the normal efforts to secure the areas around minor installations. The major results of Korean efforts were reflected in the infrequent larger scale operation of the Koreans; however, their kill ratio remained high for all operations.

Every time the Koreans performed a mission they did it well. A study of the tactical area of responsibility assigned them shows clearly that they were stretched to the limit geographically, with the job of keeping the roads open from above Phu Cat north of Qui Nhon all the way to Phan Rang down in Ninh Thuan, three provinces below Binh Dinh. They had several hundred road miles of responsibility—and they kept the roads open.

The enemy feared the Koreans both for their tactical innovations and for the soldiers' tenacity. It is of more than passing interest to note that there never was an American unit in Vietnam which was able to "smell out" small arms like the Koreans. The Koreans might not suffer many casualties, might not get too many of the enemy on an operation, but when they brought in seventy-five or a hundred weapons, the Americans wondered where in the world they got them. They appeared to have a natural nose for picking up enemy weapons that were, as far as the enemy thought, securely cached away. Considered opinion was that it was good the Koreans were "friendlies."

Evaluation of Korean Operations

Evaluation by senior U.S. officers of Korean operations during the period of the Koreans' employment in Vietnam tended to become more critical the longer the Koreans remained in Vietnam. Of several factors contributing to this trend, three were more significant than the others. First, the U.S. commanders expected more of the Koreans as they gained experience and familiarity with the terrain and the enemy. Second, the Koreans persisted in planning each operation "by the numbers," even though it would appear that previous experience could have eliminated a great deal of time and effort. Third, as time went on the Korean soldiers sent to Vietnam were of lower quality than the "cream of the crop" level of the entire Korean Army which first arrived.

General Larsen's successor as Commanding General, I Field Force, Vietnam, General William B. Rosson, in his "End of Tour Debriefing Report" presented a number of insights into the problems of establishing effective teamwork between Korean and U.S. and Korean and Vietnam forces. General Rosson stressed the "extraordinary combination of ROK aspirations, attitudes, training, political sensitivities and national pride" which culminated in the Korean characteristics of restraint and inflexibility that many U.S. officers found so difficult to comprehend and to deal with. Rosson's experience led him to employ "studied flattery," which he used liberally and with success in establishing productive rapport, "but never to the point of meting out undeserved praise."

In addition General Rosson found certain other techniques in dealing with the Korean authorities: occasional calls on Korean officials junior to himself; encouragement of staff level visits between U.S. and Korean unit headquarters; combined U.S.-Korean conferences on a no-commitment basis to consider subjects of common interest; planning and conduct of combined operations; fulfillment of Korean requests for support whenever possible; visits to Korean units during combat operations; personal, face-to-face requests for assistance from the Koreans.

One of these techniques—fulfillment of Korean requests

whenever possible—has been challenged by later commanders. One other—planning and conduct of combined operations—has been one of the chief sources of criticism of the Koreans, who are very reluctant to enter into truly combined operations.

General Peers, who succeeded General Rosson, stated that it took some learning and understanding but that he found the Koreans highly efficient and a.distinct pleasure to work with. He also stated that every effort was made to support Korean operations by providing additional artillery, helicopters, APC's, and tanks and that this practice proved of immense value in developing co-operation between the Koreans and adjacent U.S. units.

A slightly different point of view was provided by Lieutenant General Arthur S. Collins, Jr., who was Commanding General, I Field Force, Vietnam, from 15 February 1970 through 9 January 1971. General Collins stated that the Koreans made excessive demands for choppers and support and that they stood down for too long after an operation. He equated the total effort from the two Korean divisions to "what one can expect from one good US Brigade."

General Collins, for the first eight months of his time, followed the policy of his predecessors in that he went to great lengths "to ensure that the ROK forces received the support they asked for." He felt that it was in the interest of the United States to do so. His final analysis, however, was that this was a mistake in that in spite of all-out support the Koreans did not conduct the number of operations they could and should have. He felt that a less accommodating attitude might have gained more respect and co-operation from the Koreans but did not venture to guess whether such a position would have made them any more active.

General Collins' successor, Major General Charles P. Brown, deputy commander and later commanding general of I Field Force, Vietnam, and commanding general of the Second Regional Assistance Command during the period 31 March 1970– 15 May 1971 made this statement:

The ROK's spent relatively long periods planning regimental and division sized operations, but the duration of the execution phase is short.

The planning which leads to requests for helicopter assets to support airmobile operations is poor. This assessment is based on the fact that the magnitude of their requests for helicopters generally is absurdly high. Without disturbing their tactical plan one iota, their aviation requests can always be scaled down, frequently almost by a factor of one-half. . . .

Execution is methodical and thorough, and there is faithful adherence to the plan with little display of the ingenuity or flexibility that must be present to take advantage of tactical situations that may develop. In other words, reaction to tactical opportunities is slow, and this is true not only within their own operations, but also is true (to an even greater degree) when they are asked to react for others.

In terms of effort expended, they do not manage as many battalion days in the field as they should, yet they are loath to permit others to operate in their TAOR.

In summary, however, General Brown stated that "while the preceding tends to be critical, the facts are that results (especially when one considers the relatively short amount of time devoted to fighting are generally good, and this is what counts in the end."

Other senior officers noted the great political pressure the Seoul government placed on the Korean commander and its effect on Korean military operations. Since the Korean government was not fully attuned to the changing requirements of the ground situation, its policy guidance often hampered the optimum utilization of Korean resources. Specifically this resulted at times in a strong desire on the part of the Koreans to avoid casualties during periods of domestic political sensitivity as well as sudden changes in their relations with the people and government of South Vietnam.

General Creighton Abrams has indicated that from a purely professional point of view the Koreans probably outperformed all of our allied forces in South Vietnam. In response to a question from Vice President Spiro T. Agnew regarding the performance of the Koreans in comparison with the Vietnamese, General Abrams made this statement:

There were some things in which the Koreans, based purely on their professionalism, probably exceeded any of our allied forces in South Vietnam. An example of this would be when they decided to surround and attack a hill. A task of this sort would take one month of preparation time during which a lot of negotiating would be done to get the support of B-52's, artillery and tanks. Their planning is deliberate and their professional standards are high. The Korean planning is disciplined and thorough. In many other fields, however, particularly in working close to the population, the Vietnamese show much more sensitivity and flexibility than the Koreans. In short, the kind of war that we have here can be compared to an orchestra. It is sometimes appropriate to emphasize the drums or the trumpets or the bassoon, or even the flute. [The] Vietnamese, to a degree, realize this and do it. The Koreans, on the other hand, play one instrument—the bass drum.

Color Guard Displays Flags *at ceremonies commemorating third anniversary of Korean forces in Vietnam.*

In summary, it appears that Korean operations in Vietnam were highly professional, well planned, and thoroughly executed; limited in size and scope, especially in view of assets made available; generally unilateral and within the Korean tactical area of responsibility; subject to domestic political considerations; and highly successful in terms of kill ratio.

Tactics

Korean units, without exception, employed tactics in line with established U.S. Army doctrine. Squad, company, and battalion operations were characterized by skillful use of fire and maneuver and by strict fire discipline. A basic rule, which seemed to be followed in all observed instances, involved having one element cover another whenever a tactical movement was under way. During search and destroy operations, companies moved out to their assigned areas with platoons on line, separated by 150 to 200 meters, depending on the type of terrain encountered. One platoon usually remained behind as security for

GENERAL ABRAMS PRESENTS BRONZE STARS *to soldiers of the Tiger Division.*

the headquarters element and also acted as the company reaction force in the event of contact. Within platoons, a V-formation or inverted wedge was usually employed. This formation lent itself to encircling an enemy force or a village. The lead squads would envelop right and left; the remainder of the platoon would search or attack as the situation required.

The Korean troops' searching was thorough and precise. They took their time and moved only when units were ready. They prepared sound plans; everyone knew the plan; each element was mutually supporting. It was not unusual for the same area to be searched three or four times and by different platoons. Areas of operation for platoons and companies were usually smaller than those assigned to U.S. units. The units remained in each objective area until commanders were satisfied that it had been thoroughly combed. This persistence paid off time and again in rooting out the Viet Cong and finding their weapons and equipment.

As the hamlet was being searched, civilians were collected and moved to a safe central location where they were guarded and exploited for information of immediate tactical value. Civilians were segregated according to age and sex. Women and children were usually interrogated in two separate groups. Men were questioned individually. The Koreans used rewards routinely to elicit information. They fed and provided medical attention to those people from whom they sought information. They also used bribes of food, money, candy, and cigarettes to soften the more likely subjects (women and children).

Detainees were a valuable source of information. They were retained in one central area until the Koreans were convinced they had been properly exploited. There was no rush to release the people to return to their homes, the theory being that if held long enough they would provide the desired information. The villagers themselves were employed to point out Viet Cong dwellings and the location of weapons, booby traps, and enemy equipment.

Ambushes

The usual ambush force was a squad, reinforced with one or more machine guns. An on-line formation was used with the automatic weapons on the flanks, about twenty meters off the selected trail. The position had been thoroughly reconnoitered before dark and was occupied at last light or in darkness. All unnecessary equipment was left at the company base. Faces were blackened and all equipment carried was taped or tied down.

Ambush sites were not altered by cutting fields of fire or by digging in. Absolute light and noise discipline was maintained. Until contact was made, communication between squad members was accomplished through tugs on a length of rope or radio wire, strung between positions. No firing was permitted until the enemy was well within the killing zone. Troops in the ambush force remained quiet and awake throughout the period of ambush, be it all day or all night. All individuals appeared to remain awake and alert with no help from squad leaders.

In summary, the factors contributing to the success of Korean forces were the following: discipline, aggressiveness, training, patience, and physical fitness of the Korean soldiers; outstanding leadership; adherence to the same tactical doctrine taught at U.S. service schools and written in U.S. manuals; thorough planning; careful initial reconnaissance; time taken to develop tactical situations; sealing and blocking of selected areas prior to entrance; use of interpreters at company level (interpreters were the product of division school training).

The criteria listed above should not suggest that the Koreans

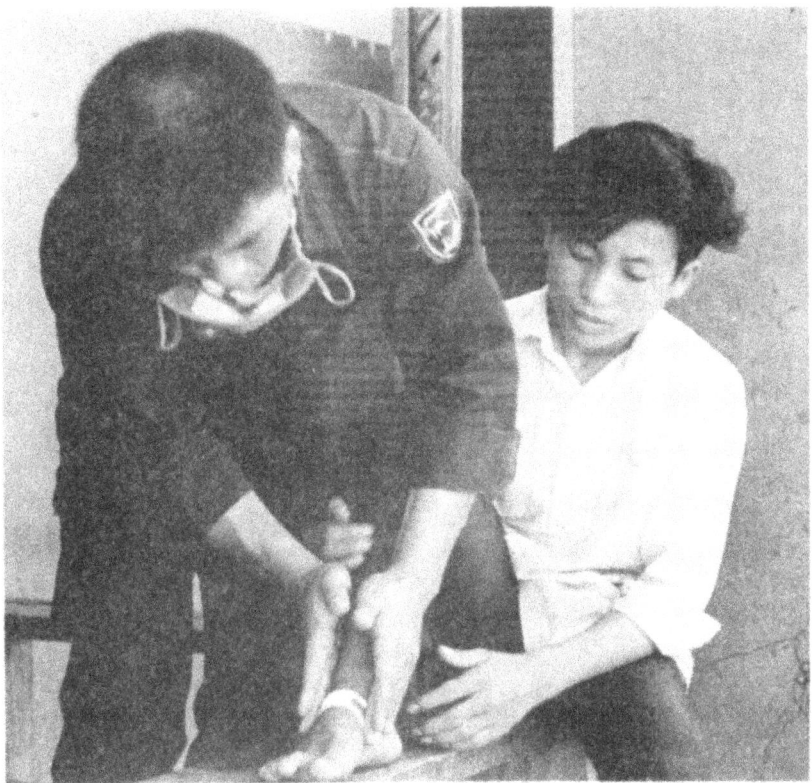

MEDIC OF TIGER DIVISION TREATS VILLAGE BOY

were outstanding in every respect; actually there were deficiencies noted, but despite these the Koreans demonstrated a sure grasp of tactical fundamentals, and their discipline, their patience, their persistence in attaining an objective, and their physical fitness, were admirable.

Pacification Efforts

Korean pacification efforts have been the subject of a certain amount of controversy over the years. Early comments by commanders of all levels were highly favorable. Later, however, questions as to the over-all effectiveness of Korean pacification efforts were raised. As a result, from 5 July to 23 August 1968, the evaluation branch of CORDS (Civil Operations Revolutionary Development Support) analyzed the influence of the Army of the Republic of Korea upon the pacification programs in the II Corps Tactical Zone which were supported by CORDS. The

Korean Instructor in Taekwondo *watches Vietnamese practice after class.*

evaluation was based on personal observations of two tactical operations and the pacification efforts of both Korean divisions, interviews of most of the district chiefs in the Koreans' area of responsibility, all U.S. district senior advisers and their deputies, both Korean division G-5's, and most regimental and battalion S-5's. The report, critical of Korean Army pacification performance in certain areas, noted that Korean units provided excellent local security but devoted scant attention to upgrading Vietnam government territorial forces and countering hamlet regression. Though devoting much effort to the attack on the Viet Cong, the Koreans' neutralization activities were shrouded in secrecy. Korean support of the National Police and revolutionary development cadre program was held to be inadequate, as were Korean civic action and psychological programs. The report also alleged corruption on the part of Korean officers and units. The Korean *Chieu Hoi*, refugee, and civilian war casualty programs were praised. These programs helped to change the somewhat unfavorable first image of the Korean troops held by the Vietnamese.

The report, however, was not totally accepted. Other evaluators emphasized the combat skill and efficiency of the Koreans and pointed to their tactical successes within their area of operations. What was not disputed was the initial report's evidence of the improved security the Koreans provided. Subsequent evaluations by CORDS tended to corroborate the initial conclusions: while the Korean Army troops provided excellent local security and operated effectively against Viet Cong forces, there was still insufficient rapport and co-ordination between the Koreans and Vietnamese (civilian and military) to maximize pacification efforts.

The pacification techniques of the Korean Army were closely linked with their combat operations. After Korean Army units occupied an area and drove out the enemy, Korean civic action teams would begin their training programs and provide medical assistance in an attempt to gain the allegiance of the people.

The Korean Marine Corps pacification program also received mixed ratings. Again the major problem was insufficient rapport with the Vietnamese people and incomplete co-ordination of efforts with the Vietnamese Army.

An analysis of the over-all Korean contribution to the pacification program leads to the conclusion that Korean combat forces had their greatest success with small unit civic action projects and security operations within their Korean tactical area of responsibility. Complete success eluded the Koreans, however, because of their insufficient co-ordination and co-operation, and the initial impression they made in dealing with the Vietnamese.

CHAPTER VII
Nonmilitary Aid to Vietnam

Various nations have provided military and nonmilitary assistance since the government of Vietnam launched an appeal for aid on 14 July 1964. By 1969 five Asian and Pacific countries —Australia, the Republic of Korea, New Zealand, the Philippines, and Thailand—had approximately 68,000 troops on the ground. Germany, Australia, Canada, Japan, the United Kingdom, New Zealand, and the Netherlands set up large continuing programs of economic, humanitarian, and technical assistance, either under the Columbo Plan or as a result of bilateral arrangements. Several other countries made smaller continuing contributions, while many others sent relief or commodity aid at varying times after 1964. All told thirty-nine nations besides the United States helped Vietnam under the Free World assistance program. The following is a list of these nations.

FAR EAST
    Australia
    Republic of China
    Japan
    Republic of Korea
    Laos
    Malaysia
    New Zealand
    Pakistan
    Philippines
    Thailand

MIDDLE EAST
    Iran
    Israel
    Turkey

AFRICA
    Liberia
    Morocco
    South Africa
    Tunisia

EUROPE
    Belgium
    Denmark
    Federal Republic of Germany
    France
    Greece
    Ireland
    Italy
    Luxembourg
    The Netherlands
    Norway
    Spain
    Switzerland
    United Kingdom

NORTH AMERICA
    Canada

LATIN AMERICA
    Argentina
    Brazil
    Costa Rica

LATIN AMERICA—Continued Honduras
  Ecuador Uruguay
  Guatemala Venezuela

Far East

Australia

Australia provided a wide and substantial range of aid to Vietnam under the Columbo Plan and by direct bilateral assistance in addition to its military aid of approximately 7,000 combat troops.

Economic and technical assistance after 1964 totaled more than $10.5 million. Australia provided three surgical teams—forty-two people; a group of civil engineers to work on water supply and road construction projects; and three experts in dairy and crop practices and radio techniques. The Australian government trained 130 Vietnamese in Australia; furnished 1,500,000 textbooks in Vietnamese for rural schools; and provided 3,300 tons of corrugated roofing for Vietnamese military dependent housing, six large community windmills, 15,750 sets of hand tools, 400 radio sets and 2,400 loudspeakers, 16,000 blankets, 14,000 cases of condensed milk, and a 50-kilowatt broadcasting station at Ban Me Thuot. In addition, approximately $650,000 in emergency assistance was provided during 1968; included were construction materials, foodstuffs, and vaccines.

Republic of China

The Republic of China provided an 80-man agricultural team, an 18-man military psychological warfare team, a 34-man electrical power mission, and a 16-man surgical team.

China financed the training of 40 Vietnamese power engineers and technicians and also provided training for more than 200 Vietnamese in Taiwan. In the way of goods and materials, it provided 26 aluminum prefabricated warehouses, agricultural tools, seeds and fertilizers, cement, medical supplies, 500,000 mathematics textbooks, and an electrical power substation. China also donated 5,000 tons of rice worth more than $1 million. There were private gifts as well.

Japan

Partly in response to a request from the Vietnam government but chiefly through reparations, Japan provided over $55 million worth of economic assistance to Vietnam. Japan sent two medical teams, considerable amounts of medical goods, 20,000 transistor radios, and 25 ambulances. In addition, Japan provided technicians and funds for the construction of a large power dam across the Da Nhim River, an electrical transmission line, and scholarships for students and technicians, and constructed a neurological ward in Saigon.

Republic of Korea

Korean military personnel constituted the majority of allied forces other than U.S. forces in South Vietnam. Korean military medical personnel provided some medical care to the local population in areas where Korean troops were stationed. In addition, seven civilian medical teams—118 doctors, nurses, and support personnel—worked in provincial health programs. Korea also donated more than $50,000 worth of relief supplies.

Laos

Laos contributed $4,167 for flood relief in 1965 and a small cash donation for refugees in 1966. An additional $5,000 in relief supplies was provided in 1968.

Malaysia

Beginning in 1964 Malaysia trained nearly 2,900 Vietnamese military and police officers. Groups of thirty to sixty men were regularly sent to Malaysia for about a month's training in counterinsurgency operations with the Malaysian Police Special Constabulary. Malaysia also provided some counterinsurgency equipment, primarily military and police transport vehicles, and medicines and relief supplies.

In early 1967 Malaysia received and accepted a formal invitation to send four experts on rural settlement and pacification to South Vietnam. The team was to make recommendations concerning hamlet security and psychological warfare. The Vietnamese did not feel that the team was very effective. At the close of 1967 there was some talk of a Malaysian proposal to increase the training staff and double the size of the training effort at the police school. While appreciative of the offer, police officials in Saigon pointed out that so many police had already been trained in Malaysia and the Philippines that there was little need for large expansion of the program.

New Zealand

In nonmilitary aid, New Zealand assistance averaged $347,500 annually. Civilian aid expenditures in 1969 were 48,000 New Zealand dollars, which financed a 15-man surgical team at Qui Nhon, scholarships for 80 Vietnamese in New Zealand, medical and teaching equipment for Hue University, equipment for a technical high school, and a contribution toward the construction of a science building at the University of Saigon. In early 1968 the government of New Zealand donated $20,000 in food and other supplies.

Pakistan

Pakistan contributed financial assistance and clothing for flood victims.

Philippines

The Philippine government provided a 1,500-man military engineering unit with its own security support, a station hospital, and rural health and civic action teams. The bulk of this force was withdrawn in 1969. A 12-man medical team was financed, and clothing, food, and medical supplies were donated. The Philippine government donated $28,700 worth of supplies as well.

Thailand

In nonmilitary aid, Thailand supplied rice for refugees, cement, and corrugated iron roofing materials. In early 1968 Thailand donated $242,170 in building materials and vaccines.

Middle East

Iran

Iran extended significant assistance to the Republic of Vietnam. Shortly after President Johnson's appeal, Iran promised petroleum products, and one thousand tons of gasoline were delivered in July of 1965. Beginning on 12 January 1966, Iran maintained in Vietnam a medical team of high quality—some twenty doctors and medical technicians, and nurses from the Red Lion and Sun Society, which is roughly equivalent to a National Red Crescent or Red Cross organization.

Israel

Israel donated pharmaceutical supplies for flood victims and trained three Vietnamese in irrigation techniques.

Turkey

Turkey provided medicines and in early 1968 supplied a quantity of vaccines. Turkey also offered to give a substantial amount of cement.

Africa

Liberia

Liberia made a gift of $50,000 for the purchase of medical supplies and hospital equipment.

Morocco

Morocco contributed 10,000 cans of sardines worth $2,000.

South Africa

The South African government contributed approximately $14,000 worth of medical supplies to Vietnam.

Tunisia

Tunisia made available fifteen to twenty scholarships for Vietnamese students.

Europe

Belgium

Belgium provided medicines and an ambulance, and granted scholarships for fifteen Vietnamese to study in Belgium.

Denmark

Denmark provided medical supplies and offered to train twelve Vietnamese nurses in Denmark.

Federal Republic of Germany

German economic and humanitarian aid, beginning in 1966, averaged about $7.5 million annually and more than 200 technical and medical personnel served in Vietnam. In 1966 the Federal Republic of Germany also contributed the 3,000-ton hospital ship S.S. *Helgoland* to provide medical assistance to the civilian population. With eight doctors, thirty other medical personnel, and a 130-bed capacity, the ship was initially stationed near Saigon where more than 21,000 out-patient treatments were given to approximately 6,700 patients from September 1966 until 30 June 1967. Over 850 major surgical cases were also treated. In October of 1967 the *Helgoland* shifted its operations to Da Nang.

In March 1967 the German government's Maltese Aid Service team for the care of refugees was increased from twenty-five to forty-seven—six doctors, two dentists, and thirty-nine nurses and vocational teachers. Operating from sites in An Hoa, Da Nang, and Hoi An, teams provided regular health and refugee care. Other Germans serving in Vietnam taught in the Technical High School at Thu Duc near Saigon and five professors served on the Hue University faculty. Twenty Vietnamese were trained in Germany to replace the seven Germans at the Technical High School, and scholarships at German schools were granted to seven Vietnamese students each year.

The German government supplied credits of $21.2 million for capital projects and commodity imports. It also provided the following credits: $3.75 million for the import of German products such as machine tools and fertilizer; $12.5 million for development of the industrial complex at An Hoa-Nong Son; $5 million for capital projects; and $3.5 million to equip a modern slaughterhouse and provide technical aid.

Other assistance included the construction and staffing, with German aid funds, of nine social centers in Saigon, a training center for experts in the social field, and a home for juvenile delinquents at Thu Duc.

Substantial quantities of pharmaceuticals and other medical supplies and equipment were donated for distribution to civilian hospitals and dispensaries and 100,000 health textbooks were provided. Germany constructed a 170-bed hospital at a cost of $2.5 million in Da Nang as a replacement for the *Helgoland*.

France

Beginning in 1956 France contributed approximately $155 million in assistance to South Vietnam. Aid averaged about $4 million per year, largely in the cultural field.

Most of the French in Vietnam were engaged in some form of cultural work; some taught in secondary schools and a few were professors on university staffs. France provided fifty-five fellowships for technical training and eighty-five academic fellowships for schooling in France in 1965; afterward the program continued but at a slightly reduced scale.

France also provided low-interest credits of 100 million francs ($20 million) for financing imports of French equipment for Vietnamese industry and a grant of 500,000 francs ($100,000) for equipment for L'Ecole Nationale d'Ingenieurs des Arts Industriels. In 1960 a low-interest credit of 70 million francs ($14 million) was made to aid construction of the major coal and chemical complex under way at An Hoa-Nong Son, south of Da Nang. A low-interest, five-year credit of 60 million francs ($12 million) was also provided for construction of Vietnam's largest cement-producing complex, with plants at Ha Tien and Thu Duc. In 1964 France made a 930,000-franc ($186,000) grant for the installation of a training center for electrical technicians and in 1965 a gift of 1.25 million francs ($250,000) for teaching equipment, primarily in the medical field.

Greece

Greece contributed $15,000 worth of medical supplies.

Ireland

Ireland contributed $2,800 to Vietnam through the Red Cross.

Italy

The Italians provided a ten-man surgical team and offered science scholarships to ten Vietnamese to study in Italy. They also gave relief commodities worth about $29,000, including some private donations.

Luxembourg

This country provided plasma and blood transfusion equipment.

The Netherlands

The Netherlands aid program, which began in 1965, financed scholarships for Vietnamese doctors, the construction and equipping of three tuberculosis centers, and the renovation and expansion of hospital facilities in Cho Lon. The government also earmarked $1 million in trust for United Nations projects in Vietnam. In October 1968 the Netherlands announced a $186,000 grant to UNICEF for relief projects in Vietnam.

Norway

Norway sent a contribution through the International Red Cross for flood victims in February 1965. Norway also contributed money in early 1968 for the homeless *Tet* refugees in South Vietnam.

Spain

In December 1965 the government of Spain announced that as a result of a request by the government of Vietnam, it would provide a medical mission of twelve to fourteen men to the Republic of Vietnam. Negotiations over support arrangements were made in co-ordination with the U.S. Agency for International Development and the Vietnamese Minister of Health. The major points of this arrangement were that the government of Spain would pay the team's salaries and allowance, plus fifty dollars a month per member for subsistence, and the United States would pay all other costs.

It was decided to locate the team of four doctors, one quartermaster, a captain, and seven nurses in Go Cong Province in the IV Corps Tactical Zone. The team arrived in Vietnam on 8 September and on 10 September it replaced the U.S. Military Provincial Health Assistance Program team at the province hospital in Go Cong.

Switzerland

The Swiss provided microscopes for the University of Saigon, as well as a medical team of eleven men through the auspices of the International Committee of the Red Cross to work in a provincial hospital in the Central Highlands in April 1966. Another team arrived in Da Nang in late 1967, and a government grant was used to finance the construction of a pediatric wing at the Da Nang hospital. In addition, the Swiss donated $200,000 in emergency supplies.

United Kingdom

In 1963 and 1964, the United Kingdom provided the following goods and materials: laboratory equipment for Saigon University; a typesetting machine for the Government Printing Office, a cobalt deep-ray therapy unit for the National Cancer Institute; equipment for the faculties of medicine, science, and pharmacy at Saigon University, the Meteorologic Service and the Agricultural School at Saigon, the Atomic Research Establishment at Dalat, and the faculty of education at Hue. A pediatric team of five British doctors and six nurses went to Saigon in August 1966 and remained for five years. The team was later expanded to twenty-six members. From 1968 through 1971 the United Kingdom supplied economic aid valued at $2.4 million. It provided police advisers, teachers, a professor of English at Hue University, and technical experts.

North America

Canada

Beginning in 1964, Canada provided more than $9.3 million in development assistance to Vietnam. At Quang Ngai a small tuberculosis clinic was constructed, with two doctors and four nurses to staff the clinic. A Canadian professor of orthopedics worked at the Cho Ray Hospital, Saigon, and a Canadian instructor taught at the University of Hue for two years. In Canada 380 trainees under the Columbo Plan and a total of 483 trainees under all programs received technical training.

Medical assistance constituted the largest portion of Canadian aid to Vietnam. Approximately 560,000 doses of polio vaccine were delivered for inoculation of school children, and Canada offered additional vaccines against polio, tuberculosis, and smallpox.

Starting in 1958, Canada provided $850,000 worth of food; the funds collected by sales of food were used for capital construction projects in Vietnam. The Canadians provided a new science building for the medical school at the University of Hue costing $333,000 and agreed to allocate about $125,000 for the construction of an auditorium at the university. In addition, $1 million was allocated for medical assistance which, in part, funded delivery of ten 200-bed emergency hospital units. Two of these units were located near Saigon.

In 1968 the government sent emergency supplies worth $200,000, provided eight doctors on short-term assignments, and donated $225,000 for housing Vietnamese left homeless by the *Tet* offensive.

Canada also printed half a million copies of a social science textbook for grade school children.

Latin America

Argentina

Argentina donated 5,000 tons of wheat flour and 20,000 doses of cholera vaccine.

Brazil

Brazil provided 5,000 sacks of coffee and a substantial quantity of medical supplies.

Costa Rica

This country contributed an ambulance for use by the Vietnamese Ministry of Health.

Ecuador

A gift of medical supplies was sent to Vietnam.

Guatemala

Approximately 15,000 doses of typhoid-paratyphoid serum were donated.

Honduras

Honduras contributed medicines and 3,100 pounds of new clothes for Vietnamese refugees. This represented contributions from the people of Honduras to the Red Cross during a campaign in October 1966. It was not until February 1967 that a Honduran Air Force plane completed the mercy flight in what was the first trans-Pacific flight for a Honduran Air Force crew.

Uruguay

A contribution of $21,500 for relief supplies and medicines was donated.

Venezuela

Two civilian doctors were sent to Vietnam, and 500 tons of rice were provided by Venezuela.

Appendix A

LEAFLET ADDRESSED TO THE VIETNAMESE PEOPLE

TO THE VIETNAMESE PEOPLE:

The Filipino people, in response to the request of the Vietnamese people for civic action assistance as expressed by the Government of Vietnam, have sent the Ist Philippine Civic Action Group, RVN (Ist PHILCAGV) to extend that assistance in all sincerity though humble it may be.

We, the members of Ist PHILCAGV therefore, are pledged to carry out the mandate of our people to the best of our ability and to the fullest extent of our capacity. We ask the Vietnamese people to understand that we are here to help build and not to destroy, to bring the Vietnamese people happiness and not sorrow, to develop good will and not hatred. We further ask the Vietnamese people cooperation in whatever manner they think best so that we can accomplish our civic action projects with the least obstacle and interference by some individuals or groups of individuals who are against the idea of the Vietnamese people being able to enjoy happiness and a better way of life.

Within the pages of this leaflet is the Vietnamese translation of the law passed by the representatives of our people, The Congress of the Philippines, and approved by the Chief Executive, President Ferdinand E Marcos. This law reflects the sentiments of the people of the Philippines and provides the basis for our being here with you today.

As our late President Magsaysay, the father of civic action in the Philippines said, "Ano po ba ang kailangan natin?" - meaning, "What sir, would you want me to do for you?" Like our late President Magsaysay, we ask the Vietnamese the same question. Please do not hesitate to tell us where we can be most useful to you, and where you think we are not doing well as you expected. Undoubtedly, you and we can attain greater achievements if we do them together.

Sixth Congress

of the

Republic of the Philippines

Second Special Session

Begun and held in the City of Manila on Friday, the twentieth day of May, nineteen hundred and sixty-six

(REPUBLIC ACT NO. 4664)

AN ACT AUTHORIZING THE INCREASE OF PHILIPPINE ECONOMIC AND TECHNICAL ASSISTANCE TO SOUTH VIETNAM.

WHEREAS, on July 21, 1964, upon request of the Government of South Vietnam, and in consonance with the stand taken by the Philippine Delegation in the Ninth SEATO Council Meeting held in Manila from April 13 to 15, 1964, the Congress of the Philippines enacted Republic Act Numbered Forty-one hundred sixty-two, authorizing the President of the Philippines to send economic and technical assistance to South Vietnam;

WHEREAS, THE Government of South Vietnam has requested the Philippine Government for more assistance with a view to carrying out socio-economic projects calculated to improve the living conditions of the people in the areas recovered from Communist control;

WHEREAS, the Government of the Philippines views the said request for more assistance with the utmost sympathy and, in consonance with the stand taken by the Philippine Delegation in the Tenth SEATO Council Meeting held in London from May 3 to 5, 1965, is ready within the limits of its capability to continue extending economic and technical assistance to South Vietnam: Now, therefore, Be it enacted by the Senate and House of Representatives of the Philippines in Congress assembled:

SECTION 1. The President of the Republic of the Philippines is hereby authorized to increase Philippine economic and technical assistance to South Vietnam as provided for under Republic Act Numbered Forty-one hundred sixty-two by sending to that country a Civic Action Group consisting of engineer construction, medical, and rural community development teams which shall undertake socio-economic projects mutually agreed upon by the Government of the Philippines and the Government of South Vietnam. The said Civic Action Group shall be provided with its own security support.

All personnel sent to South Vietnam under the authority of this Act shall be drawn from volunteers and shall at all times be under a Philippine command. No person shall be included in the Civic Action Group and the security support herein provided unless he signs a sworn statement that he has volunteered to join said group.

SEC. 2. It shall be unlawful for any person to compel, induce, or allow anyone to go to South Vietnam under this Act without the sworn statement provided for in Section one hereof. Any violation of this section shall be punishable by imprisonment of not less than one year nor more than five years.

SEC. 3. To carry out the purpose of this Act, the sum of thirty five million pesos, or so much thereof as may be necessary, is hereby appropriated out of any funds in the National Treasury not otherwise appropriated.

SEC. 4. This Act shall take effect upon its approval.

Approved.

ARTURO M. TOLENTINO
President of the Senate

CORNELIO T. VILLAREAL
Speaker of the House of
Representatives

This Act, which is a substitution by consolidation of H. No. 3411 and S. No. 391, was finally passed by the Senate and the House of Representatives on June 9, 1966.

REGINO S. EUSTAQUIO
Secretary of the Senate

INOCENCIO B. PAREJA
Secretary of the House of
Representatives

Approved: June 18, 1966.

FERDINAND E. MARCOS
President of the Philippines

Copies of this leaflet were originally made in the Vietnamese language and distributed by air and by hand in Vietnam.

Glossary

Admin	Administrative
ANZAC	Australian—New Zealand Army Corps
APC's	Armored personnel carriers
Comd	Command
CORDS	Civil Operations Revolutionary Development Support
CTZ	Corps tactical zone
DMZ	Demilitarized zone
DS	Direct support
GVN	Government of South Vietnam
JUSPAO	Joint U.S. Public Affairs Office
KANZUS	Korean, Australian, New Zealand, and U.S. (troops)
KIA	Killed in action
LRRP	Long-range reconnaissance patrol
LSM's	Landing ships, mechanized
LST's	Landing ships, tank
MAP	Military Assistance Program
MOS	Military occupational specialty
NVA	North Vietnamese Army
NZ SAS	New Zealand Special Air Services
PGM 107	Motor gunboat
PHILCAG	Philippine Civic Action Group
PHILCAGV	Philippine Civic Action Group, Vietnam
POL	Petroleum, oil, and lubricants
RCT	Regimental combat team
Repl	Replacement
RNZIR	Royal New Zealand Infantry Regiment
ROK	Republic of Korea
RVN	Republic of Vietnam
RVNAF	Republic of Vietnam armed forces
SEATO	Southeast Asia Treaty Organization
Svcs	Services
TAOR	Tactical area of responsibility
UNICEF	United Nations Children's Fund
USAID	U.S. Agency for International Development
USMACV	U.S. Military Assistance Command, Vietnam

Index

Abrams, General Creighton B.: 38, 153
Administrative support
  Australia: 14–15, 89–90, 98–99
  Free World: 19, 22
  Korea: 139
  New Zealand: 105–06, 110
  Philippines: 68, 74
Advisers
  Australia: 88–89
  China: 115–17
  Free World: 4–5, 16
  Philippines: 52, 65
  Thailand: 38
Africa: 20
Agnew, Spiro T.: 153
Agriculture, improvement of
  Australia: 96, 161
  China: 116, 119, 161
  Germany: 165
  Israel: 164
  Philippines: 85
Agricultural School: 167
Air bases, U.S.: 25
Air liaison officers
  Free World: 19
  United States: 48
Air support. *See* Strategic air support; Tactical air support.
Air units
  Australia: 15, 18, 88, 90, 92, 96–99
  China: 116
  Free World: 19
  Honduras: 169
  Korea: 124–25, 131
  New Zealand: 106–08
  Philippines: 54–56, 69
  Thailand: 17, 26–27, 49–50
Aircraft
  B-57: 96–98, 106, 108
  Bristol cargo-transport: 106, 108
  C-7: 69, 88, 90–92, 106
  C-46: 116, 131
  C-47: 27, 47, 49
  C-123: 26–27, 49, 69, 125–26
  C-130: 73
  F-4: 106, 108
  F-5: 55–56
  F-86: 124
  F-111: 97
  T-33: 26

Airfields, construction and repair
  Australia: 98
  Philippines: 76
Airlifts, of troops and supplies
  Australia: 93
  Korea: 150
  Philippines: 59–60, 62–63, 68, 71, 73–74
  Thailand: 32
Airmobile Divisions
  1st Cavalry: 130, 140
  101st Airborne: 130, 135, 138, 140
Airmobile operations and units
  Korea: 152
  Thailand: 36
Allowances. *See* Pay and allowances.
Ambulance units. *See* Medical services and units.
Ambush actions, Korean: 148, 150, 156–57
Ammunition supply
  Korea: 18
  Philippines: 58
Amnesty program. *See Chieu Hoi* program.
Amphibious Force, III Marine: 129
An Hoa: 165–66
An Khe: 130, 135–36, 140
Antiaircraft units
  Free World: 19
  Thailand: 37–38
Ap Thanh Trung: 83
Armor units
  Australia: 18, 90, 99–100
  China: 117
  Philippines: 58–59
  Thailand: 27, 29
  United States: 141
Armored personnel carriers
  Australia: 93
  Philippines: 59
  Thailand: 29–30, 36–37
Army, Department of the: 41–42
Artillery units
  Australia: 15, 18, 90, 93
  China: 117
  Korea: 131
  New Zealand: 15, 105, 108, 110
  Philippines: 20, 55, 59–62, 72, 77
  Thailand: 27, 29, 34, 36–38, 42

Assistant Secretary of Defense. *See* Gilpatric, Roswell L.
Atomic Research Establishment, Republic of Vietnam: 167–68
Aviation Company, 135th: 99
Aviation Group, 12th: 99
Awards. *See* Decorations and awards.

Ba Ria: 90
BAEK MA 9 Operation: 148
Ban Me Thuot: 96, 161
Bangkok: 48
Bao Trai (Kiem Cuong): 59, 62, 74
Base camps: 22, 29, 32
  Australia: 100
  New Zealand: 109
  Philippines: 64, 77
BAYANIHAN Task Force: 64, 83
Beach, General Dwight E.: 125–27, 131, 141
Bearcat: 32, 42, 45, 99
Ben Cam: 46
Berlin crisis: 16
Bien Hoa: 12, 14, 19, 54, 88–89, 99
Bien Hoa Province: 34, 46, 90, 123
Binh Ba: 93
Binh Dinh Province: 107–108, 120, 131, 136, 139–40, 149–50
Binh Duong Province: 52, 62
Black market operations: 82
Blackpool (New Zealand frigate): 106, 108
Bong Son: 108, 110, 140
Booby traps, enemy: 47, 64, 83
Borneo: 112
Bridge construction and repair: 64, 83, 86, 123
Brigades
  173d Airborne: 14–15, 89–90, 105
  196th Light Infantry: 60, 79, 83
Broadcasting facilities: 96, 161
BROTHERHOOD Operation: 52
Brown, Major General Charles P.: 152–53
Brown, Winthrop D.: 127
Buddhists: 27, 135
Bulldozers, combat use: 47
Bundy, McGeorge: 3, 7
Bundy, William P.: 3
Bunker, Ellsworth: 73
Butterworth, Malaysia: 97–98

Cam Ranh Bay: 16, 23, 60, 74, 130–31, 136–38, 150
Cambodia: 49, 54, 59, 91, 140
Cao Dai: 60, 78
CARE (Co-operative for American Remittances to Everywhere): 85
Casualties
  Australia: 93
  enemy: 34, 47, 93–94, 141, 145, 147–48, 150
  Korea: 141, 145, 147–48, 150
  Philippines: 64, 83–84
  Thailand: 47
Catholic Relief Service: 85
Central Highlands: 2, 120, 136, 140–41, 167
Central Training Command, Republic of Vietnam: 102
Chae Myung Shin, Major General, Republic of Korea Army: 15–16, 131–35, 138–40, 142, 146
Chau Doc Province: 103
Chi Lang National Training Center: 103
Chiang Kai-shek: 2, 115
Chief of Staff, U.S. Army. *See* Johnson, General Harold K.
Chieu Hoi program: 46–47, 79, 86, 158
China, Communist: 1, 16, 20, 115
China, Nationalist: *See* Chiang Kai-shek.
Cho Lon: 166
Cho Ray Hospital: 168
Cholard, Maj. General Hirunsiri, Royal Thai Army: 36
Chu Lai: 98, 129
Civic action programs and units
  Australia: 88, 111–12
  China: 16
  Germany: 165
  Korea: 15, 158–59
  New Zealand: 105, 111
  Philippines: 16, 20–21, 54–57, 59–60, 64–65, 68, 72, 74, 77, 79–81, 83–87, 163
  Thailand: 16, 34
Civil affairs programs and units: 5
  Australia: 96
  Philippines: 52
Civil Operations Revolutionary Development Support (CORDS): 82, 85, 157, 159

Civilians
    employment and pay: 125–27
    Korean exploitation of: 155–56
    medical care. *See* Civic action programs and units; Medical services and units.
    refugees, assistance to: 162–68
Clarke, Lieutenant General Bruce C.: 121
Clear and hold operations
    Australia: 111
    New Zealand: 111
Club facilities: 58, 98
Co, Lieutenant General Nguyen Huu: 59–60
Collins, Lieutenant General Arthur S., Jr.: 152
Collins, Brigadier General James L., Jr.: 14
Columbo Plan: 88, 160–61, 168
Combat effectiveness
    Australia: 93, 112–13
    Koreas: 141–45, 147, 149–51, 156, 159
    Thailand: 34
Combat service support units. *See* Support units.
Combat support units. *See* Support units.
Command and control. *See under* Troop units, command and control.
Commander in Chief, Pacific. *See* Felt, Admiral Harry D.; Sharp, Admiral U. S. Grant.
Commissary facilities
    Australia: 101
    New Zealand: 110
    Philippines: 58
Communications services
    Australia: 96, 101, 161
    Japan: 162
    Korea: 125–26, 131
    New Zealand: 109
Constabulary, Republic of Vietnam: 65
Construction programs and supplies
    Australia: 100, 112, 161
    Canada: 168
    China: 116, 161
    France: 166
    Germany: 165

Construction programs and supplies—Continued
    Japan: 162
    Korea: 122–23, 127, 129, 144
    Netherlands: 166
    New Zealand: 109, 163
    Philippines: 59, 64, 72, 76–78, 85
    Switzerland: 167
    Thailand: 34, 163
    Turkey: 164
Cooper, Chester: 5
Cordon and search operations: 149
Corps tactical zones
    I: 10, 22, 129
    II: 10, 120, 133, 138–39, 148–49, 157
    III: 52, 99–100, 108
    IV: 167
Counterinsurgency plans: 9–10, 13, 21, 53, 139

Da Nang: 7–8, 74, 165, 167
Da Nhim River: 162
Dalat: 116, 168
Dams, construction by Japan: 162
Death gratuities
    Korea: 17, 124–26
    Philippines: 58
    Thailand: 28
Decorations and awards
    Philippines: 86
    Thailand: 51
Defense, Department of: 2, 18, 21, 28, 121, 125. *See also* McNamara, Robert S.
Demilitarized zone: 9–10, 13, 21–22
Democratic Republic of Vietnam. *See* North Vietnam.
Dental services and units
    Australia: 101
    New Zealand: 109
    Philippines: 60, 71, 74, 76–77, 80
Di An: 15
Diem, Ngo Dinh: 2
Dinh Tuong Province: 62
Disability compensation: 17
Discipline, Korean: 145–46, 156–57
Documents, enemy, exploitation of: 93
Dong Bo 7 Operation
Don Son: 110

Eaton, Air Vice Marshal Brian Alexander, Royal Australian Air Force: 97
Ecole Nationale d'Ingenieurs des Arts Industriels: 166
Economic assistance: 4–5
  Australia: 96, 103, 161
  Canada: 168
  China: 119
  France: 165
  Germany: 164
  Ireland: 166
  Italy: 166
  Japan: 161–62
  Korea: 162
  Laos: 162
  Netherlands: 166
  New Zealand: 110, 163
  Norway: 167
  Pakistan: 163
  Philippines: 52, 85
  Switzerland: 167
  United Kingdom: 167–68
Economy of force, application of: 149
Education, contributions to
  Australia: 151
  Belgium: 164
  Canada: 168
  China: 161
  France: 165–66
  Italy: 166
  Japan: 162
  Netherlands: 166
  Tunisia: 164
Edwards, Major General Norman B.: 121
Eighth Army: 56
Electric power. *See* Utilities, development of.
Engineer operations and units. *See also* Construction programs and supplies.
  Australia: 15, 88, 90, 96, 99, 161
  China: 115, 117
  Free World: 19
  Korea: 15, 18, 122, 131, 143
  New Zealand: 105, 108
  Philippines: 20, 54–55, 64, 68–71, 76, 81, 83–87, 163
  Thailand: 29, 32, 34, 36, 38, 47
  United Kingdom: 22
England. *See* United Kingdom; Wilson, J. Harold.

Equipment, allotment and supply. *See* Matériel, allotment and supply; *also by name.*
Explosive ordnance demolition teams: 64, 83

"Face" problem: 135, 145 151
Felt, Admiral Harry D.: 115. *See also* United States Pacific Command.
Field Forces
  I: 134, 138–40, 146, 151–52
  II: 45, 60, 90–92, 108
Financial assistance. *See* Economic assistance.
Fire Support Base Tak: 46
Flood relief
  Laos: 162
  Norway: 167
FLYING TIGER Operation: 145
Food contributions
  Argentina: 168
  Australia: 161
  Brazil: 169
  Canada: 168
  China: 161
  Morocco: 164
  New Zealand: 163
  Thailand: 163
  Venezuela: 169
Formosa Strait: 16, 115
Fort Magsaysay: 56, 67
Forward air control units
  Free World: 19
  New Zealand: 106, 108
Forward observers, Philippines: 64, 83
France, policy in Vietnam: 3
Free World Military Assistance Policy Council: 15, 59, 119, 122–23, 133–34

GAME WARDEN Operation: 108
Geneva Accords: 2
Gia Dinh Province: 52
Gilpatric, Roswell L.: 1
Go Cong District: 167
Gomes, Major General Lloyd H.: 54, 65, 68, 70–71
Government Printing Office, Republic of Vietnam: 167
Grenade assaults, enemy: 64, 83
Guerrilla operations
  Australian experience: 112–13
  enemy: 46, 87, 136

INDEX 181

Gunboats: 30, 69
Gurkha Brigade: 22–23
Gurr, Lieutenant Colonel Robert M., New Zealand Army: 104–05

Ha Tien: 166
Hainan: 115
Hau Nghia Province: 59–62
Headquarters. *See* Staffs and staff officers.
Helgoland, SS: 165
Helicopters
  H–34: 65, 98
  OH–1: 65–66
  UH–1: 90–91, 99, 106, 108
Helicopters, allocation and supply
  Australia: 90–91, 98–100
  Korea: 152
  New Zealand: 106, 108
  Philippines: 56, 65–66
  Thailand: 48
Hiep Hoa: 66, 86
Hieu, General Nguyen Van: 140
Highway 1: 23, 130–31, 136, 140, 143, 148
Highway 13: 83
Highway 15: 91–93
Highway 19: 120, 130, 135–36, 140, 148
Highway 21: 23, 131
Highway 22: 83
Highway 25: 46
Hobart, HMAS: 96–98
Hoi An: 165
Holyoake, Keith J.: 104–105
Hong Kil Dong Operation: 148
Honolulu conference: 12–13, 19
Hospitals and hospital teams. *See* Medical services and units.
Housing facilities
  Australia: 100, 161
  China: 119
  New Zealand: 109
  Philippines: 58
Howze, General Hamilton H.: 121–22, 124
Hue University: 110, 163, 165, 168
Huk insurgency: 72
Hydrographic survey: 19

Indonesia: 53

Infantry Divisions, U.S.
  1st: 90
  4th: 130, 140
  7th: 125
  9th: 29, 31–32
  25th: 59–60, 128
Infantry units. *See also* Troop units, combat missions and operations; Troop units, command and control; Troop units deployments; Troop units, strength; Troop units, withdrawals.
  Australia: 14, 21, 88–89, 99
  Free World: 19
  Korea: 16–18, 21, 128, 131
  New Zealand: 21, 106–108, 110
  Philippines: 54
  Thailand: 27, 29, 34, 36, 38, 41–42, 47
  United Kingdom: 22
  United States: 21
Information programs: 42
Intelligence operations and specialists
  Australia: 93
  China: 117
  Korea: 138–49
  New Zealand: 108
  Thailand: 47
International Control Commission: 17, 21
International Red Cross: 166–67, 169
Interpreters, Korean use: 156
Iron Triangle: 93
Irrigation projects. *See* Agriculture, improvement of.

Jackson, Brigadier Oliver D., Australian Army: 90, 94, 97
JEFFERSON Operation: 145
Johnson, General Harold K.: 8–9
Johnson, Lyndon B.: 2–4, 9, 11–12, 18, 25–26, 53, 67, 124, 127, 163
Johnson, U. Alexis: 2
Joint Chiefs of Staff: 1–2, 7–8, 10, 12, 18–19, 21, 30–31, 35, 41–42, 56, 92, 98–99, 128. *See also* Wheeler, General Earle G.
Joint General Staff, Republic of Vietnam: 14–15, 17, 34, 74, 123. *See also* Vien, Brigadier General Cao Van.

KANZUS Project: 21–22

Karate instructors: 121
Keelung: 116
Khanh, Major General Nguyen: 4
Khoman, Thanat: 48–49, 73
Kiem Cuong (Bao Trai): 59
Kim Sung Eun: 121–22, 124 141
Kit Carson Scouts: 46
Korea forces, evaluation of: 142–46, 151–54
Korean War experience: 1, 4
Ky, Nguyen Cao: 67

Labor unions, Australian: 101
Land-clearing operations, Philippines: 64, 76, 78, 81, 83–87
Landing craft, mechanized: 69
Landing ship, mechanized: 122, 124
Landing ship, tank: 50, 69, 73–74, 116, 122
Language barrier: 19, 135, 143, 145
Laos: 2, 9, 13, 25, 49, 82
Larsen, Lieutenant General Stanley R.: 134, 139, 151. *See also* Field Forces, I.
Latin America: 5–6
Leadership, Korean: 156
Lee Sae Ho, Major General: 123
Legal services, Thailand: 42
Lew Byong Hion, General, ROKA: 139
Liaison procedures and personnel
  Australia: 112
  Korea: 122, 125, 138–39, 152
  Philippines: 60, 79, 81
  Thailand: 31, 42, 47
Lines of communication: 22
Loc, General Vinh: 139
Lodge, Henry Cabot: 21, 49. *See also* United States Embassy, Vietnam.
Logistical lift ships: 19
Logistical support and units
  Australia: 14, 88–89, 97–98, 100
  China: 116
  Free World: 7–8, 12, 19, 22
  Korea: 121, 123 125, 127, 131, 143
  New Zealand: 15, 106, 108–10
  Philippines: 20, 55–57, 68, 74
  Thailand: 28, 32, 36, 48
  United States: 54, 90, 97–98
  Vietnamese: 16, 18, 54
Long An Province: 52, 59
Long Binh: 74
Long Ha: 78

Long Le District: 111
Long Xuyen Province: 88
Lost Crusade: 5

Macapagal, Diosdada: 20, 53–54
McCown, Major General Hal D.: 34, 37. *See also* United States Military Assistance Command, Thailand.
Machine guns, allocation and supply, Philippines: 55
McMahon, William: 101–03
McNamara, Robert S.: 8–9, 25, 28, 53, 66. *See also* Defense, Department of.
Maintenance and repair
  Australia: 18, 90, 97, 99, 101, 112
  Korea: 123, 128
  New Zealand: 105, 110
  Philippines: 57, 65–66
  Thailand: 29
Malaysia: 19, 72, 97, 106–08, 112
Maltese Aid Service: 165
Manila International Airport: 62
Manpower procurement, retention, and use, Republic of Vietnam: 10, 12
Marcos, Ferdinand E.: 54–56, 58, 62, 64–65, 67, 69–71, 73
Marine corps units
  Korea: 16, 122, 124, 127–28, 131, 136–38, 146–47, 159
  United States. *See* United States Marine Corps.
MARKET TIME Operation: 30, 69, 108
Martin, Graham: 36, 40. *See also* United States Embassy, Thailand.
Mata, General Ernesto S., Philippine Army: 58–59, 67, 70–71
Matériel, allocation and supply. *See also* by name.
  Korea: 123–24, 126–27, 129
  Malaysia: 162
  Philippines: 54, 57–59, 74
  Thailand: 32, 37
Matériel, losses
  enemy: 47, 93, 140, 147–48, 151
  Korea: 143
  Philippines: 84
Mechanized units, Thailand: 37
Medical services and units
  Argentina: 168
  Australia: 18, 88, 96, 101, 161
  Belgium: 164

Medical services and units—Continued
  Brazil: 169
  Canada: 168
  China: 116–17, 119, 161
  Costa Rica: 169
  Denmark: 164
  Ecuador: 169
  France: 166
  Free World: 16, 18
  Germany: 164–65
  Greece: 166
  Guatemala: 169
  Honduras: 169
  Iran: 163
  Israel: 164
  Italy: 166
  Japan: 162
  Korea: 18, 121–23, 125, 131, 143, 156, 159, 162
  Liberia: 164
  Luxembourg: 166
  Malaysia: 162
  Netherlands: 166
  New Zealand: 105–10, 163
  Philippines: 20, 52, 55, 59–62, 70–74, 76–77, 80, 163
  South Africa: 164
  Spain: 167
  Switzerland: 167
  Thailand: 29, 34, 37, 42, 163
  Turkey: 164
  United Kingdom: 167–68
  Uruguay: 169
  Venezuela: 169
Medical Civic Action Program: 76
Mekong River: 9
Mess facilities
  Australia: 98, 100
  New Zealand: 109
  Philippines: 58
Meteorologic Service, Republic of Vietnam: 167
Military assistance
  Australia: 4, 6, 88
  Canada: 4, 16
  China: 4, 16, 20, 115
  criticism of and protests against: 48, 71–72, 82, 90, 94, 101, 103
  Free World: 2–14, 19
  India: 16
  Korea: 4, 17, 19, 120–22, 134–35
  Latin America: 6

  New Zealand: 4, 105–107
  Philippines: 52–57, 66–73, 171–73
  Thailand: 19, 25–45 48–50
  United Kingdom: 4
  U.S. initiative and funding: 1, 4–5, 7, 12, 16–18, 25–26, 53–54, 88–89, 115, 126–27
Military police
  Korea: 146
  Thailand: 29
Mine warfare, enemy: 64, 83
Minh, Major General Duong Van: 11, 14
Ministry of Defense: 59–60. *See also* Co, Lieutenant General Nguyen Huu; Vy, Nguyen Van.
Ministry of Public Health: 59, 167, 169
Miscellaneous Environmental Improvement Program: 76
Missile units, to Thailand: 37
Mobile training teams
  Philippines: 68
  United States: 56–57
Monsoons. *See* Weather, effect on operations.
Morale, national: 136–38
Moreno-Salcedo, Luis: 86
Mortar assaults, enemy: 64, 83
Mortar units
  Philippines: 58–59
  Thailand: 29, 36
Muy Ba Mountain. *See* Phu Cat Mountain.
My Tho: 62, 74

NARASUAN Operation: 32–34
National Cancer Institute, Republic of Vietnam: 167
National Police: 158
National Security Council, U.S.: 1–2
Nationalities, problems of: 19
Naval assistance and forces
  Australia: 9, 96–99
  China: 116
  command and control: 97
  Free World: 19
  Korea: 122, 125
  New Zealand: 105–108
  Philippines: 54–56, 69
  Thailand: 30, 32, 50
Naval gunfire support: 19, 97

Newport Army Terminal: 32
Nha Trang: 138
Nhon Trach District: 34, 46
Night operations
  Korea: 136, 141, 156–57
  Thailand: 47
Ninh Hoa: 23, 131
Ninh Thuan Province: 149–50
Nolting, Frederick C., Jr.: 2. *See also* United States Embassy Vietnam.
Nong Son: 165–66
North Atlantic Treaty Organization: 20
North Vietnam: 1, 12
North Vietnamese Army: 2, 93, 120. *See also* Viet Cong.
  3d Division: 140
  5th Division: 150
  324-B Division: 21
  325th Division: 10
  12th Regiment: 140, 148
  22d Regiment: 140
  95th Regiment: 130, 136, 148
  101st Regiment: 141
Norton, Major General John: 140
Nui Dat: 99, 110

Observers, military: 20–21
Office facilities
  Australia: 101
  China: 119
  New Zealand: 110
Oh Jac Kyo Operation: 148
On-the-job training
  China: 117
  Philippines: 68
Ordnance services and units
  Australia: 18, 90
  China: 117
  Korea: 18

Pacification programs
  Korea: 157–59
  Malaysia: 162
  Philippines: 76–87
Park, Chung Hee: 17, 124, 141–42, 146
  Patrol actions: 11, 13
  Australia: 89
  Korea: 135–36, 141
  New Zealand: 107
Patrol craft
  Free World: 19
  New Zealand: 108

Philippines: 55, 69
Pay and allowances
  Australia: 98
  Korea: 121, 124–27, 129
  Philippines: 57
  Thailand: 48
Peers, Lieutenant General William R.: 149, 152
Petroleum, oil, and lubricants supply
  Australia: 97, 101
  Free World: 19
  Iran: 163
  Korea: 127–28
  New Zealand: 110
  Philippines: 57–58
Phan Rang: 97–98, 131, 138, 140, 149–50
Phan Thiet: 116
Phu Cat Mountain: 136, 140, 148, 150
Phu Cuong: 62, 74
Phu Khuong District: 83
Phu Yen Province: 136, 140, 148
Phuoc Dien: 83
Phuoc Ninh District: 83
Phuoc Tuy Province: 18, 90, 92, 103, 105, 110–12
Pilots, assignment and training
  Australian: 98–99
  New Zealand: 106, 108
  Philippines: 65–66
  Thailand: 26–27
Pleiku City and Province: 120
Police training
  Malaysia and Philippines: 162
  United Kingdom: 168
Political crises, Republic of Vietnam: 2, 7, 20
Political Warfare College and Directorate, Republic of Vietnam: 116
Popular Forces: 64, 81, 83, 85, 103, 145
Port units: 19
Post exchange facilities
  Australia: 98, 101
  New Zealand: 109–10
  Philippines: 58
Postal service
  Australia: 101
  New Zealand: 109
  Philippines: 58
Power plants. *See* Utilities, development of.

Press reports: 48
Prisoners of war, enemy: 47
Psychological operations and teams
  China: 115–17, 161
  enemy: 66, 87
  Korea: 125–26, 158
  Malaysia: 162
  Philippines: 52, 64, 79, 81
  Thailand: 29, 47
Psychological Warfare Directorate, Republic of Vietnam: 52
Public works programs, Philippines: 59
Publicity programs. *See* Information programs; Press reports.

Quang Ngai: 10, 12, 129, 168
Quang Tri Province: 22
Quartermaster services and units. *See also* Logistical support and units.
  Australia: 18, 90
  Korea: 18
  Thailand: 27, 29, 35
Quat Phan Huy: 89
Qui Nhon: 16, 18, 74, 105, 110, 120, 130–31, 135–38, 140, 149–50, 163

Ralliers. *See Chieu Hoi* program.
Rations supply
  Australia: 97
  Korea: 121, 123, 129, 131
  Philippines: 57
Reconnaissance operations and units: 13
  Australia: 90
  Korea: 136
  New Zealand: 106–08
  Philippines: 58
  Thailand: 29, 36–38
Recreation facilities and programs, Philippines: 58
Red Lion and Sun Society: 163
Refugees, assistance to
  Canada: 168
  Germany: 165
  Israel: 164
  Italy: 166
  Korea: 162
  Laos: 162
  Netherlands: 166
  New Zealand: 163
  Norway: 167
  Thailand: 163

Regional Forces: 8, 64, 81, 83, 85, 89, 103, 145
Rehabilitation programs, Philippines: 59
Religions, problems of: 19
Religious groups: 27, 60, 78–79
Religious services
  Korea: 135
  Philippines: 58
Repair parts. *See* Maintenance and repair.
Repatriation program. *See Chieu Hoi* program.
Replacement systems
  Korea: 125, 142
  Philippines: 67, 71
  Thailand: 37
Republic of Vietnam Air Force: 26–27, 49, 122
Republic of Vietnam Armed Forces: 10–11, 13
Republic of Vietnam Army: 8, 120, 123, 140
  1st Division: 21
  22d Division: 140
  1st Psychological Warfare Battalion: 52
Republic of Vietnam Navy: 30
Resettlement programs
  Australia: 96
  Malaysia: 162
  Philippines: 66, 76–77, 81, 83–87
Rest and recreation programs
  Australia: 101
  New Zealand: 110
Revolutionary Development Program: 107
Rhee, Syngman: 120
Rifles, allocation and supply
  Korea: 31
  Philippines: 55, 59
  Thailand: 30–31
Road construction and repair
  Australia: 96, 161
  Philippines: 64, 76–78, 80, 83
  Thailand: 34
Rockefeller International Rice Research Institute: 85
Romulo, Carlos P.: 73
Rosson, General William B.: 122–23, 151–52
Rostow, Walt W.: 2

Rotation programs
    Korea: 125
    New Zealand: 108
    Philippines: 58, 68
    Thailand: 45, 48–50
Rung Sat Special Zone: 92
Rural development
    Australian: 88
    Philippine: 52–53
Rusk, Dean: 4, 17 21, 28, 66. *See also*
    State, Department of.
Russia. *See* Soviet Union.

Sabah crises: 72
Saigon: 74, 89, 100, 110, 138, 162, 165, 167-68
Saigon conference: 97–98
Saigon University: 110, 163, 167–68
Scholarships. *See* Education, contributions to.
Search and clear operations
    Korea: 148, 150, 154–56
    New Zealand: 107
    Thailand: 46
Secretary of Defense, U.S. *See* McNamara, Robert S.
Secretary of State. *See* Rusk, Dean.
Security measures and units: 2–3, 7, 10–11, 13, 16, 20
    Australia: 89
    Cambodia: 49
    Korea: 122, 148, 154–55, 158–59
    Laos: 49
    Malaysia: 162
    New Zealand: 104, 107
    Philippines: 55–56, 58, 60, 64, 69, 71–72, 74, 76, 81, 83, 163
    Thailand: 34, 40, 42, 47
Seoul: 17
Seventh Fleet: 9, 98, 106, 108
Sharp, Admiral U. S. Grant: 10, 18–19, 28, 30–31, 35, 41–42, 56, 66, 89, 92, 107, 126–28, 133–34. *See also* United States Pacific Command.
Shop units: *See* Maintenance and repair.
Signal units
    Australian: 14–15, 18, 89–90
    Korea: 18, 125–26
    Thailand: 36
    United Kingdom: 22

Singapore: 106
Snipers, enemy: 64, 83
Social programs. *See by type.*
South China Sea: 9
Southeast Asia Treaty Organization: 1–3, 8–9
Soviet Union: 1, 16
Special Air Services. *See* Special forces units, New Zealand.
Special forces units
    New Zealand: 106–107, 109
    Philippines: 54
Staffs and staff officers: 10–11, 14
    Korea: 134, 138, 142
    Thailand: 29, 42
State, Department of: 1, 5, 8–9, 21, 40, 53–54, 69, 73, 92–93, 117, 121, 125–27. *See also* Rusk, Dean.
Stilwell, Major General Richard G.: 15
Strategic air support: 92–93
Supply services and units: 22. *See also* Quartermaster services and units.
Support units
    Australia: 90, 100
    Korea: 122, 127, 131, 143–44
    New Zealand: 108
    Philippines: 54, 60, 69
    Thailand: 37, 45
    U.S. battalion: 35
Surgical teams. *See* Medical services and units.
Survey ships: 19
Symington Subcommittee: 48

Tactical air support
    Australia: 99
    Korea: 124, 131
    New Zealand: 108
    Thailand: 47–48
Tactics, Korean: 154–57
Taiwan: 116, 119 161
Tam Ky: 129
Tan Son Nhut: 49
Tank units. *See* Armor units.
Tao Mountain: 150
Tay Ninh: 21, 54, 64, 67, 72, 74, 77, 79, 83
Tay Ninh Friendship Council: 79
Tay Ninh Province: 59–62, 64, 77, 79, 81–87
Tay Ninh West airfield: 62, 77
Taylor, General Maxwell D.: 4, 8–9,

Taylor, General Maxwell D.—
Continued
   11–12, 89–90. *See also* United
   States Embassy, Vietnam.
Technical assistance: 4
   Australia: 96, 161
   China: 119, 161
   France: 166
   Germany: 164
   Japan: 162
   Philippines: 52, 59
   United Kingdom: 167–68
Tet offensive: 119, 167–68
Textbooks, supply of. *See* Education, contributions to.
Thanh, Tran Chan: 48
Thanh Dien Forest area: 64, 66–67, 77–78, 81, 83–87
Thanom, Kittikachorn: 25, 28, 34
Thieu, Nguyen Van: 11, 76
Thu Duc: 116, 165–66
Tobias, Brigadier General Gaudencio V.: 60–62, 67
Tra Vo: 64
Training literature. *See* Education, contributions to.
Training programs
   Australia: 89, 96, 103, 161
   Canada: 168
   China: 119, 161
   Denmark: 164
   Free World: 40
   Germany: 165
   Korea: 128–30, 145, 159
   Malaysia: 162
   New Zealand: 103
   Philippines: 56–57, 65, 68, 76
   Thailand: 26–27, 29, 31–32, 34–35, 37–41
   United Kingdom: 167–68
Transportation services and units
   Australia: 18, 90, 100–101
   China: 119
   Free World: 19
   Korea: 18, 122, 125–26, 128–29, 131
   Malaysia: 162
   New Zealand: 106, 109
   Philippines: 57–58
   Thailand: 29, 35
Troop units, combat missions and operations
   Australia: 89–94, 97–98, 110–11
   China: 117, 119
   Korea: 122, 129–54
   New Zealand: 105, 107–08, 110–11
   Philippines: 72, 74
   Thailand: 32–34, 36, 45–48
Troop units, command and control
   Australia: 11, 14–15, 18, 89–92, 96–98
   China: 119
   Free World: 7–8, 10–11, 13–17, 19, 21, 23
   Korea: 10, 15, 122–23, 125, 127, 131–35, 138, 146
   New Zealand: 15, 105, 108
   Philippines: 59, 62, 68
   Thailand: 17, 45
   United Kingdom: 23
   United States: 13
   Vietnam: 13
Troop units, deployments
   Australia: 3, 8–9, 12, 14–15, 18, 88–90, 92, 94, 96–97, 99–100.
   China: 2, 116–17
   Free World: 1–3, 5, 7–10, 19
   Korea: 7–9, 11–13, 15–17, 20, 23, 120–24, 127–28, 131
   New Zealand: 3, 8–9, 12, 15, 18, 103, 105–06, 108–09
   Philippines: 3, 12, 20, 52, 54–56, 60–62, 66–68, 74, 76–77
   Thailand: 3, 17, 27–29, 31–32, 34–42, 45
   United Kingdom: 22–23
   United States: 1–2, 7–9, 11–12, 40–42
Troop units, strength
   Australia: 15, 18, 24, 89–90, 98–99, 1 3, 161
   China: 24, 116, 119
   Free World: 24, 160
   Korea: 16, 18, 24, 123–24, 128, 131, 146
   New Zealand: 15, 24, 109–10
   Philippines: 21, 24, 54, 58, 64, 70, 74
   Spain: 24
   Thailand: 24, 29, 34, 38, 49–50
Troop units, withdrawals
   Australia: 93, 101–03
   Korea: 129
   New Zealand: 103–04
   Philippines: 48, 68–73
   Thailand: 48–50
   United States: 124, 127–29

Truck units. *See* Transportation services and units.
Tugboat crews: 19
Tunnel systems, enemy: 93
Tuy Hoa: 23, 120, 130–31, 136–38, 140

Under Secretary of State. *See* Johnson, U. Alexis.
United Kingdom: 4, 22, 23, 167–68
United Nations projects: 166
United States
 military assistance, initiative in: 1, 4–5, 7, 12, 16–18, 25–26, 53–54, 88–89, 115, 126–27
 mission and objective: 2–3, 7, 9–10, 13
United States Agency for International Development: 7, 59, 79, 112, 116, 167
United States Air Force: 7, 19, 47
 Pacific Air Forces: 26
 Seventh Air Force: 92, 97
 315th Air Commando Wing: 26–27
 19th Tactical Airlift Squadron: 49
United States Army: 7
United States Army, Pacific: 42, 128
United States Army, Vietnam: 38, 41–42, 56, 70
United States Embassy, China: 117
United States Embassy, Korea: 127. *See also* Brown, Winthrop D.
United States Embassy, Philippines: 54, 65, 68, 71–73
United States Embassy, Thailand: 27–28, 34, 38, 42. *See also* Martin, Graham.
United States Embassy, Vietnam: 54, 116–17. *See also* Bunker, Ellsworth; Lodge, Henry Cabot; Nolting, Frederick C., Jr.; Taylor, General Maxwell D.
United States Forces, Korea. *See* Howze, General Hamilton H.
United States Joint Military Advisory Group, Korea: 121
United States Joint Military Assistance Group, Philippines: 54. *See also* Gomes, Major General Lloyd H.
United States Joint Public Affairs Office: 79, 112

United States Marine Corps: 7–8, 10, 21
United States Military Assistance Advisory Group, China: 117, 119
United States Military Assistance Command, Thailand: 28, 30, 32, 34, 37–40, 42. *See also* McCown, Major General Hal D.
United States Military Assistance Command, Vietnam: 3, 5, 8, 10–11, 19–20. *See also* Westmoreland, General William C.
 and Australian forces: 89–91, 97–98, 102
 and China forces: 116–19
 and Korean forces: 121, 123, 128, 133, 146-49
 and New Zealand forces: 104–05, 107
 and Philippines forces: 52, 54, 56, 58–59, 66, 68, 72, 74
 and Thai forces: 26–30, 35, 37–38, 41
United States Military Provincial Health Assistance Program: 167
United States Naval Forces, Vietnam: 97–98. *See also* Ward, Rear Admiral Norvell G.
United States Navy: 19, 30, 97
United States Operations Mission: 5, 20–21
United States Pacific Command: 8, 10. *See also* Felt, Admiral Harry D.; Sharp, Admiral U. S. Grant.
Unity of command. *See* Troop units, command and control.
Utilities, development of
 China: 116, 119, 161
 Japan: 162
 Philippines: 59, 77

Vam Co Dong River: 83
Vien, Brigadier General Cao Van: 4, 15, 134. *See also* Joint General Staff, Republic of Vietnam.
Viet Cong: 1–3 12–13, 45, 47, 60, 64, 66, 78, 81, 83, 93, 111, 120, 122, 136, 147, 158–59. *See also* North Vietnamese Army.
 2d Regiment: 140
 C–40 Company: 83

Vietnam War, as test against communism: 1
Vietnamization program: 48
Villereal, Cornelio T.: 67
Vocational training. *See also* On-the-job training.
  Australia: 96
  Germany: 165
  New Zealand: 110
  Philippines: 76
Vung Tau: 12, 96, 99, 107
Vy, Nguyen Van: 86. *See also* Ministry of Defense.

War Zone C: 59
Ward, Rear Admiral Norvell G.: 97–98. *See also* United States Naval Forces, Vietnam.
Water supply improvements
  Australia: 96, 161
Philippines: 76
Weather, effect on operations: 22, 64, 93
Western Pacific Transportation Office: 71
Westmoreland, General William C.: 7–8, 10–11, 13–16, 21–23, 26, 28, 35–42, 54, 58–59, 65, 67–68, 89–90, 92, 98–99, 105, 108, 116–17, 123, 127, 129, 131–34, 138, 145–47. *See also* United States Military Assistance Command, Vietnam.
Wheeler, General Earle G.: 7–8, 34. *See also* Joint Chiefs of Staff.
White House. *See* Johnson, Lyndon B.
Wilson, J. Harold: 3
Wright, Admiral Jerauld: 115

Yan, Manuel: 71
Yu Tai-wei: 115, 119

www.ingramcontent.com/pod-product-compliance
Lightning Source LLC
Chambersburg PA
CBHW061306110426
42742CB00012BA/2080